ITALIAN
VOCABULARY

FOR ENGLISH SPEAKERS

ENGLISH-ITALIAN

The most useful words
To expand your lexicon and sharpen
your language skills

9000 words

Italian vocabulary for English speakers - 9000 words

By Andrey Taranov

T&P Books vocabularies are intended for helping you learn, memorize and review foreign words. The dictionary is divided into themes, covering all major spheres of everyday activities, business, science, culture, etc.

The process of learning words using T&P Books' theme-based dictionaries gives you the following advantages:

- Correctly grouped source information predetermines success at subsequent stages of word memorization
- Availability of words derived from the same root allowing memorization of word units (rather than separate words)
- Small units of words facilitate the process of establishing associative links needed for consolidation of vocabulary
- Level of language knowledge can be estimated by the number of learned words

T&P Books Publishing
www.tpbooks.com

ISBN: 978-1-78071-294-9

This book is also available in E-book formats.
Please visit www.tpbooks.com or the major online bookstores.

ITALIAN VOCABULARY
for English speakers

T&P Books vocabularies are intended to help you learn, memorize, and review foreign words. The vocabulary contains over 9000 commonly used words arranged thematically.

- Vocabulary contains the most commonly used words
- Recommended as an addition to any language course
- Meets the needs of beginners and advanced learners of foreign languages
- Convenient for daily use, revision sessions, and self-testing activities
- Allows you to assess your vocabulary

Special features of the vocabulary

- Words are organized according to their meaning, not alphabetically
- Words are presented in three columns to facilitate the reviewing and self-testing processes
- Words in groups are divided into small blocks to facilitate the learning process
- The vocabulary offers a convenient and simple transcription of each foreign word

The vocabulary has 256 topics including:

Basic Concepts, Numbers, Colors, Months, Seasons, Units of Measurement, Clothing & Accessories, Food & Nutrition, Restaurant, Family Members, Relatives, Character, Feelings, Emotions, Diseases, City, Town, Sightseeing, Shopping, Money, House, Home, Office, Working in the Office, Import & Export, Marketing, Job Search, Sports, Education, Computer, Internet, Tools, Nature, Countries, Nationalities and more ...

T&P BOOKS' THEME-BASED DICTIONARIES

The Correct System for Memorizing Foreign Words

Acquiring vocabulary is one of the most important elements of learning a foreign language, because words allow us to express our thoughts, ask questions, and provide answers. An inadequate vocabulary can impede communication with a foreigner and make it difficult to understand a book or movie well.

The pace of activity in all spheres of modern life, including the learning of modern languages, has increased. Today, we need to memorize large amounts of information (grammar rules, foreign words, etc.) within a short period. However, this does not need to be difficult. All you need to do is to choose the right training materials, learn a few special techniques, and develop your individual training system.

Having a system is critical to the process of language learning. Many people fail to succeed in this regard; they cannot master a foreign language because they fail to follow a system comprised of selecting materials, organizing lessons, arranging new words to be learned, and so on. The lack of a system causes confusion and eventually, lowers self-confidence.

T&P Books' theme-based dictionaries can be included in the list of elements needed for creating an effective system for learning foreign words. These dictionaries were specially developed for learning purposes and are meant to help students effectively memorize words and expand their vocabulary.

Generally speaking, the process of learning words consists of three main elements:

- Reception (creation or acquisition) of a training material, such as a word list
- Work aimed at memorizing new words
- Work aimed at reviewing the learned words, such as self-testing

All three elements are equally important since they determine the quality of work and the final result. All three processes require certain skills and a well-thought-out approach.

New words are often encountered quite randomly when learning a foreign language and it may be difficult to include them all in a unified list. As a result, these words remain written on scraps of paper, in book margins, textbooks, and so on. In order to systematize such words, we have to create and continually update a "book of new words." A paper notebook, a netbook, or a tablet PC can be used for these purposes.

This "book of new words" will be your personal, unique list of words. However, it will only contain the words that you came across during the learning process. For example, you might have written down the words "Sunday," "Tuesday," and "Friday." However, there are additional words for days of the week, for example, "Saturday," that are missing, and your list of words would be incomplete. Using a theme dictionary, in addition to the "book of new words," is a reasonable solution to this problem.

The theme-based dictionary may serve as the basis for expanding your vocabulary.

It will be your big "book of new words" containing the most frequently used words of a foreign language already included. There are quite a few theme-based dictionaries available, and you should ensure that you make the right choice in order to get the maximum benefit from your purchase.

Therefore, we suggest using theme-based dictionaries from T&P Books Publishing as an aid to learning foreign words. Our books are specially developed for effective use in the sphere of vocabulary systematization, expansion and review.

Theme-based dictionaries are not a magical solution to learning new words. However, they can serve as your main database to aid foreign-language acquisition. Apart from theme dictionaries, you can have copybooks for writing down new words, flash cards, glossaries for various texts, as well as other resources; however, a good theme dictionary will always remain your primary collection of words.

T&P Books' theme-based dictionaries are specialty books that contain the most frequently used words in a language.

The main characteristic of such dictionaries is the division of words into themes. For example, the *City* theme contains the words "street," "crossroads," "square," "fountain," and so on. The *Talking* theme might contain words like "to talk," "to ask," "question," and "answer".

All the words in a theme are divided into smaller units, each comprising 3–5 words. Such an arrangement improves the perception of words and makes the learning process less tiresome. Each unit contains a selection of words with similar meanings or identical roots. This allows you to learn words in small groups and establish other associative links that have a positive effect on memorization.

The words on each page are placed in three columns: a word in your native language, its translation, and its transcription. Such positioning allows for the use of techniques for effective memorization. After closing the translation column, you can flip through and review foreign words, and vice versa. "This is an easy and convenient method of review – one that we recommend you do often."

Our theme-based dictionaries contain transcriptions for all the foreign words. Unfortunately, none of the existing transcriptions are able to convey the exact nuances of foreign pronunciation. That is why we recommend using the transcriptions only as a supplementary learning aid. Correct pronunciation can only be acquired with the help of sound. Therefore our collection includes audio theme-based dictionaries.

The process of learning words using T&P Books' theme-based dictionaries gives you the following advantages:

- You have correctly grouped source information, which predetermines your success at subsequent stages of word memorization
- Availability of words derived from the same root (lazy, lazily, lazybones), allowing you to memorize word units instead of separate words
- Small units of words facilitate the process of establishing associative links needed for consolidation of vocabulary
- You can estimate the number of learned words and hence your level of language knowledge
- The dictionary allows for the creation of an effective and high-quality revision process
- You can revise certain themes several times, modifying the revision methods and techniques
- Audio versions of the dictionaries help you to work out the pronunciation of words and develop your skills of auditory word perception

The T&P Books' theme-based dictionaries are offered in several variants differing in the number of words: 1.500, 3.000, 5.000, 7.000, and 9.000 words. There are also dictionaries containing 15,000 words for some language combinations. Your choice of dictionary will depend on your knowledge level and goals.

We sincerely believe that our dictionaries will become your trusty assistant in learning foreign languages and will allow you to easily acquire the necessary vocabulary.

TABLE OF CONTENTS

PRONUNCIATION GUIDE

T&P phonetic alphabet	Italian example	English example
[a]	**casco** ['kasko]	shorter than in ask
[e]	**sfera** ['sfera]	elm, medal
[i]	**filo** ['filo]	shorter than in feet
[o]	**dolce** ['doltʃe]	pod, John
[u]	**siluro** [si'luro]	book
[y]	**würstel** ['vyrstel]	fuel, tuna
[b]	**busta** ['busta]	baby, book
[d]	**andare** [an'dare]	day, doctor
[ʣ]	**zinco** ['ʣinko]	beads, kids
[ʤ]	**Norvegia** [nor'veʤa]	joke, general
[ʒ]	**garage** [ga'raʒ]	forge, pleasure
[f]	**ferrovia** [ferro'via]	face, food
[g]	**ago** ['ago]	game, gold
[k]	**cocktail** ['koktejl]	clock, kiss
[j]	**piazza** ['pjattsa]	yes, New York
[l]	**olive** [o'live]	lace, people
[ʎ]	**figlio** ['fiʎʎo]	daily, million
[m]	**mosaico** [mo'zaiko]	magic, milk
[n]	**treno** ['treno]	name, normal
[ŋ]	**granchio** ['graŋkio]	English, ring
[ɲ]	**magnete** [ma'ɲete]	canyon, new
[p]	**pallone** [pal'lone]	pencil, private
[r]	**futuro** [fu'turo]	rice, radio
[s]	**triste** ['triste]	city, boss
[ʃ]	**piscina** [pi'ʃina]	machine, shark
[t]	**estintore** [estin'tore]	tourist, trip
[ʦ]	**spezie** ['spetsie]	cats, tsetse fly
[ʧ]	**lancia** ['lanʧa]	church, French
[v]	**volo** ['volo]	very, river
[w]	**whisky** ['wiski]	vase, winter
[z]	**deserto** [de'zerto]	zebra, please

ABBREVIATIONS
used in the vocabulary

English abbreviations

ab.	-	about
adj	-	adjective
adv	-	adverb
anim.	-	animate
as adj	-	attributive noun used as adjective
e.g.	-	for example
etc.	-	et cetera
fam.	-	familiar
fem.	-	feminine
form.	-	formal
inanim.	-	inanimate
masc.	-	masculine
math	-	mathematics
mil.	-	military
n	-	noun
pl	-	plural
pron.	-	pronoun
sb	-	somebody
sing.	-	singular
sth	-	something
v aux	-	auxiliary verb
vi	-	intransitive verb
vi, vt	-	intransitive, transitive verb
vt	-	transitive verb

Italian abbreviations

agg	-	adjective
f	-	feminine noun
f pl	-	feminine plural
m	-	masculine noun
m pl	-	masculine plural
m, f	-	masculine, feminine
pl	-	plural

v aus	-	auxiliary verb
vi	-	intransitive verb
vi, vt	-	intransitive, transitive verb
vr	-	reflexive verb
vt	-	transitive verb

BASIC CONCEPTS

Basic concepts. Part 1

1. Pronouns

I, me	**io**	['io]
you	**tu**	['tu]
he	**lui**	['luj]
she	**lei**	['lej]
we	**noi**	['noj]
you (to a group)	**voi**	['voi]
they	**loro, essi**	['loro], ['essi]

2. Greetings. Salutations. Farewells

Hello! (fam.)	**Buongiorno!**	[buon'ʤorno]
Hello! (form.)	**Salve!**	['salve]
Good morning!	**Buongiorno!**	[buon'ʤorno]
Good afternoon!	**Buon pomeriggio!**	[bu'on pome'riʤo]
Good evening!	**Buonasera!**	[buona'sera]
to say hello	**salutare** (vt)	[salu'tare]
Hi! (hello)	**Ciao! Salve!**	['ʧao], ['salve]
greeting (n)	**saluto** (m)	[sa'luto]
to greet (vt)	**salutare** (vt)	[salu'tare]
How are you?	**Come va?**	['kome 'va]
What's new?	**Che c'è di nuovo?**	[ke ʧe di nu'ovo]
Bye-Bye! Goodbye!	**Arrivederci!**	[arrive'derʧi]
See you soon!	**A presto!**	[a 'presto]
Farewell!	**Addio!**	[ad'dio]
to say goodbye	**congedarsi** (vr)	[konʤe'darsi]
So long!	**Ciao!**	['ʧao]
Thank you!	**Grazie!**	['gratsie]
Thank you very much!	**Grazie mille!**	['gratsie 'mille]
You're welcome	**Prego**	['prego]
Don't mention it!	**Non c'è di che!**	[non ʧe di 'ke]
It was nothing	**Di niente**	[di 'njente]
Excuse me! (fam.)	**Scusa!**	['skuza]

Excuse me! (form.)	**Scusi!**	['skuzi]
to excuse (forgive)	**scusare** (vt)	[sku'zare]
to apologize (vi)	**scusarsi** (vr)	[sku'zarsi]
My apologies	**Chiedo scusa**	['kjedo 'skuza]
I'm sorry!	**Mi perdoni!**	[mi per'doni]
to forgive (vt)	**perdonare** (vt)	[perdo'nare]
It's okay! (that's all right)	**Non fa niente**	[non fa 'njente]
please (adv)	**per favore**	[per fa'vore]
Don't forget!	**Non dimentichi!**	[non di'mentiki]
Certainly!	**Certamente!**	[ʧerta'mente]
Of course not!	**Certamente no!**	[ʧerta'mente no]
Okay! (I agree)	**D'accordo!**	[dak'kordo]
That's enough!	**Basta!**	['basta]

3. How to address

mister, sir	**signore**	[si'ɲore]
ma'am	**signora**	[si'ɲora]
miss	**signorina**	[siɲo'rina]
young man	**signore**	[si'ɲore]
young man (little boy, kid)	**ragazzo**	[ra'gattso]
miss (little girl)	**ragazza**	[ra'gattsa]

4. Cardinal numbers. Part 1

0 zero	**zero** (m)	['ʣero]
1 one	**uno**	['uno]
2 two	**due**	['due]
3 three	**tre**	['tre]
4 four	**quattro**	['kwattro]
5 five	**cinque**	['ʧinkwe]
6 six	**sei**	['sej]
7 seven	**sette**	['sette]
8 eight	**otto**	['otto]
9 nine	**nove**	['nove]
10 ten	**dieci**	['djeʧi]
11 eleven	**undici**	['undiʧi]
12 twelve	**dodici**	['dodiʧi]
13 thirteen	**tredici**	['trediʧi]
14 fourteen	**quattordici**	[kwat'tordiʧi]
15 fifteen	**quindici**	['kwindiʧi]
16 sixteen	**sedici**	['sediʧi]
17 seventeen	**diciassette**	[diʧas'sette]

18 eighteen	**diciotto**	[di'ʧotto]
19 nineteen	**diciannove**	[diʧan'nove]
20 twenty	**venti**	['venti]
21 twenty-one	**ventuno**	[ven'tuno]
22 twenty-two	**ventidue**	['venti 'due]
23 twenty-three	**ventitre**	['venti 'tre]
30 thirty	**trenta**	['trenta]
31 thirty-one	**trentuno**	[tren'tuno]
32 thirty-two	**trentadue**	[trenta 'due]
33 thirty-three	**trentatre**	[trenta 'tre]
40 forty	**quaranta**	[kwa'ranta]
41 forty-one	**quarantuno**	[kwa'rant'uno]
42 forty-two	**quarantadue**	[kwa'ranta 'due]
43 forty-three	**quarantatre**	[kwa'ranta 'tre]
50 fifty	**cinquanta**	[ʧin'kwanta]
51 fifty-one	**cinquantuno**	[ʧin'kwant'uno]
52 fifty-two	**cinquantadue**	[ʧin'kwanta 'due]
53 fifty-three	**cinquantatre**	[ʧin'kwanta 'tre]
60 sixty	**sessanta**	[ses'santa]
61 sixty-one	**sessantuno**	[sessan'tuno]
62 sixty-two	**sessantadue**	[ses'santa 'due]
63 sixty-three	**sessantatre**	[ses'santa 'tre]
70 seventy	**settanta**	[set'tanta]
71 seventy-one	**settantuno**	[settan'tuno]
72 seventy-two	**settantadue**	[set'tanta 'due]
73 seventy-three	**settantatre**	[set'tanta 'tre]
80 eighty	**ottanta**	[ot'tanta]
81 eighty-one	**ottantuno**	[ottan'tuno]
82 eighty-two	**ottantadue**	[ot'tanta 'due]
83 eighty-three	**ottantatre**	[ot'tanta 'tre]
90 ninety	**novanta**	[no'vanta]
91 ninety-one	**novantuno**	[novan'tuno]
92 ninety-two	**novantadue**	[no'vanta 'due]
93 ninety-three	**novantatre**	[no'vanta 'tre]

5. Cardinal numbers. Part 2

100 one hundred	**cento**	['ʧento]
200 two hundred	**duecento**	[due'ʧento]
300 three hundred	**trecento**	[tre'ʧento]
400 four hundred	**quattrocento**	[kwattro'ʧento]
500 five hundred	**cinquecento**	[ʧinkwe'ʧento]

600 six hundred	**seicento**	[sej'tʃento]
700 seven hundred	**settecento**	[sette'tʃento]
800 eight hundred	**ottocento**	[otto'tʃento]
900 nine hundred	**novecento**	[nove'tʃento]
1000 one thousand	**mille**	['mille]
2000 two thousand	**duemila**	[due'mila]
3000 three thousand	**tremila**	[tre'mila]
10000 ten thousand	**diecimila**	['djetʃi 'mila]
one hundred thousand	**centomila**	[tʃento'mila]
million	**milione** (m)	[mi'ljone]
billion	**miliardo** (m)	[mi'ljardo]

6. Ordinal numbers

first (adj)	**primo**	['primo]
second (adj)	**secondo**	[se'kondo]
third (adj)	**terzo**	['tertso]
fourth (adj)	**quarto**	['kwarto]
fifth (adj)	**quinto**	['kwinto]
sixth (adj)	**sesto**	['sesto]
seventh (adj)	**settimo**	['settimo]
eighth (adj)	**ottavo**	[ot'tavo]
ninth (adj)	**nono**	['nono]
tenth (adj)	**decimo**	['detʃimo]

7. Numbers. Fractions

fraction	**frazione** (f)	[fra'tsjone]
one half	**un mezzo**	[un 'meddzo]
one third	**un terzo**	[un 'tertso]
one quarter	**un quarto**	[un 'kwarto]
one eighth	**un ottavo**	[un ot'tavo]
one tenth	**un decimo**	[un 'detʃimo]
two thirds	**due terzi**	['due 'tertsi]
three quarters	**tre quarti**	[tre 'kwarti]

8. Numbers. Basic operations

subtraction	**sottrazione** (f)	[sottra'tsjone]
to subtract (vi, vt)	**sottrarre** (vt)	[sot'trarre]
division	**divisione** (f)	[divi'zjone]
to divide (vt)	**dividere** (vt)	[di'videre]
addition	**addizione** (f)	[addi'tsjone]

to add up (vt)	**addizionare** (vt)	[additsjo'nare]
to add (vi, vt)	**addizionare** (vt)	[additsjo'nare]
multiplication	**moltiplicazione** (f)	[moltiplika'tsjone]
to multiply (vt)	**moltiplicare** (vt)	[moltipli'kare]

9. Numbers. Miscellaneous

digit, figure	**cifra** (f)	['ʧifra]
number	**numero** (m)	['numero]
numeral	**numerale** (m)	[nume'rale]
minus sign	**meno** (m)	['meno]
plus sign	**più** (m)	['pju]
formula	**formula** (f)	['formula]
calculation	**calcolo** (m)	['kalkolo]
to count (vi, vt)	**contare** (vt)	[kon'tare]
to count up	**calcolare** (vt)	[kalko'lare]
to compare (vt)	**comparare** (vt)	[kompa'rare]
How much?	**Quanto?**	['kwanto]
How many?	**Quanti?**	['kwanti]
sum, total	**somma** (f)	['somma]
result	**risultato** (m)	[rizul'tato]
remainder	**resto** (m)	['resto]
a few (e.g., ~ years ago)	**qualche ...**	['kwalke]
little (I had ~ time)	**un po'di ...**	[un po di]
the rest	**resto** (m)	['resto]
one and a half	**uno e mezzo**	['uno e 'meddzo]
dozen	**dozzina** (f)	[dod'dzina]
in half (adv)	**in due**	[in 'due]
equally (evenly)	**in parti uguali**	[in 'parti u'gwali]
half	**metà** (f), **mezzo** (m)	[me'ta], ['meddzo]
time (three ~s)	**volta** (f)	['volta]

10. The most important verbs. Part 1

to advise (vt)	**consigliare** (vt)	[konsiʎ'ʎare]
to agree (say yes)	**essere d'accordo**	['essere dak'kordo]
to answer (vi, vt)	**rispondere** (vi, vt)	[ris'pondere]
to apologize (vi)	**scusarsi** (vr)	[sku'zarsi]
to arrive (vi)	**arrivare** (vi)	[arri'vare]
to ask (~ oneself)	**chiedere, domandare**	['kjedere], [doman'dare]
to ask (~ sb to do sth)	**chiedere, domandare**	['kjedere], [doman'dare]
to be (vi)	**essere** (vi)	['essere]

to be afraid	**avere paura**	[a'vere pa'ura]
to be hungry	**avere fame**	[a'vere 'fame]
to be interested in ...	**interessarsi di ...**	[interes'sarsi di]
to be needed	**occorrere**	[ok'korrere]
to be surprised	**stupirsi** (vr)	[stu'pirsi]
to be thirsty	**avere sete**	[a'vere 'sete]
to begin (vt)	**cominciare** (vt)	[komin'ʧare]
to belong to ...	**appartenere** (vi)	[apparte'nere]
to boast (vi)	**vantarsi** (vr)	[van'tarsi]
to break (split into pieces)	**rompere** (vt)	['rompere]
to call (~ for help)	**chiamare** (vt)	[kja'mare]
can (v aux)	**potere** (v aus)	[po'tere]
to catch (vt)	**afferrare** (vt)	[affer'rare]
to change (vt)	**cambiare** (vt)	[kam'bjare]
to choose (select)	**scegliere** (vt)	['ʃeʎʎere]
to come down (the stairs)	**scendere** (vi)	['ʃendere]
to compare (vt)	**comparare** (vt)	[kompa'rare]
to complain (vi, vt)	**lamentarsi** (vr)	[lamen'tarsi]
to confuse (mix up)	**confondere** (vt)	[kon'fondere]
to continue (vt)	**continuare** (vt)	[kontinu'are]
to control (vt)	**controllare** (vt)	[kontrol'lare]
to cook (dinner)	**cucinare** (vi)	[kuʧi'nare]
to cost (vt)	**costare** (vt)	[ko'stare]
to count (add up)	**contare** (vt)	[kon'tare]
to count on ...	**contare su ...**	[kon'tare su]
to create (vt)	**creare** (vt)	[kre'are]
to cry (weep)	**piangere** (vi)	['pjanʤere]

11. The most important verbs. Part 2

to deceive (vi, vt)	**ingannare** (vt)	[ingan'nare]
to decorate (tree, street)	**decorare** (vt)	[deko'rare]
to defend (a country, etc.)	**difendere** (vt)	[di'fendere]
to demand (request firmly)	**esigere** (vt)	[e'ziʤere]
to dig (vt)	**scavare** (vt)	[ska'vare]
to discuss (vt)	**discutere** (vt)	[di'skutere]
to do (vt)	**fare** (vt)	['fare]
to doubt (have doubts)	**dubitare** (vi)	[dubi'tare]
to drop (let fall)	**lasciar cadere**	[la'ʃar ka'dere]
to enter (room, house, etc.)	**entrare** (vi)	[en'trare]
to excuse (forgive)	**battaglia** (f)	[bat'taʎʎa]
to exist (vi)	**esistere** (vi)	[e'zistere]
to expect (foresee)	**prevedere** (vt)	[preve'dere]

to explain (vt)	**spiegare** (vt)	[spje'gare]
to fall (vi)	**cadere** (vi)	[ka'dere]
to find (vt)	**trovare** (vt)	[tro'vare]
to finish (vt)	**finire** (vt)	[fi'nire]
to fly (vi)	**volare** (vi)	[vo'lare]
to follow ... (come after)	**seguire** (vt)	[se'gwire]
to forget (vi, vt)	**dimenticare** (vt)	[dimenti'kare]
to forgive (vt)	**perdonare** (vt)	[perdo'nare]
to give (vt)	**dare** (vt)	['dare]
to give a hint	**dare un suggerimento**	[dare un sudʒeri'mento]
to go (on foot)	**andare** (vi)	[an'dare]
to go for a swim	**fare il bagno**	['fare il 'baɲo]
to go out (for dinner, etc.)	**uscire** (vi)	[u'ʃire]
to guess (the answer)	**indovinare** (vt)	[indovi'nare]
to have (vt)	**avere** (vt)	[a'vere]
to have breakfast	**fare colazione**	['fare kola'tsjone]
to have dinner	**cenare** (vi)	[ʧe'nare]
to have lunch	**pranzare** (vi)	[pran'tsare]
to hear (vt)	**sentire** (vt)	[sen'tire]
to help (vt)	**aiutare** (vt)	[aju'tare]
to hide (vt)	**nascondere** (vt)	[na'skondere]
to hope (vi, vt)	**sperare** (vi, vt)	[spe'rare]
to hunt (vi, vt)	**cacciare** (vt)	[ka'ʧare]
to hurry (vi)	**avere fretta**	[a'vere 'fretta]

12. The most important verbs. Part 3

to inform (vt)	**informare** (vt)	[infor'mare]
to insist (vi, vt)	**insistere** (vi)	[in'sistere]
to insult (vt)	**insultare** (vt)	[insul'tare]
to invite (vt)	**invitare** (vt)	[invi'tare]
to joke (vi)	**scherzare** (vi)	[sker'tsare]
to keep (vt)	**conservare** (vt)	[konser'vare]
to keep silent, to hush	**tacere** (vi)	[ta'ʧere]
to kill (vt)	**uccidere** (vt)	[u'ʧidere]
to know (sb)	**conoscere**	[ko'noʃere]
to know (sth)	**sapere** (vt)	[sa'pere]
to laugh (vi)	**ridere** (vi)	['ridere]
to liberate (city, etc.)	**liberare** (vt)	[libe'rare]
to like (I like ...)	**piacere** (vi)	[pja'ʧere]
to look for ... (search)	**cercare** (vt)	[ʧer'kare]
to love (sb)	**amare qn**	[a'mare]
to make a mistake	**sbagliare** (vi)	[zbaʎ'ʎare]

to manage, to run	**dirigere** (vt)	[di'ridʒere]
to mean (signify)	**significare** (vt)	[siɲifi'kare]
to mention (talk about)	**menzionare** (vt)	[mentsjo'nare]
to miss (school, etc.)	**mancare le lezioni**	[man'kare le le'tsjoni]
to notice (see)	**accorgersi** (vr)	[ak'kordʒersi]
to object (vi, vt)	**obiettare** (vt)	[objet'tare]
to observe (see)	**osservare** (vt)	[osser'vare]
to open (vt)	**aprire** (vt)	[a'prire]
to order (meal, etc.)	**ordinare** (vt)	[ordi'nare]
to order (mil.)	**ordinare** (vt)	[ordi'nare]
to own (possess)	**possedere** (vt)	[posse'dere]
to participate (vi)	**partecipare** (vi)	[partetʃi'pare]
to pay (vi, vt)	**pagare** (vi, vt)	[pa'gare]
to permit (vt)	**permettere** (vt)	[per'mettere]
to plan (vt)	**pianificare** (vt)	[pjanifi'kare]
to play (children)	**giocare** (vi)	[dʒo'kare]
to pray (vi, vt)	**pregare** (vi, vt)	[pre'gare]
to prefer (vt)	**preferire** (vt)	[prefe'rire]
to promise (vt)	**promettere** (vt)	[pro'mettere]
to pronounce (vt)	**pronunciare** (vt)	[pronun'tʃare]
to propose (vt)	**proporre** (vt)	[pro'porre]
to punish (vt)	**punire** (vt)	[pu'nire]

13. The most important verbs. Part 4

to read (vi, vt)	**leggere** (vi, vt)	['ledʒere]
to recommend (vt)	**raccomandare** (vt)	[rakkoman'dare]
to refuse (vi, vt)	**rifiutarsi** (vr)	[rifju'tarsi]
to regret (be sorry)	**rincrescere** (vi)	[rin'kreʃere]
to rent (sth from sb)	**affittare** (vt)	[affit'tare]
to repeat (say again)	**ripetere** (vt)	[ri'petere]
to reserve, to book	**riservare** (vt)	[rizer'vare]
to run (vi)	**correre** (vi)	['korrere]
to save (rescue)	**salvare** (vt)	[sal'vare]
to say (~ thank you)	**dire** (vt)	['dire]
to scold (vt)	**sgridare** (vt)	[zgri'dare]
to see (vt)	**vedere** (vt)	[ve'dere]
to sell (vt)	**vendere** (vt)	['vendere]
to send (vt)	**mandare** (vt)	[man'dare]
to shoot (vi)	**sparare** (vi)	[spa'rare]
to shout (vi)	**gridare** (vi)	[gri'dare]
to show (vt)	**mostrare** (vt)	[mo'strare]
to sign (document)	**firmare** (vt)	[fir'mare]
to sit down (vi)	**sedersi** (vr)	[se'dersi]

to smile (vi)	**sorridere** (vi)	[sor'ridere]
to speak (vi, vt)	**parlare** (vi, vt)	[par'lare]
to steal (money, etc.)	**rubare** (vt)	[ru'bare]
to stop (for pause, etc.)	**fermarsi** (vr)	[fer'marsi]
to stop (please ~ calling me)	**cessare** (vt)	[ʧes'sare]

to study (vt)	**studiare** (vt)	[stu'djare]
to swim (vi)	**nuotare** (vi)	[nuo'tare]
to take (vt)	**prendere** (vt)	['prendere]
to think (vi, vt)	**pensare** (vi, vt)	[pen'sare]
to threaten (vt)	**minacciare** (vt)	[mina'ʧare]

to touch (with hands)	**toccare** (vt)	[tok'kare]
to translate (vt)	**tradurre** (vt)	[tra'durre]
to trust (vt)	**fidarsi** (vr)	[fi'darsi]
to try (attempt)	**tentare** (vt)	[ten'tare]
to turn (e.g., ~ left)	**girare** (vi)	[ʤi'rare]

to underestimate (vt)	**sottovalutare** (vt)	[sottovalu'tare]
to understand (vt)	**capire** (vt)	[ka'pire]
to unite (vt)	**unire** (vt)	[u'nire]
to wait (vt)	**aspettare** (vt)	[aspet'tare]

to want (wish, desire)	**volere** (vt)	[vo'lere]
to warn (vt)	**avvertire** (vt)	[avver'tire]
to work (vi)	**lavorare** (vi)	[lavo'rare]
to write (vt)	**scrivere** (vt)	['skrivere]
to write down	**annotare** (vt)	[anno'tare]

14. Colors

color	**colore** (m)	[ko'lore]
shade (tint)	**sfumatura** (f)	[sfuma'tura]
hue	**tono** (m)	['tono]
rainbow	**arcobaleno** (m)	[arkoba'leno]

white (adj)	**bianco**	['bjanko]
black (adj)	**nero**	['nero]
gray (adj)	**grigio**	['griʤo]

green (adj)	**verde**	['verde]
yellow (adj)	**giallo**	['ʤallo]
red (adj)	**rosso**	['rosso]

blue (adj)	**blu**	['blu]
light blue (adj)	**azzurro**	[ad'ʣurro]
pink (adj)	**rosa**	['roza]
orange (adj)	**arancione**	[aran'ʧone]
violet (adj)	**violetto**	[vio'letto]

brown (adj)	**marrone**	[mar'rone]
golden (adj)	**d'oro**	['doro]
silvery (adj)	**argenteo**	[ar'dʒenteo]
beige (adj)	**beige**	[beʒ]
cream (adj)	**color crema**	[ko'lor 'krema]
turquoise (adj)	**turchese**	[tur'keze]
cherry red (adj)	**rosso ciliegia** (f)	['rosso ʧi'ljedʒa]
lilac (adj)	**lilla**	['lilla]
crimson (adj)	**rosso lampone**	['rosso lam'pone]
light (adj)	**chiaro**	['kjaro]
dark (adj)	**scuro**	['skuro]
bright, vivid (adj)	**vivo, vivido**	['vivo], ['vivido]
colored (pencils)	**colorato**	[kolo'rato]
color (e.g., ~ film)	**a colori**	[a ko'lori]
black-and-white (adj)	**bianco e nero**	['bjanko e 'nero]
plain (one-colored)	**in tinta unita**	[in 'tinta u'nita]
multicolored (adj)	**multicolore**	[multiko'lore]

15. Questions

Who?	**Chi?**	[ki]
What?	**Che cosa?**	[ke 'koza]
Where? (at, in)	**Dove?**	['dove]
Where (to)?	**Dove?**	['dove]
From where?	**Di dove?, Da dove?**	[di 'dove], [da 'dove]
When?	**Quando?**	['kwando]
Why? (What for?)	**Perché?**	[per'ke]
Why? (~ are you crying?)	**Perché?**	[per'ke]
What for?	**Per che cosa?**	[per ke 'koza]
How? (in what way)	**Come?**	['kome]
What? (What kind of ...?)	**Che?**	[ke]
Which?	**Quale?**	['kwale]
To whom?	**A chi?**	[a 'ki]
About whom?	**Di chi?**	[di 'ki]
About what?	**Di che cosa?**	[di ke 'koza]
With whom?	**Con chi?**	[kon 'ki]
How many?	**Quanti?**	['kwanti]
How much?	**Quanto?**	['kwanto]
Whose?	**Di chi?**	[di 'ki]

16. Prepositions

with (accompanied by)	**con**	[kon]
without	**senza**	['sentsa]

to (indicating direction)	**a**	[a]
about (talking ~ ...)	**di**	[di]
before (in time)	**prima di ...**	['prima di]
in front of ...	**di fronte a ...**	[di 'fronte a]
under (beneath, below)	**sotto**	['sotto]
above (over)	**sopra**	['sopra]
on (atop)	**su**	[su]
from (off, out of)	**da, di**	[da], [di]
of (made from)	**di**	[di]
in (e.g., ~ ten minutes)	**fra ...**	[fra]
over (across the top of)	**attraverso**	[attra'verso]

17. Function words. Adverbs. Part 1

Where? (at, in)	**Dove?**	['dove]
here (adv)	**qui**	[kwi]
there (adv)	**lì**	[li]
somewhere (to be)	**da qualche parte**	[da 'kwalke 'parte]
nowhere (not in any place)	**da nessuna parte**	[da nes'suna 'parte]
by (near, beside)	**vicino a ...**	[vi'ʧino a]
by the window	**vicino alla finestra**	[vi'ʧino 'alla fi'nestra]
Where (to)?	**Dove?**	['dove]
here (e.g., come ~!)	**di qui**	[di kwi]
there (e.g., to go ~)	**ci**	[ʧi]
from here (adv)	**da qui**	[da kwi]
from there (adv)	**da lì**	[da 'li]
close (adv)	**vicino, accanto**	[vi'ʧino], [a'kanto]
far (adv)	**lontano**	[lon'tano]
near (e.g., ~ Paris)	**vicino a ...**	[vi'ʧino a]
nearby (adv)	**vicino**	[vi'ʧino]
not far (adv)	**non lontano**	[non lon'tano]
left (adj)	**sinistro**	[si'nistro]
on the left	**a sinistra**	[a si'nistra]
to the left	**a sinistra**	[a si'nistra]
right (adj)	**destro**	['destro]
on the right	**a destra**	[a 'destra]
to the right	**a destra**	[a 'destra]
in front (adv)	**davanti**	[da'vanti]
front (as adj)	**anteriore**	[ante'rjore]
ahead (the kids ran ~)	**avanti**	[a'vanti]

behind (adv)	**dietro**	['djetro]
from behind	**da dietro**	[da 'djetro]
back (towards the rear)	**indietro**	[in'djetro]
middle	**mezzo** (m), **centro** (m)	['meddzo], ['tʃentro]
in the middle	**in mezzo, al centro**	[in 'meddzo], [al 'tʃentro]
at the side	**di fianco**	[di 'fjanko]
everywhere (adv)	**dappertutto**	[dapper'tutto]
around (in all directions)	**attorno**	[at'torno]
from inside	**da dentro**	[da 'dentro]
somewhere (to go)	**da qualche parte**	[da 'kwalke 'parte]
straight (directly)	**dritto**	['dritto]
back (e.g., come ~)	**indietro**	[in'djetro]
from anywhere	**da qualsiasi parte**	[da kwal'siazi 'parte]
from somewhere	**da qualche posto**	[da 'kwalke 'posto]
firstly (adv)	**in primo luogo**	[in 'primo lu'ogo]
secondly (adv)	**in secondo luogo**	[in se'kondo lu'ogo]
thirdly (adv)	**in terzo luogo**	[in 'tertso lu'ogo]
suddenly (adv)	**all'improvviso**	[all improv'vizo]
at first (in the beginning)	**all'inizio**	[all i'nitsio]
for the first time	**per la prima volta**	[per la 'prima 'volta]
long before ...	**molto tempo prima di ...**	['molto 'tempo 'prima di]
anew (over again)	**di nuovo**	[di nu'ovo]
for good (adv)	**per sempre**	[per 'sempre]
never (adv)	**mai**	[maj]
again (adv)	**ancora**	[an'kora]
now (at present)	**adesso**	[a'desso]
often (adv)	**spesso**	['spesso]
then (adv)	**allora**	[al'lora]
urgently (quickly)	**urgentemente**	[urdʒente'mente]
usually (adv)	**di solito**	[di 'solito]
by the way, ...	**a proposito, ...**	[a pro'pozito]
possibly	**è possibile**	[e pos'sibile]
probably (adv)	**probabilmente**	[probabil'mente]
maybe (adv)	**forse**	['forse]
besides ...	**inoltre ...**	[i'noltre]
that's why ...	**ecco perché ...**	['ekko per'ke]
in spite of ...	**nonostante**	[nono'stante]
thanks to ...	**grazie a ...**	['gratsie a]
what (pron.)	**che cosa**	[ke 'koza]
that (conj.)	**che**	[ke]
something	**qualcosa**	[kwal'koza]
anything (something)	**qualcosa**	[kwal'koza]
nothing	**niente**	['njente]

who (pron.)	**chi**	[ki]
someone	**qualcuno**	[kwal'kuno]
somebody	**qualcuno**	[kwal'kuno]
nobody	**nessuno**	[nes'suno]
nowhere (a voyage to ~)	**da nessuna parte**	[da nes'suna 'parte]
nobody's	**di nessuno**	[di nes'suno]
somebody's	**di qualcuno**	[di kwal'kuno]
so (I'm ~ glad)	**così**	[ko'zi]
also (as well)	**anche**	['aŋke]
too (as well)	**anche, pure**	['aŋke], ['pure]

18. Function words. Adverbs. Part 2

Why?	**Perché?**	[per'ke]
for some reason	**per qualche ragione**	[per 'kwalke ra'ʤone]
because ...	**perché ...**	[per'ke]
for some purpose	**per qualche motivo**	[per 'kwalke mo'tivo]
and	**e**	[e]
or	**o ...**	[o]
but	**ma**	[ma]
for (e.g., ~ me)	**per**	[per]
too (~ many people)	**troppo**	['troppo]
only (exclusively)	**solo**	['solo]
exactly (adv)	**esattamente**	[ezatta'mente]
about (more or less)	**circa**	['ʧirka]
approximately (adv)	**approssimativamente**	[approsimativa'mente]
approximate (adj)	**approssimativo**	[approssima'tivo]
almost (adv)	**quasi**	['kwazi]
the rest	**resto** (m)	['resto]
each (adj)	**ogni**	['oɲi]
any (no matter which)	**qualsiasi**	[kwal'siazi]
many (adj)	**molti**	['molti]
much (adv)	**molto**	['molto]
many people	**molta gente**	['molta 'ʤente]
all (everyone)	**tutto, tutti**	['tutto], ['tutti]
in return for ...	**in cambio di ...**	[in 'kambio di]
in exchange (adv)	**in cambio**	[in 'kambio]
by hand (made)	**a mano**	[a 'mano]
hardly (negative opinion)	**poco probabile**	['poko pro'babile]
probably (adv)	**probabilmente**	[probabil'mente]
on purpose (intentionally)	**apposta**	[ap'posta]
by accident (adv)	**per caso**	[per 'kazo]

very (adv)	**molto**	['molto]
for example (adv)	**per esempio**	[per e'zempjo]
between	**fra**	[fra]
among	**fra**	[fra]
so much (such a lot)	**tanto**	['tanto]
especially (adv)	**soprattutto**	[sopra'tutto]

Basic concepts. Part 2

19. Weekdays

Monday	**lunedì** (m)	[lune'di]
Tuesday	**martedì** (m)	[marte'di]
Wednesday	**mercoledì** (m)	[merkole'di]
Thursday	**giovedì** (m)	[dʒove'di]
Friday	**venerdì** (m)	[vener'di]
Saturday	**sabato** (m)	['sabato]
Sunday	**domenica** (f)	[do'menika]
today (adv)	**oggi**	['odʒi]
tomorrow (adv)	**domani**	[do'mani]
the day after tomorrow	**dopodomani**	[dopodo'mani]
yesterday (adv)	**ieri**	['jeri]
the day before yesterday	**l'altro ieri**	['laltro 'jeri]
day	**giorno** (m)	['dʒorno]
working day	**giorno** (m) **lavorativo**	['dʒorno lavora'tivo]
public holiday	**giorno** (m) **festivo**	['dʒorno fes'tivo]
day off	**giorno** (m) **di riposo**	['dʒorno di ri'pozo]
weekend	**fine** (m) **settimana**	['fine setti'mana]
all day long	**tutto il giorno**	['tutto il 'dʒorno]
the next day (adv)	**l'indomani**	[lindo'mani]
two days ago	**due giorni fa**	['due 'dʒorni fa]
the day before	**il giorno prima**	[il 'dʒorno 'prima]
daily (adj)	**quotidiano**	[kwoti'djano]
every day (adv)	**ogni giorno**	['oɲi 'dʒorno]
week	**settimana** (f)	[setti'mana]
last week (adv)	**la settimana scorsa**	[la setti'mana 'skorsa]
next week (adv)	**la settimana prossima**	[la setti'mana 'prossima]
weekly (adj)	**settimanale**	[settima'nale]
every week (adv)	**ogni settimana**	['oɲi setti'mana]
twice a week	**due volte alla settimana**	['due 'volte 'alla setti'mana]
every Tuesday	**ogni martedì**	['oɲi marte'di]

20. Hours. Day and night

morning	**mattina** (f)	[mat'tina]
in the morning	**di mattina**	[di mat'tina]

noon, midday	**mezzogiorno** (m)	[meddzo'dʒorno]
in the afternoon	**nel pomeriggio**	[nel pome'ridʒo]
evening	**sera** (f)	['sera]
in the evening	**di sera**	[di 'sera]
night	**notte** (f)	['notte]
at night	**di notte**	[di 'notte]
midnight	**mezzanotte** (f)	[meddza'notte]
second	**secondo** (m)	[se'kondo]
minute	**minuto** (m)	[mi'nuto]
hour	**ora** (f)	['ora]
half an hour	**mezzora** (f)	[med'dzora]
a quarter-hour	**un quarto d'ora**	[un 'kwarto 'dora]
fifteen minutes	**quindici minuti**	['kwinditʃi mi'nuti]
24 hours	**ventiquattro ore**	[venti'kwattro 'ore]
sunrise	**levata** (f) **del sole**	[le'vata del 'sole]
dawn	**alba** (f)	['alba]
early morning	**mattutino** (m)	[mattu'tino]
sunset	**tramonto** (m)	[tra'monto]
early in the morning	**di buon mattino**	[di bu'on mat'tino]
this morning	**stamattina**	[stamat'tina]
tomorrow morning	**domattina**	[domat'tina]
this afternoon	**oggi pomeriggio**	['odʒi pome'ridʒo]
in the afternoon	**nel pomeriggio**	[nel pome'ridʒo]
tomorrow afternoon	**domani pomeriggio**	[do'mani pome'ridʒo]
tonight (this evening)	**stasera**	[sta'sera]
tomorrow night	**domani sera**	[do'mani 'sera]
at 3 o'clock sharp	**alle tre precise**	['alle tre pre'tʃize]
about 4 o'clock	**verso le quattro**	['verso le 'kwattro]
by 12 o'clock	**per le dodici**	[per le 'doditʃi]
in 20 minutes	**fra venti minuti**	[fra 'venti mi'nuti]
in an hour	**fra un'ora**	[fra un 'ora]
on time (adv)	**puntualmente**	[puntual'mente]
a quarter to ...	**un quarto di ...**	[un 'kwarto di]
within an hour	**entro un'ora**	['entro un 'ora]
every 15 minutes	**ogni quindici minuti**	['oɲi 'kwinditʃi mi'nuti]
round the clock	**giorno e notte**	['dʒorno e 'notte]

21. Months. Seasons

January	**gennaio** (m)	[dʒen'najo]
February	**febbraio** (m)	[feb'brajo]

March	**marzo** (m)	['martso]
April	**aprile** (m)	[a'prile]
May	**maggio** (m)	['madʒo]
June	**giugno** (m)	['dʒuɲo]
July	**luglio** (m)	['luʎʎo]
August	**agosto** (m)	[a'gosto]
September	**settembre** (m)	[set'tembre]
October	**ottobre** (m)	[ot'tobre]
November	**novembre** (m)	[no'vembre]
December	**dicembre** (m)	[di'tʃembre]
spring	**primavera** (f)	[prima'vera]
in spring	**in primavera**	[in prima'vera]
spring (as adj)	**primaverile**	[primave'rile]
summer	**estate** (f)	[e'state]
in summer	**in estate**	[in e'state]
summer (as adj)	**estivo**	[e'stivo]
fall	**autunno** (m)	[au'tunno]
in fall	**in autunno**	[in au'tunno]
fall (as adj)	**autunnale**	[autun'nale]
winter	**inverno** (m)	[in'verno]
in winter	**in inverno**	[in in'verno]
winter (as adj)	**invernale**	[inver'nale]
month	**mese** (m)	['meze]
this month	**questo mese**	['kwesto 'meze]
next month	**il mese prossimo**	[il 'meze 'prossimo]
last month	**il mese scorso**	[il 'meze 'skorso]
a month ago	**un mese fa**	[un 'meze fa]
in a month (a month later)	**fra un mese**	[fra un 'meze]
in 2 months (2 months later)	**fra due mesi**	[fra 'due 'mezi]
the whole month	**un mese intero**	[un 'meze in'tero]
all month long	**per tutto il mese**	[per 'tutto il 'meze]
monthly (~ magazine)	**mensile**	[men'sile]
monthly (adv)	**mensilmente**	[mensil'mente]
every month	**ogni mese**	['oɲi 'meze]
twice a month	**due volte al mese**	['due 'volte al 'meze]
year	**anno** (m)	['anno]
this year	**quest'anno**	[kwest'anno]
next year	**l'anno prossimo**	['lanno 'prossimo]
last year	**l'anno scorso**	['lanno 'skorso]
a year ago	**un anno fa**	[un 'anno fa]
in a year	**fra un anno**	[fra un 'anno]

in two years	**fra due anni**	[fra 'due 'anni]
the whole year	**un anno intero**	[un 'anno in'tero]
all year long	**per tutto l'anno**	[per 'tutto 'lanno]
every year	**ogni anno**	['oɲi 'anno]
annual (adj)	**annuale**	[annu'ale]
annually (adv)	**annualmente**	[annual'mente]
4 times a year	**quattro volte all'anno**	['kwattro 'volte all 'anno]
date (e.g., today's ~)	**data** (f)	['data]
date (e.g., ~ of birth)	**data** (f)	['data]
calendar	**calendario** (m)	[kalen'dario]
half a year	**mezz'anno** (m)	[med'dzanno]
six months	**semestre** (m)	[se'mestre]
season (summer, etc.)	**stagione** (f)	[sta'dʒone]
century	**secolo** (m)	['sekolo]

22. Time. Miscellaneous

time	**tempo** (m)	['tempo]
moment	**istante** (m)	[i'stante]
instant (n)	**momento** (m)	[mo'mento]
instant (adj)	**istantaneo**	[istan'taneo]
lapse (of time)	**periodo** (m)	[pe'riodo]
life	**vita** (f)	['vita]
eternity	**eternità** (f)	[eterni'ta]
epoch	**epoca** (f)	['epoka]
era	**era** (f)	['era]
cycle	**ciclo** (m)	['tʃiklo]
period	**periodo** (m)	[pe'riodo]
term (short-~)	**scadenza** (f)	[ska'dentsa]
the future	**futuro** (m)	[fu'turo]
future (as adj)	**futuro**	[fu'turo]
next time	**la prossima volta**	[la 'prossima 'volta]
the past	**passato** (m)	[pas'sato]
past (recent)	**scorso**	['skorso]
last time	**la volta scorsa**	[la 'volta 'skorsa]
later (adv)	**più tardi**	[pju 'tardi]
after (prep.)	**dopo**	['dopo]
nowadays (adv)	**oggigiorno**	[odʒi'dʒorno]
now (at this moment)	**adesso, ora**	[a'desso], [ora]
immediately (adv)	**subito**	['subito]
soon (adv)	**fra poco, presto**	[fra 'poko], ['presto]
in advance (beforehand)	**in anticipo**	[in an'titʃipo]
a long time ago	**tanto tempo fa**	['tanto 'tempo fa]
recently (adv)	**di recente**	[di re'tʃente]

destiny	**destino** (m)	[de'stino]
memories (childhood ~)	**ricordi** (m pl)	[ri'kordi]
archives	**archivio** (m)	[ar'kiwio]
during ...	**durante ...**	[du'rante]
long, a long time (adv)	**a lungo**	[a 'lungo]
not long (adv)	**per poco tempo**	[per 'poko 'tempo]
early (in the morning)	**presto**	['presto]
late (not early)	**tardi**	['tardi]
forever (for good)	**per sempre**	[per 'sempre]
to start (begin)	**cominciare** (vt)	[komin'ʧare]
to postpone (vt)	**posticipare** (vt)	[postiʧi'pare]
at the same time	**simultaneamente**	[simultanea'mento]
permanently (adv)	**tutto il tempo**	['tutto il 'tempo]
constant (noise, pain)	**costante**	[ko'stante]
temporary (adj)	**temporaneo**	[tempo'raneo]
sometimes (adv)	**a volte**	[a 'volte]
rarely (adv)	**raramente**	[rara'mente]
often (adv)	**spesso**	['spesso]

23. Opposites

rich (adj)	**ricco**	['rikko]
poor (adj)	**povero**	['povero]
ill, sick (adj)	**malato**	[ma'lato]
well (not sick)	**sano**	['sano]
big (adj)	**grande**	['grande]
small (adj)	**piccolo**	['pikkolo]
quickly (adv)	**rapidamente**	[rapida'mente]
slowly (adv)	**lentamente**	[lenta'mente]
fast (adj)	**veloce**	[ve'loʧe]
slow (adj)	**lento**	['lento]
glad (adj)	**allegro**	[al'legro]
sad (adj)	**triste**	['triste]
together (adv)	**insieme**	[in'sjeme]
separately (adv)	**separatamente**	[separata'mente]
aloud (to read)	**ad alta voce**	[ad 'alta 'voʧe]
silently (to oneself)	**in silenzio**	[in si'lentsio]
tall (adj)	**alto**	['alto]
low (adj)	**basso**	['basso]

deep (adj)	**profondo**	[pro'fondo]
shallow (adj)	**basso**	['basso]
yes	**sì**	[si]
no	**no**	[no]
distant (in space)	**lontano**	[lon'tano]
nearby (adj)	**vicino**	[vi'tʃino]
far (adv)	**lontano**	[lon'tano]
nearby (adv)	**vicino**	[vi'tʃino]
long (adj)	**lungo**	['lungo]
short (adj)	**corto**	['korto]
good (kindhearted)	**buono**	[bu'ono]
evil (adj)	**cattivo**	[kat'tivo]
married (adj)	**sposato**	[spo'zato]
single (adj)	**celibe**	['tʃelibe]
to forbid (vt)	**vietare** (vt)	[vje'tare]
to permit (vt)	**permettere** (vt)	[per'mettere]
end	**fine** (f)	['fine]
beginning	**inizio** (m)	[i'nitsio]
left (adj)	**sinistro**	[si'nistro]
right (adj)	**destro**	['destro]
first (adj)	**primo**	['primo]
last (adj)	**ultimo**	['ultimo]
crime	**delitto** (m)	[de'litto]
punishment	**punizione** (f)	[puni'tsjone]
to order (vt)	**ordinare** (vt)	[ordi'nare]
to obey (vi, vt)	**obbedire** (vi)	[obbe'dire]
straight (adj)	**dritto**	['dritto]
curved (adj)	**curvo**	['kurvo]
paradise	**paradiso** (m)	[para'dizo]
hell	**inferno** (m)	[in'ferno]
to be born	**nascere** (vi)	['naʃere]
to die (vi)	**morire** (vi)	[mo'rire]
strong (adj)	**forte**	['forte]
weak (adj)	**debole**	['debole]
old (adj)	**vecchio**	['vekkio]
young (adj)	**giovane**	['dʒovane]

old (adj)	**vecchio**	['vekkio]
new (adj)	**nuovo**	[nu'ovo]
hard (adj)	**duro**	['duro]
soft (adj)	**morbido**	['morbido]
warm (tepid)	**caldo**	['kaldo]
cold (adj)	**freddo**	['freddo]
fat (adj)	**grasso**	['grasso]
thin (adj)	**magro**	['magro]
narrow (adj)	**stretto**	['stretto]
wide (adj)	**largo**	['largo]
good (adj)	**buono**	[bu'ono]
bad (adj)	**cattivo**	[kat'tivo]
brave (adj)	**valoroso**	[valo'rozo]
cowardly (adj)	**codardo**	[ko'dardo]

24. Lines and shapes

square	**quadrato** (m)	[kwa'drato]
square (as adj)	**quadrato**	[kwa'drato]
circle	**cerchio** (m)	['ʧerkio]
round (adj)	**rotondo**	[ro'tondo]
triangle	**triangolo** (m)	[tri'angolo]
triangular (adj)	**triangolare**	[triango'lare]
oval	**ovale** (m)	[o'vale]
oval (as adj)	**ovale**	[o'vale]
rectangle	**rettangolo** (m)	[ret'tangolo]
rectangular (adj)	**rettangolare**	[rettango'lare]
pyramid	**piramide** (f)	[pi'ramide]
rhombus	**rombo** (m)	['rombo]
trapezoid	**trapezio** (m)	[tra'petsio]
cube	**cubo** (m)	['kubo]
prism	**prisma** (m)	['prizma]
circumference	**circonferenza** (f)	[ʧirkonfe'rentsa]
sphere	**sfera** (f)	['sfera]
ball (solid sphere)	**palla** (f)	['palla]
diameter	**diametro** (m)	[di'ametro]
radius	**raggio** (m)	['raʤo]
perimeter (circle's ~)	**perimetro** (m)	[pe'rimetro]
center	**centro** (m)	['ʧentro]
horizontal (adj)	**orizzontale**	[oriddzon'tale]
vertical (adj)	**verticale**	[verti'kale]

parallel (n)	**parallela** (f)	[paral'lela]
parallel (as adj)	**parallelo**	[paral'lelo]
line	**linea** (f)	['linea]
stroke	**tratto** (m)	['tratto]
straight line	**linea** (f) **retta**	['linea 'retta]
curve (curved line)	**linea** (f) **curva**	['linea 'kurva]
thin (line, etc.)	**sottile**	[sot'tile]
contour (outline)	**contorno** (m)	[kon'torno]
intersection	**intersezione** (f)	[interse'tsjone]
right angle	**angolo** (m) **retto**	['angolo 'retto]
segment	**segmento**	[seg'mento]
sector (circular ~)	**settore** (m)	[set'tore]
side (of triangle)	**lato** (m)	['lato]
angle	**angolo** (m)	['angolo]

25. Units of measurement

weight	**peso** (m)	['pezo]
length	**lunghezza** (f)	[lun'gettsa]
width	**larghezza** (f)	[lar'gettsa]
height	**altezza** (f)	[al'tettsa]
depth	**profondità** (f)	[profondi'ta]
volume	**volume** (m)	[vo'lume]
area	**area** (f)	['area]
gram	**grammo** (m)	['grammo]
milligram	**milligrammo** (m)	[milli'grammo]
kilogram	**chilogrammo** (m)	[kilo'grammo]
ton	**tonnellata** (f)	[tonnel'lata]
pound	**libbra** (f)	['libbra]
ounce	**oncia** (f)	['ontʃa]
meter	**metro** (m)	['metro]
millimeter	**millimetro** (m)	[mil'limetro]
centimeter	**centimetro** (m)	[tʃen'timetro]
kilometer	**chilometro** (m)	[ki'lometro]
mile	**miglio** (m)	['miʎʎo]
inch	**pollice** (m)	['pollitʃe]
foot	**piede** (f)	['pjede]
yard	**iarda** (f)	[jarda]
square meter	**metro** (m) **quadro**	['metro 'kwadro]
hectare	**ettaro** (m)	['ettaro]
liter	**litro** (m)	['litro]
degree	**grado** (m)	['grado]
volt	**volt** (m)	[volt]

ampere	**ampere** (m)	[am'pere]
horsepower	**cavallo vapore** (m)	[ka'vallo va'pore]
quantity	**quantità** (f)	[kwanti'ta]
a little bit of ...	**un po'di ...**	[un po di]
half	**metà** (f)	[me'ta]
dozen	**dozzina** (f)	[dod'dzina]
piece (item)	**pezzo** (m)	['pettso]
size	**dimensione** (f)	[dimen'sjone]
scale (map ~)	**scala** (f)	['skala]
minimal (adj)	**minimo**	['minimo]
the smallest (adj)	**minore**	[mi'nore]
medium (adj)	**medio**	['medio]
maximal (adj)	**massimo**	['massimo]
the largest (adj)	**maggiore**	[ma'dʒore]

26. Containers

canning jar (glass ~)	**barattolo** (m) **di vetro**	[ba'rattolo di 'vetro]
can	**latta** (f), **lattina** (f)	['latta], [lat'tina]
bucket	**secchio** (m)	['sekkio]
barrel	**barile** (m), **botte** (f)	[ba'rile], ['botte]
wash basin (e.g., plastic ~)	**catino** (m)	[ka'tino]
tank (100L water ~)	**serbatoio** (m)	[serba'tojo]
hip flask	**fiaschetta** (f)	[fias'ketta]
jerrycan	**tanica** (f)	['tanika]
tank (e.g., tank car)	**cisterna** (f)	[tʃi'sterna]
mug	**tazza** (f)	['tattsa]
cup (of coffee, etc.)	**tazzina** (f)	[tat'tsina]
saucer	**piattino** (m)	[pjat'tino]
glass (tumbler)	**bicchiere** (m)	[bik'kjere]
wine glass	**calice** (m)	['kalitʃe]
stock pot (soup pot)	**casseruola** (f)	[kasseru'ola]
bottle (~ of wine)	**bottiglia** (f)	[bot'tiʎʎa]
neck (of the bottle, etc.)	**collo** (m)	['kollo]
carafe (decanter)	**caraffa** (f)	[ka'raffa]
pitcher	**brocca** (f)	['brokka]
vessel (container)	**recipiente** (m)	[retʃi'pjente]
pot (crock, stoneware ~)	**vaso** (m) **di coccio**	['vazo di 'kotʃo]
vase	**vaso** (m)	['vazo]
flacon, bottle (perfume ~)	**boccetta** (f)	[bo'tʃetta]
vial, small bottle	**fiala** (f)	[fi'ala]

tube (of toothpaste)	**tubetto** (m)	[tu'betto]
sack (bag)	**sacco** (m)	['sakko]
bag (paper ~, plastic ~)	**sacchetto** (m)	[sak'ketto]
pack (of cigarettes, etc.)	**pacchetto** (m)	[pak'ketto]
box (e.g., shoebox)	**scatola** (f)	['skatola]
crate	**cassa** (f)	['kassa]
basket	**cesta** (f)	['ʧesta]

27. Materials

material	**materiale** (m)	[mate'rjale]
wood (n)	**legno** (m)	['leɲo]
wood-, wooden (adj)	**di legno**	[di 'leɲo]
glass (n)	**vetro** (m)	['vetro]
glass (as adj)	**di vetro**	[di 'vetro]
stone (n)	**pietra** (f)	['pjetra]
stone (as adj)	**di pietra**	[di 'pjetra]
plastic (n)	**plastica** (f)	['plastika]
plastic (as adj)	**di plastica**	[di 'plastika]
rubber (n)	**gomma** (f)	['gomma]
rubber (as adj)	**di gomma**	[di 'gomma]
cloth, fabric (n)	**stoffa** (f)	['stoffa]
fabric (as adj)	**di stoffa**	[di 'stoffa]
paper (n)	**carta** (f)	['karta]
paper (as adj)	**di carta**	[di 'karta]
cardboard (n)	**cartone** (m)	[kar'tone]
cardboard (as adj)	**di cartone**	[di kar'tone]
polyethylene	**polietilene** (m)	[polieti'lene]
cellophane	**cellofan** (m)	['ʧellofan]
linoleum	**linoleum** (m)	[li'noleum]
plywood	**legno** (m) **compensato**	['leɲo kompen'sato]
porcelain (n)	**porcellana** (f)	[porʧel'lana]
porcelain (as adj)	**di porcellana**	[di porʧel'lana]
clay (n)	**argilla** (f)	[ar'ʤilla]
clay (as adj)	**d'argilla**	[dar'ʤilla]
ceramic (n)	**ceramica** (f)	[ʧe'ramika]
ceramic (as adj)	**ceramico**	[ʧe'ramiko]

28. Metals

metal (n)	**metallo** (m)	[me'tallo]
metal (as adj)	**metallico**	[me'talliko]
alloy (n)	**lega** (f)	['lega]
gold (n)	**oro** (m)	['oro]
gold, golden (adj)	**d'oro**	['doro]
silver (n)	**argento** (m)	[ar'ʤento]
silver (as adj)	**d'argento**	[dar'ʤento]
iron (n)	**ferro** (m)	['ferro]
iron-, made of iron (adj)	**di ferro**	[di 'ferro]
steel (n)	**acciaio** (m)	[a'ʧajo]
steel (as adj)	**d'acciaio**	[da'ʧajo]
copper (n)	**rame** (m)	['rame]
copper (as adj)	**di rame**	[di 'rame]
aluminum (n)	**alluminio** (m)	[allu'minio]
aluminum (as adj)	**di alluminio**	[allu'minio]
bronze (n)	**bronzo** (m)	['bronʣo]
bronze (as adj)	**di bronzo**	[di 'bronʣo]
brass	**ottone** (m)	[ot'tone]
nickel	**nichel** (m)	['nikel]
platinum	**platino** (m)	['platino]
mercury	**mercurio** (m)	[mer'kurio]
tin	**stagno** (m)	['staɲo]
lead	**piombo** (m)	['pjombo]
zinc	**zinco** (m)	['ʣinko]

HUMAN BEING

Human being. The body

29. Humans. Basic concepts

human being	**uomo** (m), **essere umano** (m)	[u'omo], ['essere u'mano]
man (adult male)	**uomo** (m)	[u'omo]
woman	**donna** (f)	['donna]
child	**bambino** (m)	[bam'bino]
girl	**bambina** (f)	[bam'bina]
boy	**bambino** (m)	[bam'bino]
teenager	**adolescente** (m, f)	[adole'ʃente]
old man	**vecchio** (m)	['vekkio]
old woman	**vecchia** (f)	['vekkia]

30. Human anatomy

organism (body)	**organismo** (m)	[orga'nizmo]
heart	**cuore** (m)	[ku'ore]
blood	**sangue** (m)	['sangue]
artery	**arteria** (f)	[ar'teria]
vein	**vena** (f)	['vena]
brain	**cervello** (m)	[tʃer'vello]
nerve	**nervo** (m)	['nervo]
nerves	**nervi** (m pl)	['nervi]
vertebra	**vertebra** (f)	['vertebra]
spine (backbone)	**colonna** (f) **vertebrale**	[ko'lonna verte'brale]
stomach (organ)	**stomaco** (m)	['stomako]
intestines, bowels	**intestini** (m pl)	[inte'stini]
intestine (e.g., large ~)	**intestino** (m)	[inte'stino]
liver	**fegato** (m)	['fegato]
kidney	**rene** (m)	['rene]
bone	**osso** (m)	['osso]
skeleton	**scheletro** (m)	['skeletro]
rib	**costola** (f)	['kostola]
skull	**cranio** (m)	['kranio]
muscle	**muscolo** (m)	['muskolo]

biceps	**bicipite** (m)	[bitʃi'pite]
triceps	**tricipite** (m)	[tritʃi'pite]
tendon	**tendine** (m)	['tendine]
joint	**articolazione** (f)	[artikola'tsjone]
lungs	**polmoni** (m pl)	[pol'moni]
genitals	**genitali** (m pl)	[dʒeni'tali]
skin	**pelle** (f)	['pelle]

31. Head

head	**testa** (f)	['testa]
face	**viso** (m)	['vizo]
nose	**naso** (m)	['nazo]
mouth	**bocca** (f)	['bokka]
eye	**occhio** (m)	['okkio]
eyes	**occhi** (m pl)	['okki]
pupil	**pupilla** (f)	[pu'pilla]
eyebrow	**sopracciglio** (m)	[sopra'tʃiʎʎo]
eyelash	**ciglio** (m)	['tʃiʎʎo]
eyelid	**palpebra** (f)	['palpebra]
tongue	**lingua** (f)	['lingua]
tooth	**dente** (m)	['dente]
lips	**labbra** (f pl)	['labbra]
cheekbones	**zigomi** (m pl)	['dzigomi]
gum	**gengiva** (f)	[dʒen'dʒiva]
palate	**palato** (m)	[pa'lato]
nostrils	**narici** (f pl)	[na'ritʃi]
chin	**mento** (m)	['mento]
jaw	**mascella** (f)	[ma'ʃella]
cheek	**guancia** (f)	['gwantʃa]
forehead	**fronte** (f)	['fronte]
temple	**tempia** (f)	['tempia]
ear	**orecchio** (m)	[o'rekkio]
back of the head	**nuca** (f)	['nuka]
neck	**collo** (m)	['kollo]
throat	**gola** (f)	['gola]
hair	**capelli** (m pl)	[ka'pelli]
hairstyle	**pettinatura** (f)	[pettina'tura]
haircut	**taglio** (m)	['taʎʎo]
wig	**parrucca** (f)	['parrukka]
mustache	**baffi** (m pl)	['baffi]
beard	**barba** (f)	['barba]
to have (a beard, etc.)	**portare** (vt)	[por'tare]

braid	**treccia** (f)	['tretʃa]
sideburns	**basette** (f pl)	[ba'zette]
red-haired (adj)	**rosso**	['rosso]
gray (hair)	**brizzolato**	[brittso'lato]
bald (adj)	**calvo**	['kalvo]
bald patch	**calvizie** (f)	[kal'vitsie]
ponytail	**coda** (f) **di cavallo**	['koda di ka'vallo]
bangs	**frangetta** (f)	[fran'dʒetta]

32. Human body

hand	**mano** (f)	['mano]
arm	**braccio** (m)	['bratʃo]
finger	**dito** (m)	['dito]
toe	**dito** (m) **del piede**	['dito del 'pjede]
thumb	**pollice** (m)	['pollitʃe]
little finger	**mignolo** (m)	[mi'ɲolo]
nail	**unghia** (f)	['ungia]
fist	**pugno** (m)	['puɲo]
palm	**palmo** (m)	['palmo]
wrist	**polso** (m)	['polso]
forearm	**avambraccio** (m)	[avam'bratʃo]
elbow	**gomito** (m)	['gomito]
shoulder	**spalla** (f)	['spalla]
leg	**gamba** (f)	['gamba]
foot	**pianta** (f) **del piede**	['pjanta del 'pjede]
knee	**ginocchio** (m)	[dʒi'nokkio]
calf (part of leg)	**polpaccio** (m)	[pol'patʃo]
hip	**anca** (f)	['anka]
heel	**tallone** (m)	[tal'lone]
body	**corpo** (m)	['korpo]
stomach	**pancia** (f)	['pantʃa]
chest	**petto** (m)	['petto]
breast	**seno** (m)	['seno]
flank	**fianco** (m)	['fjanko]
back	**schiena** (f)	['skjena]
lower back	**zona** (f) **lombare**	['dzona lom'bare]
waist	**vita** (f)	['vita]
navel (belly button)	**ombelico** (m)	[ombe'liko]
buttocks	**natiche** (f pl)	['natike]
bottom	**sedere** (m)	[se'dere]
beauty mark	**neo** (m)	['neo]
birthmark (café au lait spot)	**voglia** (f)	['voʎʎa]

tattoo	**tatuaggio** (m)	[tatu'adʒo]
scar	**cicatrice** (f)	[ʧika'triʧe]

Clothing & Accessories

33. Outerwear. Coats

clothes	**vestiti** (m pl)	[ve'stiti]
outerwear	**soprabito** (m)	[so'prabito]
winter clothing	**abiti** (m pl) **invernali**	['abiti inver'nali]
coat (overcoat)	**cappotto** (m)	[kap'potto]
fur coat	**pelliccia** (f)	[pel'litʃa]
fur jacket	**pellicciotto** (m)	[pelli'tʃotto]
down coat	**piumino** (m)	[pju'mino]
jacket (e.g., leather ~)	**giubbotto** (m), **giaccha** (f)	[dʒub'botto], ['dʒakka]
raincoat (trenchcoat, etc.)	**impermeabile** (m)	[imperme'abile]
waterproof (adj)	**impermeabile**	[imperme'abile]

34. Men's & women's clothing

shirt (button shirt)	**camicia** (f)	[ka'mitʃa]
pants	**pantaloni** (m pl)	[panta'loni]
jeans	**jeans** (m pl)	['dʒins]
suit jacket	**giacca** (f)	['dʒakka]
suit	**abito** (m) **da uomo**	['abito da u'omo]
dress (frock)	**abito** (m)	['abito]
skirt	**gonna** (f)	['gonna]
blouse	**camicetta** (f)	[kami'tʃetta]
knitted jacket (cardigan, etc.)	**giacca** (f) **a maglia**	['dʒakka a 'maʎʎa]
jacket (of woman's suit)	**giacca** (f) **tailleur**	['dʒakka ta'jer]
T-shirt	**maglietta** (f)	[maʎ'ʎetta]
shorts (short trousers)	**pantaloni** (m pl) **corti**	[panta'loni 'korti]
tracksuit	**tuta** (f) **sportiva**	['tuta spor'tiva]
bathrobe	**accappatoio** (m)	[akkappa'tojo]
pajamas	**pigiama** (m)	[pi'dʒama]
sweater	**maglione** (m)	[maʎ'ʎone]
pullover	**pullover** (m)	[pul'lover]
vest	**gilè** (m)	[dʒi'le]
tailcoat	**frac** (m)	[frak]
tuxedo	**smoking** (m)	['zmoking]

uniform	**uniforme** (f)	[uni'forme]
workwear	**tuta** (f) **da lavoro**	['tuta da la'voro]
overalls	**salopette** (f)	[salo'pett]
coat (e.g., doctor's smock)	**camice** (m)	[ka'mitʃe]

35. Clothing. Underwear

underwear	**intimo** (m)	['intimo]
boxers, briefs	**boxer briefs** (m)	['bokser brifs]
panties	**mutandina** (f)	[mutan'dina]
undershirt (A-shirt)	**maglietta** (f) **intima**	[maʎ'ʎetta 'intima]
socks	**calzini** (m pl)	[kal'tsini]
nightdress	**camicia** (f) **da notte**	[ka'mitʃa da 'notte]
bra	**reggiseno** (m)	[redʒi'seno]
knee highs (knee-high socks)	**calzini** (m pl) **alti**	[kal'tsini 'alti]
pantyhose	**collant** (m)	[kol'lant]
stockings (thigh highs)	**calze** (f pl)	['kaltse]
bathing suit	**costume** (m) **da bagno**	[ko'stume da 'baɲo]

36. Headwear

hat	**cappello** (m)	[kap'pello]
fedora	**cappello** (m) **di feltro**	[kap'pello di feltro]
baseball cap	**cappello** (m) **da baseball**	[kap'pello da 'bejzbol]
flatcap	**coppola** (f)	['koppola]
beret	**basco** (m)	['basko]
hood	**cappuccio** (m)	[kap'putʃo]
panama hat	**panama** (m)	['panama]
knit cap (knitted hat)	**berretto** (m) **a maglia**	[ber'retto a 'maʎʎa]
headscarf	**fazzoletto** (m) **da capo**	[fattso'letto da 'kapo]
women's hat	**cappellino** (m) **donna**	[kappel'lino 'donna]
hard hat	**casco** (m)	['kasko]
garrison cap	**bustina** (f)	[bu'stina]
helmet	**casco** (m)	['kasko]
derby	**bombetta** (f)	[bom'betta]
top hat	**cilindro** (m)	[tʃi'lindro]

37. Footwear

footwear	**calzature** (f pl)	[kaltsa'ture]
shoes (men's shoes)	**stivaletti** (m pl)	[stiva'letti]

shoes (women's shoes)	**scarpe** (f pl)	['skarpe]
boots (e.g., cowboy ~)	**stivali** (m pl)	[sti'vali]
slippers	**pantofole** (f pl)	[pan'tofole]
tennis shoes (e.g., Nike ~)	**scarpe** (f pl) **da tennis**	['skarpe da 'tennis]
sneakers (e.g., Converse ~)	**scarpe** (f pl) **da ginnastica**	['skarpe da dʒin'nastika]
sandals	**sandali** (m pl)	['sandali]
cobbler (shoe repairer)	**calzolaio** (m)	[kaltso'lajo]
heel	**tacco** (m)	['takko]
pair (of shoes)	**paio** (m)	['pajo]
shoestring	**laccio** (m)	['latʃo]
to lace (vt)	**allacciare** (vt)	[ala'tʃare]
shoehorn	**calzascarpe** (m)	[kaltsa'skarpe]
shoe polish	**lucido** (m) **per le scarpe**	['lutʃido per le 'skarpe]

38. Textile. Fabrics

cotton (n)	**cotone** (m)	[ko'tone]
cotton (as adj)	**di cotone**	[di ko'tone]
flax (n)	**lino** (m)	['lino]
flax (as adj)	**di lino**	[di 'lino]
silk (n)	**seta** (f)	['seta]
silk (as adj)	**di seta**	[di 'seta]
wool (n)	**lana** (f)	['lana]
wool (as adj)	**di lana**	[di 'lana]
velvet	**velluto** (m)	[vel'luto]
suede	**camoscio** (m)	[ka'moʃo]
corduroy	**velluto** (m) **a coste**	[vel'luto a 'koste]
nylon (n)	**nylon** (m)	['najlon]
nylon (as adj)	**di nylon**	[di 'najlon]
polyester (n)	**poliestere** (m)	[poli'estere]
polyester (as adj)	**di poliestere**	[di poli'estere]
leather (n)	**pelle** (f)	['pelle]
leather (as adj)	**di pelle**	[di 'pelle]
fur (n)	**pelliccia** (f)	[pel'litʃa]
fur (e.g., ~ coat)	**di pelliccia**	[di pel'litʃa]

39. Personal accessories

gloves	**guanti** (m pl)	['gwanti]
mittens	**manopole** (f pl)	[ma'nopole]

scarf (muffler)	**sciarpa** (f)	['ʃarpa]
glasses (eyeglasses)	**occhiali** (m pl)	[ok'kjali]
frame (eyeglass ~)	**montatura** (f)	[monta'tura]
umbrella	**ombrello** (m)	[om'brello]
walking stick	**bastone** (m)	[ba'stone]
hairbrush	**spazzola** (f) **per capelli**	['spattsola per ka'pelli]
fan	**ventaglio** (m)	[ven'taʎʎo]
tie (necktie)	**cravatta** (f)	[kra'vatta]
bow tie	**cravatta** (f) **a farfalla**	[kra'vatta a far'falla]
suspenders	**bretelle** (f pl)	[bre'telle]
handkerchief	**fazzoletto** (m)	[fattso'letto]
comb	**pettine** (m)	['pettine]
barrette	**fermaglio** (m)	[fer'maʎʎo]
hairpin	**forcina** (f)	[for'ʧina]
buckle	**fibbia** (f)	['fibbia]
belt	**cintura** (f)	[ʧin'tura]
shoulder strap	**spallina** (f)	[spal'lina]
bag (handbag)	**borsa** (f)	['borsa]
purse	**borsetta** (f)	[bor'setta]
backpack	**zaino** (m)	['ʤajno]

40. Clothing. Miscellaneous

fashion	**moda** (f)	['moda]
in vogue (adj)	**di moda**	[di 'moda]
fashion designer	**stilista** (m)	[sti'lista]
collar	**collo** (m)	['kollo]
pocket	**tasca** (f)	['taska]
pocket (as adj)	**tascabile**	[ta'skabile]
sleeve	**manica** (f)	['manika]
hanging loop	**asola** (f) **per appendere**	['azola per ap'pendere]
fly (on trousers)	**patta** (f)	['patta]
zipper (fastener)	**cerniera** (f) **lampo**	[ʧer'njera 'lampo]
fastener	**chiusura** (f)	[kju'zura]
button	**bottone** (m)	[bot'tone]
buttonhole	**occhiello** (m)	[ok'kjello]
to come off (ab. button)	**staccarsi** (vr)	[stak'karsi]
to sew (vi, vt)	**cucire** (vi, vt)	[ku'ʧire]
to embroider (vi, vt)	**ricamare** (vi, vt)	[rika'mare]
embroidery	**ricamo** (m)	[ri'kamo]
sewing needle	**ago** (m)	['ago]
thread	**filo** (m)	['filo]
seam	**cucitura** (f)	[kuʧi'tura]

to get dirty (vi)	**sporcarsi** (vr)	[spor'karsi]
stain (mark, spot)	**macchia** (f)	['makkia]
to crease, crumple (vi)	**sgualcirsi** (vr)	[zgwal'tʃirsi]
to tear, to rip (vt)	**strappare** (vt)	[strap'pare]
clothes moth	**tarma** (f)	['tarma]

41. Personal care. Cosmetics

toothpaste	**dentifricio** (m)	[denti'fritʃo]
toothbrush	**spazzolino** (m) **da denti**	[spatso'lino da 'denti]
to brush one's teeth	**lavarsi i denti**	[la'varsi i 'denti]
razor	**rasoio** (m)	[ra'zojo]
shaving cream	**crema** (f) **da barba**	['krema da 'barba]
to shave (vi)	**rasarsi** (vr)	[ra'zarsi]
soap	**sapone** (m)	[sa'pone]
shampoo	**shampoo** (m)	['ʃampo]
scissors	**forbici** (f pl)	['forbitʃi]
nail file	**limetta** (f)	[li'metta]
nail clippers	**tagliaunghie** (m)	[taʎʎa'ungje]
tweezers	**pinzette** (f pl)	[pin'tsette]
cosmetics	**cosmetica** (f)	[ko'zmetika]
face mask	**maschera** (f) **di bellezza**	['maskera di bel'lettsa]
manicure	**manicure** (m)	[mani'kure]
to have a manicure	**fare la manicure**	['fare la mani'kure]
pedicure	**pedicure** (m)	[pedi'kure]
make-up bag	**borsa** (f) **del trucco**	['borsa del 'trukko]
face powder	**cipria** (f)	['tʃipria]
powder compact	**portacipria** (m)	[porta·'tʃipria]
blusher	**fard** (m)	[far]
perfume (bottled)	**profumo** (m)	[pro'fumo]
toilet water (lotion)	**acqua** (f) **da toeletta**	['akwa da toe'letta]
lotion	**lozione** (f)	[lo'tsjone]
cologne	**acqua** (f) **di Colonia**	['akwa di ko'lonia]
eyeshadow	**ombretto** (m)	[om'bretto]
eyeliner	**eyeliner** (m)	[aj'lajner]
mascara	**mascara** (m)	[ma'skara]
lipstick	**rossetto** (m)	[ros'setto]
nail polish, enamel	**smalto** (m)	['zmalto]
hair spray	**lacca** (f) **per capelli**	['lakka per ka'pelli]
deodorant	**deodorante** (m)	[deodo'rante]
cream	**crema** (f)	['krema]
face cream	**crema** (f) **per il viso**	['krema per il 'vizo]

hand cream	**crema** (f) **per le mani**	['krema per le 'mani]
anti-wrinkle cream	**crema** (f) **antirughe**	['krema anti'ruge]
day cream	**crema** (f) **da giorno**	['krema da 'dʒorno]
night cream	**crema** (f) **da notte**	['krema da 'notte]
day (as adj)	**da giorno**	[da 'dʒorno]
night (as adj)	**da notte**	[da 'notte]
tampon	**tampone** (m)	[tam'pone]
toilet paper (toilet roll)	**carta** (f) **igienica**	['karta i'dʒenika]
hair dryer	**fon** (m)	[fon]

42. Jewelry

jewelry, jewels	**gioielli** (m pl)	[dʒo'jelli]
precious (e.g., ~ stone)	**prezioso**	[pre'tsjozo]
hallmark stamp	**marchio** (m)	['markio]
ring	**anello** (m)	[a'nello]
wedding ring	**anello** (m) **nuziale**	[a'nello nu'tsjale]
bracelet	**braccialetto** (m)	[bratʃa'letto]
earrings	**orecchini** (m pl)	[orek'kini]
necklace (~ of pearls)	**collana** (f)	[kol'lana]
crown	**corona** (f)	[ko'rona]
bead necklace	**perline** (f pl)	[per'line]
diamond	**diamante** (m)	[dia'mante]
emerald	**smeraldo** (m)	[zme'raldo]
ruby	**rubino** (m)	[ru'bino]
sapphire	**zaffiro** (m)	[dzaf'firo]
pearl	**perle** (f pl)	['perle]
amber	**ambra** (f)	['ambra]

43. Watches. Clocks

watch (wristwatch)	**orologio** (m)	[oro'lodʒo]
dial	**quadrante** (m)	[kwa'drante]
hand (of clock, watch)	**lancetta** (f)	[lan'tʃetta]
metal watch band	**braccialetto** (m)	[bratʃa'letto]
watch strap	**cinturino** (m)	[tʃintu'rino]
battery	**pila** (f)	['pila]
to be dead (battery)	**essere scarico**	['essere 'skariko]
to change a battery	**cambiare la pila**	[kam'bjare la 'pila]
to run fast	**andare avanti**	[an'dare a'vanti]
to run slow	**andare indietro**	[an'dare in'djetro]
wall clock	**orologio** (m) **da muro**	[oro'lodʒo da 'muro]
hourglass	**clessidra** (f)	['klessidra]

sundial	**orologio** (m) **solare**	[oro'lodʒo so'lare]
alarm clock	**sveglia** (f)	['zveʎʎa]
watchmaker	**orologiaio** (m)	[orolo'dʒajo]
to repair (vt)	**riparare** (vt)	[ripa'rare]

Food. Nutricion

44. Food

meat	**carne** (f)	['karne]
chicken	**pollo** (m)	['pollo]
Rock Cornish hen (poussin)	**pollo** (m) **novello**	['pollo no'vello]
duck	**anatra** (f)	['anatra]
goose	**oca** (f)	['oka]
game	**cacciagione** (f)	[katʃa'dʒone]
turkey	**tacchino** (m)	[tak'kino]
pork	**maiale** (m)	[ma'jale]
veal	**vitello** (m)	[vi'tello]
lamb	**agnello** (m)	[a'ɲello]
beef	**manzo** (m)	['mandzo]
rabbit	**coniglio** (m)	[ko'niʎʎo]
sausage (bologna, etc.)	**salame** (m)	[sa'lame]
vienna sausage (frankfurter)	**würstel** (m)	['vyrstel]
bacon	**pancetta** (f)	[pan'tʃetta]
ham	**prosciutto** (m)	[pro'ʃutto]
gammon	**prosciutto** (m) **affumicato**	[pro'ʃutto affumi'kato]
pâté	**pâté** (m)	[pa'te]
liver	**fegato** (m)	['fegato]
hamburger (ground beef)	**carne** (f) **trita**	['karne 'trita]
tongue	**lingua** (f)	['lingua]
egg	**uovo** (m)	[u'ovo]
eggs	**uova** (f pl)	[u'ova]
egg white	**albume** (m)	[al'bume]
egg yolk	**tuorlo** (m)	[tu'orlo]
fish	**pesce** (m)	['peʃe]
seafood	**frutti** (m pl) **di mare**	['frutti di 'mare]
crustaceans	**crostacei** (m pl)	[kro'statʃei]
caviar	**caviale** (m)	[ka'vjale]
crab	**granchio** (m)	['graŋkio]
shrimp	**gamberetto** (m)	[gambe'retto]
oyster	**ostrica** (f)	['ostrika]
spiny lobster	**aragosta** (f)	[ara'gosta]
octopus	**polpo** (m)	['polpo]

squid	**calamaro** (m)	[kala'maro]
sturgeon	**storione** (m)	[sto'rjone]
salmon	**salmone** (m)	[sal'mone]
halibut	**ippoglosso** (m)	[ippo'glosso]
cod	**merluzzo** (m)	[mer'luttso]
mackerel	**scombro** (m)	['skombro]
tuna	**tonno** (m)	['tonno]
eel	**anguilla** (f)	[an'gwilla]
trout	**trota** (f)	['trota]
sardine	**sardina** (f)	[sar'dina]
pike	**luccio** (m)	['lutʃo]
herring	**aringa** (f)	[a'ringa]
bread	**pane** (m)	['pane]
cheese	**formaggio** (m)	[for'madʒo]
sugar	**zucchero** (m)	['dzukkero]
salt	**sale** (m)	['sale]
rice	**riso** (m)	['rizo]
pasta (macaroni)	**pasta** (f)	['pasta]
noodles	**tagliatelle** (f pl)	[taʎʎa'telle]
butter	**burro** (m)	['burro]
vegetable oil	**olio** (m) **vegetale**	['oljo vedʒe'tale]
sunflower oil	**olio** (m) **di girasole**	['oljo di dʒira'sole]
margarine	**margarina** (f)	[marga'rina]
olives	**olive** (f pl)	[o'live]
olive oil	**olio** (m) **d'oliva**	['oljo do'liva]
milk	**latte** (m)	['latte]
condensed milk	**latte** (m) **condensato**	['latte konden'sato]
yogurt	**yogurt** (m)	['jogurt]
sour cream	**panna** (f) **acida**	['panna 'atʃida]
cream (of milk)	**panna** (f)	['panna]
mayonnaise	**maionese** (m)	[majo'neze]
buttercream	**crema** (f)	['krema]
groats (barley ~, etc.)	**cereali** (m pl)	[tʃere'ali]
flour	**farina** (f)	[fa'rina]
canned food	**cibi** (m pl) **in scatola**	['tʃibi in 'skatola]
cornflakes	**fiocchi** (m pl) **di mais**	['fjokki di 'mais]
honey	**miele** (m)	['mjele]
jam	**marmellata** (f)	[marmel'lata]
chewing gum	**gomma** (f) **da masticare**	['gomma da masti'kare]

45. Drinks

water	**acqua** (f)	['akwa]
drinking water	**acqua** (f) **potabile**	['akwa po'tabile]
mineral water	**acqua** (f) **minerale**	['akwa mine'rale]
still (adj)	**liscia, non gassata**	['liʃa], [non gas'sata]
carbonated (adj)	**gassata**	[gas'sata]
sparkling (adj)	**frizzante**	[frid'dzante]
ice	**ghiaccio** (m)	['gjatʃo]
with ice	**con ghiaccio**	[kon 'gjatʃo]
non-alcoholic (adj)	**analcolico**	[anal'koliko]
soft drink	**bevanda** (f) **analcolica**	[be'vanda anal'kolika]
refreshing drink	**bibita** (f)	['bibita]
lemonade	**limonata** (f)	[limo'nata]
liquors	**bevande** (f pl) **alcoliche**	[be'vande al'kolike]
wine	**vino** (m)	['vino]
white wine	**vino** (m) **bianco**	['vino 'bjanko]
red wine	**vino** (m) **rosso**	['vino 'rosso]
liqueur	**liquore** (m)	[li'kwore]
champagne	**champagne** (m)	[ʃam'paɲ]
vermouth	**vermouth** (m)	['vermut]
whiskey	**whisky**	['wiski]
vodka	**vodka** (f)	['vodka]
gin	**gin** (m)	[dʒin]
cognac	**cognac** (m)	['koɲak]
rum	**rum** (m)	[rum]
coffee	**caffè** (m)	[kaf'fe]
black coffee	**caffè** (m) **nero**	[kaf'fe 'nero]
coffee with milk	**caffè latte** (m)	[kaf'fe 'latte]
cappuccino	**cappuccino** (m)	[kappu'tʃino]
instant coffee	**caffè** (m) **solubile**	[kaf'fe so'lubile]
milk	**latte** (m)	['latte]
cocktail	**cocktail** (m)	['koktejl]
milkshake	**frullato** (m)	[frul'lato]
juice	**succo** (m)	['sukko]
tomato juice	**succo** (m) **di pomodoro**	['sukko di pomo'doro]
orange juice	**succo** (m) **d'arancia**	['sukko da'rantʃa]
freshly squeezed juice	**spremuta** (f)	[spre'muta]
beer	**birra** (f)	['birra]
light beer	**birra** (f) **chiara**	['birra 'kjara]
dark beer	**birra** (f) **scura**	['birra 'skura]
tea	**tè** (m)	[te]

black tea	**tè** (m) **nero**	[te 'nero]
green tea	**tè** (m) **verde**	[te 'verde]

46. Vegetables

vegetables	**ortaggi** (m pl)	[or'tadʒi]
greens	**verdura** (f)	[ver'dura]
tomato	**pomodoro** (m)	[pomo'doro]
cucumber	**cetriolo** (m)	[tʃetri'olo]
carrot	**carota** (f)	[ka'rota]
potato	**patata** (f)	[pa'tata]
onion	**cipolla** (f)	[tʃi'polla]
garlic	**aglio** (m)	['aʎʎo]
cabbage	**cavolo** (m)	['kavolo]
cauliflower	**cavolfiore** (m)	[kavol'fjore]
Brussels sprouts	**cavoletti** (m pl) **di Bruxelles**	[kavo'letti di bruk'sel]
broccoli	**broccolo** (m)	['brokkolo]
beet	**barbabietola** (f)	[barba'bjetola]
eggplant	**melanzana** (f)	[melan'tsana]
zucchini	**zucchina** (f)	[dzuk'kina]
pumpkin	**zucca** (f)	['dzukka]
turnip	**rapa** (f)	['rapa]
parsley	**prezzemolo** (m)	[pret'tsemolo]
dill	**aneto** (m)	[a'neto]
lettuce	**lattuga** (f)	[lat'tuga]
celery	**sedano** (m)	['sedano]
asparagus	**asparago** (m)	[a'sparago]
spinach	**spinaci** (m pl)	[spi'natʃi]
pea	**pisello** (m)	[pi'zello]
beans	**fave** (f pl)	['fave]
corn (maize)	**mais** (m)	['mais]
kidney bean	**fagiolo** (m)	[fa'dʒolo]
bell pepper	**peperone** (m)	[pepe'rone]
radish	**ravanello** (m)	[rava'nello]
artichoke	**carciofo** (m)	[kar'tʃofo]

47. Fruits. Nuts

fruit	**frutto** (m)	['frutto]
apple	**mela** (f)	['mela]
pear	**pera** (f)	['pera]

lemon	**limone** (m)	[li'mone]
orange	**arancia** (f)	[a'rantʃa]
strawberry (garden ~)	**fragola** (f)	['fragola]
mandarin	**mandarino** (m)	[manda'rino]
plum	**prugna** (f)	['pruɲa]
peach	**pesca** (f)	['peska]
apricot	**albicocca** (f)	[albi'kokka]
raspberry	**lampone** (m)	[lam'pone]
pineapple	**ananas** (m)	[ana'nas]
banana	**banana** (f)	[ba'nana]
watermelon	**anguria** (f)	[an'guria]
grape	**uva** (f)	['uva]
sour cherry	**amarena** (f)	[ama'rena]
sweet cherry	**ciliegia** (f)	[tʃi'ljedʒa]
melon	**melone** (m)	[me'lone]
grapefruit	**pompelmo** (m)	[pom'pelmo]
avocado	**avocado** (m)	[avo'kado]
papaya	**papaia** (f)	[pa'paja]
mango	**mango** (m)	['mango]
pomegranate	**melagrana** (f)	[mela'grana]
redcurrant	**ribes** (m) **rosso**	['ribes 'rosso]
blackcurrant	**ribes** (m) **nero**	['ribes 'nero]
gooseberry	**uva** (f) **spina**	['uva 'spina]
bilberry	**mirtillo** (m)	[mir'tillo]
blackberry	**mora** (f)	['mora]
raisin	**uvetta** (f)	[u'vetta]
fig	**fico** (m)	['fiko]
date	**dattero** (m)	['dattero]
peanut	**arachide** (f)	[a'rakide]
almond	**mandorla** (f)	['mandorla]
walnut	**noce** (f)	['notʃe]
hazelnut	**nocciola** (f)	[no'tʃola]
coconut	**noce** (f) **di cocco**	['notʃe di 'kokko]
pistachios	**pistacchi** (m pl)	[pi'stakki]

48. Bread. Candy

bakers' confectionery (pastry)	**pasticceria** (f)	[pastitʃe'ria]
bread	**pane** (m)	['pane]
cookies	**biscotti** (m pl)	[bi'skotti]
chocolate (n)	**cioccolato** (m)	[tʃokko'lato]
chocolate (as adj)	**al cioccolato**	[al tʃokko'lato]

candy (wrapped)	**caramella** (f)	[kara'mella]
cake (e.g., cupcake)	**tortina** (f)	[tor'tina]
cake (e.g., birthday ~)	**torta** (f)	['torta]
pie (e.g., apple ~)	**crostata** (f)	[kro'stata]
filling (for cake, pie)	**ripieno** (m)	[ri'pjeno]
jam (whole fruit jam)	**marmellata** (f)	[marmel'lata]
marmalade	**marmellata** (f) **di agrumi**	[marmel'lata di a'grumi]
wafers	**wafer** (m)	['vafer]
ice-cream	**gelato** (m)	[ʤe'lato]
pudding	**budino** (m)	[bu'dino]

49. Cooked dishes

course, dish	**piatto** (m)	['pjatto]
cuisine	**cucina** (f)	[ku'ʧina]
recipe	**ricetta** (f)	[ri'ʧetta]
portion	**porzione** (f)	[por'tsjone]
salad	**insalata** (f)	[insa'lata]
soup	**minestra** (f)	[mi'nestra]
clear soup (broth)	**brodo** (m)	['brodo]
sandwich (bread)	**panino** (m)	[pa'nino]
fried eggs	**uova** (f pl) **al tegamino**	[u'ova al tega'mino]
hamburger (beefburger)	**hamburger** (m)	[am'burger]
beefsteak	**bistecca** (f)	[bi'stekka]
side dish	**contorno** (m)	[kon'torno]
spaghetti	**spaghetti** (m pl)	[spa'getti]
mashed potatoes	**purè** (m) **di patate**	[pu're di pa'tate]
pizza	**pizza** (f)	['pittsa]
porridge (oatmeal, etc.)	**porridge** (m)	[por'riʤe]
omelet	**frittata** (f)	[frit'tata]
boiled (e.g., ~ beef)	**bollito**	[bol'lito]
smoked (adj)	**affumicato**	[affumi'kato]
fried (adj)	**fritto**	['fritto]
dried (adj)	**secco**	['sekko]
frozen (adj)	**congelato**	[konʤe'lato]
pickled (adj)	**sottoaceto**	[sottoa'ʧeto]
sweet (sugary)	**dolce**	['dolʧe]
salty (adj)	**salato**	[sa'lato]
cold (adj)	**freddo**	['freddo]
hot (adj)	**caldo**	['kaldo]
bitter (adj)	**amaro**	[a'maro]
tasty (adj)	**buono, gustoso**	[bu'ono], [gu'stozo]

to cook in boiling water	**cuocere, preparare** (vt)	[ku'otʃere], [prepa'rare]
to cook (dinner)	**cucinare** (vi)	[kutʃi'nare]
to fry (vt)	**friggere** (vt)	['fridʒere]
to heat up (food)	**riscaldare** (vt)	[riskal'dare]
to salt (vt)	**salare** (vt)	[sa'lare]
to pepper (vt)	**pepare** (vt)	[pe'pare]
to grate (vt)	**grattugiare** (vt)	[grattu'dʒare]
peel (n)	**buccia** (f)	['butʃa]
to peel (vt)	**sbucciare** (vt)	[zbu'tʃare]

50. Spices

salt	**sale** (m)	['sale]
salty (adj)	**salato**	[sa'lato]
to salt (vt)	**salare** (vt)	[sa'lare]
black pepper	**pepe** (m) **nero**	['pepe 'nero]
red pepper (milled ~)	**peperoncino** (m)	[peperon'tʃino]
mustard	**senape** (f)	[se'nape]
horseradish	**cren** (m)	['kren]
condiment	**condimento** (m)	[kondi'mento]
spice	**spezie** (f pl)	['spetsie]
sauce	**salsa** (f)	['salsa]
vinegar	**aceto** (m)	[a'tʃeto]
anise	**anice** (m)	['anitʃe]
basil	**basilico** (m)	[ba'ziliko]
cloves	**chiodi** (m pl) **di garofano**	['kjodi di ga'rofano]
ginger	**zenzero** (m)	['dzendzero]
coriander	**coriandolo** (m)	[kori'andolo]
cinnamon	**cannella** (f)	[kan'nella]
sesame	**sesamo** (m)	[sezamo]
bay leaf	**alloro** (m)	[al'loro]
paprika	**paprica** (f)	['paprika]
caraway	**cumino, comino** (m)	[ku'mino], [ko'mino]
saffron	**zafferano** (m)	[dzaffe'rano]

51. Meals

food	**cibo** (m)	['tʃibo]
to eat (vi, vt)	**mangiare** (vi, vt)	[man'dʒare]
breakfast	**colazione** (f)	[kola'tsjone]
to have breakfast	**fare colazione**	['fare kola'tsjone]
lunch	**pranzo** (m)	['prantso]

to have lunch	**pranzare** (vi)	[pran'tsare]
dinner	**cena** (f)	['tʃena]
to have dinner	**cenare** (vi)	[tʃe'nare]
appetite	**appetito** (m)	[appe'tito]
Enjoy your meal!	**Buon appetito!**	[bu'on appe'tito]
to open (~ a bottle)	**aprire** (vt)	[a'prire]
to spill (liquid)	**rovesciare** (vt)	[rove'ʃare]
to spill out (vi)	**rovesciarsi** (vi)	[rove'ʃarsi]
to boil (vi)	**bollire** (vi)	[bol'lire]
to boil (vt)	**far bollire**	[far bol'lire]
boiled (~ water)	**bollito**	[bol'lito]
to chill, cool down (vt)	**raffreddare** (vt)	[raffred'dare]
to chill (vi)	**raffreddarsi** (vr)	[raffred'darsi]
taste, flavor	**gusto** (m)	['gusto]
aftertaste	**retrogusto** (m)	[retro'gusto]
to slim down (lose weight)	**essere a dieta**	['essere a di'eta]
diet	**dieta** (f)	[di'eta]
vitamin	**vitamina** (f)	[vita'mina]
calorie	**caloria** (f)	[kalo'ria]
vegetarian (n)	**vegetariano** (m)	[vedʒeta'rjano]
vegetarian (adj)	**vegetariano**	[vedʒeta'rjano]
fats (nutrient)	**grassi** (m pl)	['grassi]
proteins	**proteine** (f pl)	[prote'ine]
carbohydrates	**carboidrati** (m pl)	[karboi'drati]
slice (of lemon, ham)	**fetta** (f), **fettina** (f)	['fetta], [fet'tina]
piece (of cake, pie)	**pezzo** (m)	['pettso]
crumb (of bread, cake, etc.)	**briciola** (f)	['britʃola]

52. Table setting

spoon	**cucchiaio** (m)	[kuk'kjajo]
knife	**coltello** (m)	[kol'tello]
fork	**forchetta** (f)	[for'ketta]
cup (e.g., coffee ~)	**tazza** (f)	['tattsa]
plate (dinner ~)	**piatto** (m)	['pjatto]
saucer	**piattino** (m)	[pjat'tino]
napkin (on table)	**tovagliolo** (m)	[tovaʎ'ʎolo]
toothpick	**stuzzicadenti** (m)	[stuttsika'denti]

53. Restaurant

restaurant	**ristorante** (m)	[risto'rante]
coffee house	**caffè** (m)	[kaf'fe]
pub, bar	**pub** (m), **bar** (m)	[pab], [bar]
tearoom	**sala** (f) **da tè**	['sala da 'te]
waiter	**cameriere** (m)	[kame'rjere]
waitress	**cameriera** (f)	[kame'rjera]
bartender	**barista** (m)	[ba'rista]
menu	**menù** (m)	[me'nu]
wine list	**lista** (f) **dei vini**	['lista 'dei 'vini]
to book a table	**prenotare un tavolo**	[preno'tare un 'tavolo]
course, dish	**piatto** (m)	['pjatto]
to order (meal)	**ordinare** (vt)	[ordi'nare]
to make an order	**fare un'ordinazione**	['fare unordina'tsjone]
aperitif	**aperitivo** (m)	[aperi'tivo]
appetizer	**antipasto** (m)	[anti'pasto]
dessert	**dolce** (m)	['doltʃe]
check	**conto** (m)	['konto]
to pay the check	**pagare il conto**	[pa'gare il 'konto]
to give change	**dare il resto**	['dare il 'resto]
tip	**mancia** (f)	['mantʃa]

Family, relatives and friends

54. Personal information. Forms

name (first name)	**nome** (m)	['nome]
surname (last name)	**cognome** (m)	[ko'ɲome]
date of birth	**data** (f) **di nascita**	['data di 'naʃita]
place of birth	**luogo** (m) **di nascita**	[lu'ogo di 'naʃita]
nationality	**nazionalità** (f)	[natsjonali'ta]
place of residence	**domicilio** (m)	[domi'ʧilio]
country	**paese** (m)	[pa'eze]
profession (occupation)	**professione** (f)	[profes'sjone]
gender, sex	**sesso** (m)	['sesso]
height	**statura** (f)	[sta'tura]
weight	**peso** (m)	['pezo]

55. Family members. Relatives

mother	**madre** (f)	['madre]
father	**padre** (m)	['padre]
son	**figlio** (m)	['fiʎʎo]
daughter	**figlia** (f)	['fiʎʎa]
younger daughter	**figlia** (f) **minore**	['fiʎʎa mi'nore]
younger son	**figlio** (m) **minore**	['fiʎʎo mi'nore]
eldest daughter	**figlia** (f) **maggiore**	['fiʎʎa ma'ʤore]
eldest son	**figlio** (m) **maggiore**	['fiʎʎo ma'ʤore]
brother	**fratello** (m)	[fra'tello]
sister	**sorella** (f)	[so'rella]
cousin (masc.)	**cugino** (m)	[ku'ʤino]
cousin (fem.)	**cugina** (f)	[ku'ʤina]
mom, mommy	**mamma** (f)	['mamma]
dad, daddy	**papà** (m)	[pa'pa]
parents	**genitori** (m pl)	[ʤeni'tori]
child	**bambino** (m)	[bam'bino]
children	**bambini** (m pl)	[bam'bini]
grandmother	**nonna** (f)	['nonna]
grandfather	**nonno** (m)	['nonno]
grandson	**nipote** (m)	[ni'pote]

granddaughter	**nipote** (f)	[ni'pote]
grandchildren	**nipoti** (pl)	[ni'poti]
uncle	**zio** (m)	['tsio]
aunt	**zia** (f)	['tsia]
nephew	**nipote** (m)	[ni'pote]
niece	**nipote** (f)	[ni'pote]
mother-in-law (wife's mother)	**suocera** (f)	[su'otʃera]
father-in-law (husband's father)	**suocero** (m)	[su'otʃero]
son-in-law (daughter's husband)	**genero** (m)	['dʒenero]
stepmother	**matrigna** (f)	[ma'triɲa]
stepfather	**patrigno** (m)	[pa'triɲo]
infant	**neonato** (m)	[neo'nato]
baby (infant)	**infante** (m)	[in'fante]
little boy, kid	**bimbo** (m)	['bimbo]
wife	**moglie** (f)	['moʎʎe]
husband	**marito** (m)	[ma'rito]
spouse (husband)	**coniuge** (m)	['konjudʒe]
spouse (wife)	**coniuge** (f)	['konjudʒe]
married (masc.)	**sposato**	[spo'zato]
married (fem.)	**sposata**	[spo'zata]
single (unmarried)	**celibe**	['tʃelibe]
bachelor	**scapolo** (m)	['skapolo]
divorced (masc.)	**divorziato**	[divortsi'ato]
widow	**vedova** (f)	['vedova]
widower	**vedovo** (m)	['vedovo]
relative	**parente** (m)	[pa'rente]
close relative	**parente** (m) **stretto**	[pa'rente 'stretto]
distant relative	**parente** (m) **lontano**	[pa'rente lon'tano]
relatives	**parenti** (m pl)	[pa'renti]
orphan (boy)	**orfano** (m)	['orfano]
orphan (girl)	**orfana** (f)	['orfana]
guardian (of a minor)	**tutore** (m)	[tu'tore]
to adopt (a boy)	**adottare** (vt)	[adot'tare]
to adopt (a girl)	**adottare** (vt)	[adot'tare]

56. Friends. Coworkers

friend (masc.)	**amico** (m)	[a'miko]
friend (fem.)	**amica** (f)	[a'mika]
friendship	**amicizia** (f)	[ami'tʃitsia]

to be friends	**essere amici**	['essere a'mitʃi]
buddy (masc.)	**amico** (m)	[a'miko]
buddy (fem.)	**amica** (f)	[a'mika]
partner	**partner** (m)	['partner]
chief (boss)	**capo** (m)	['kapo]
superior (n)	**capo** (m), **superiore** (m)	['kapo], [supe'rjore]
subordinate (n)	**subordinato** (m)	[subordi'nato]
colleague	**collega** (m)	[kol'lega]
acquaintance (person)	**conoscente** (m)	[kono'ʃente]
fellow traveler	**compagno** (m) **di viaggio**	[kom'paɲo di 'vjadʒo]
classmate	**compagno** (m) **di classe**	[kom'paɲo di 'klasse]
neighbor (masc.)	**vicino** (m)	[vi'tʃino]
neighbor (fem.)	**vicina** (f)	[vi'tʃina]
neighbors	**vicini** (m pl)	[vi'tʃini]

57. Man. Woman

woman	**donna** (f)	['donna]
girl (young woman)	**ragazza** (f)	[ra'gattsa]
bride	**sposa** (f)	['spoza]
beautiful (adj)	**bella**	['bella]
tall (adj)	**alta**	['alta]
slender (adj)	**snella**	['znella]
short (adj)	**bassa**	['bassa]
blonde (n)	**bionda** (f)	['bjonda]
brunette (n)	**bruna** (f)	['bruna]
ladies' (adj)	**da donna**	[da 'donna]
virgin (girl)	**vergine** (f)	['verdʒine]
pregnant (adj)	**incinta**	[in'tʃinta]
man (adult male)	**uomo** (m)	[u'omo]
blond (n)	**biondo** (m)	['bjondo]
brunet (n)	**bruno** (m)	['bruno]
tall (adj)	**alto**	['alto]
short (adj)	**basso**	['basso]
rude (rough)	**sgarbato**	[sgar'bato]
stocky (adj)	**tozzo**	['tottso]
robust (adj)	**robusto**	[ro'busto]
strong (adj)	**forte**	['forte]
strength	**forza** (f)	['fortsa]
stout, fat (adj)	**grasso**	['grasso]
swarthy (adj)	**bruno**	['bruno]

slender (well-built)	**snello**	['znello]
elegant (adj)	**elegante**	[ele'gante]

58. Age

age	**età** (f)	[e'ta]
youth (young age)	**giovinezza** (f)	[dʒovi'nettsa]
young (adj)	**giovane**	['dʒovane]
younger (adj)	**più giovane**	[pju 'dʒovane]
older (adj)	**più vecchio**	[pju 'vekkio]
young man	**giovane** (m)	['dʒovane]
teenager	**adolescente** (m, f)	[adole'ʃente]
guy, fellow	**ragazzo** (m)	[ra'gattso]
old man	**vecchio** (m)	['vekkio]
old woman	**vecchia** (f)	['vekkia]
adult (adj)	**adulto** (m)	[a'dulto]
middle-aged (adj)	**di mezza età**	[di 'meddza e'ta]
elderly (adj)	**anziano**	[an'tsjano]
old (adj)	**vecchio**	['vekkio]
retirement	**pensionamento** (m)	[pensjona'mento]
to retire (from job)	**andare in pensione**	[an'dare in pen'sjone]
retiree	**pensionato** (m)	[pensjo'nato]

59. Children

child	**bambino** (m)	[bam'bino]
children	**bambini** (m pl)	[bam'bini]
twins	**gemelli** (m pl)	[dʒe'melli]
cradle	**culla** (f)	['kulla]
rattle	**sonaglio** (m)	[so'naʎʎo]
diaper	**pannolino** (m)	[panno'lino]
pacifier	**tettarella** (f)	[tetta'rella]
baby carriage	**carrozzina** (f)	[karrot'tsina]
kindergarten	**scuola** (f) **materna**	['skwola ma'terna]
babysitter	**baby-sitter** (f)	[bebi'siter]
childhood	**infanzia** (f)	[in'fantsia]
doll	**bambola** (f)	['bambola]
toy	**giocattolo** (m)	[dʒo'kattolo]
construction set (toy)	**gioco** (m) **di costruzione**	['dʒoko di konstru'tsjone]
well-bred (adj)	**educato**	[edu'kato]

ill-bred (adj)	**maleducato**	[maledu'kato]
spoiled (adj)	**viziato**	[vitsi'ato]
to be naughty	**essere disubbidiente**	['essere dizubi'djente]
mischievous (adj)	**birichino**	[biri'kino]
mischievousness	**birichinata** (f)	[biriki'nata]
mischievous child	**monello** (m)	[mo'nello]
obedient (adj)	**ubbidiente**	[ubidi'ente]
disobedient (adj)	**disubbidiente**	[dizubi'djente]
docile (adj)	**docile**	['dotʃile]
clever (smart)	**intelligente**	[intelli'dʒente]
child prodigy	**bambino** (m) **prodigio**	[bam'bino pro'didʒo]

60. Married couples. Family life

to kiss (vt)	**baciare** (vt)	[ba'tʃare]
to kiss (vi)	**baciarsi** (vr)	[ba'tʃarsi]
family (n)	**famiglia** (f)	[fa'miʎʎa]
family (as adj)	**familiare**	[fami'ljare]
couple	**coppia** (f)	['koppia]
marriage (state)	**matrimonio** (m)	[matri'monio]
hearth (home)	**focolare** (m) **domestico**	[foko'lare do'mestiko]
dynasty	**dinastia** (f)	[dina'stia]
date	**appuntamento** (m)	[appunta'mento]
kiss	**bacio** (m)	['batʃo]
love (for sb)	**amore** (m)	[a'more]
to love (sb)	**amare**	[a'mare]
beloved	**amato**	[a'mato]
tenderness	**tenerezza** (f)	[tene'rettsa]
tender (affectionate)	**dolce, tenero**	['doltʃe], ['tenero]
faithfulness	**fedeltà** (f)	[fedel'ta]
faithful (adj)	**fedele**	[fe'dele]
care (attention)	**premura** (f)	[pre'mura]
caring (~ father)	**premuroso**	[premu'rozo]
newlyweds	**sposi** (m pl) **novelli**	['spozi no'velli]
honeymoon	**luna** (f) **di miele**	['luna di 'mjele]
to get married (ab. woman)	**sposarsi** (vr)	[spo'zarsi]
to get married (ab. man)	**sposarsi** (vr)	[spo'zarsi]
wedding	**nozze** (f pl)	['nottse]
golden wedding	**nozze** (f pl) **d'oro**	['nottse 'doro]
anniversary	**anniversario** (m)	[anniver'sario]
lover (masc.)	**amante** (m)	[a'mante]

mistress (lover)	**amante** (f)	[a'mante]
adultery	**adulterio** (m)	[adul'terio]
to cheat on ... (commit adultery)	**tradire**	[tra'dire]
jealous (adj)	**geloso**	[dʒe'lozo]
to be jealous	**essere geloso**	['essere dʒe'lozo]
divorce	**divorzio** (m)	[di'vortsio]
to divorce (vi)	**divorziare** (vi)	[divor'tsjare]
to quarrel (vi)	**litigare** (vi)	[liti'gare]
to be reconciled (after an argument)	**fare pace**	['fare 'patʃe]
together (adv)	**insieme**	[in'sjeme]
sex	**sesso** (m)	['sesso]
happiness	**felicità** (f)	[felitʃi'ta]
happy (adj)	**felice**	[fe'litʃe]
misfortune (accident)	**disgrazia** (f)	[dis'gratsia]
unhappy (adj)	**infelice**	[infe'litʃe]

Character. Feelings. Emotions

61. Feelings. Emotions

feeling (emotion)	**sentimento** (m)	[senti'mento]
feelings	**sentimenti** (m pl)	[senti'menti]
to feel (vt)	**sentire** (vt)	[sen'tire]
hunger	**fame** (f)	['fame]
to be hungry	**avere fame**	[a'vere 'fame]
thirst	**sete** (f)	['sete]
to be thirsty	**avere sete**	[a'vere 'sete]
sleepiness	**sonnolenza** (f)	[sonno'lentsa]
to feel sleepy	**avere sonno**	[a'vere 'sonno]
tiredness	**stanchezza** (f)	[staŋ'kettsa]
tired (adj)	**stanco**	['stanko]
to get tired	**stancarsi** (vr)	[stan'karsi]
mood (humor)	**umore** (m)	[u'more]
boredom	**noia** (f)	['noja]
to be bored	**annoiarsi** (vr)	[anno'jarsi]
seclusion	**isolamento** (f)	[izola'mento]
to seclude oneself	**isolarsi** (vr)	[izo'larsi]
to worry (make anxious)	**preoccupare** (vt)	[preokku'pare]
to be worried	**essere preoccupato**	['essere preokku'pato]
worrying (n)	**agitazione** (f)	[adʒita'tsjone]
anxiety	**preoccupazione** (f)	[preokkupa'tsjone]
preoccupied (adj)	**preoccupato**	[preokku'pato]
to be nervous	**essere nervoso**	['essere ner'vozo]
to panic (vi)	**andare in panico**	[an'dare in 'paniko]
hope	**speranza** (f)	[spe'rantsa]
to hope (vi, vt)	**sperare** (vi, vt)	[spe'rare]
certainty	**certezza** (f)	[ʧer'tettsa]
certain, sure (adj)	**sicuro**	[si'kuro]
uncertainty	**incertezza** (f)	[inʧer'tettsa]
uncertain (adj)	**incerto**	[in'ʧerto]
drunk (adj)	**ubriaco**	[ubri'ako]
sober (adj)	**sobrio**	['sobrio]
weak (adj)	**debole**	['debole]
happy (adj)	**fortunato**	[fortu'nato]
to scare (vt)	**spaventare** (vt)	[spaven'tare]

fury (madness)	**rabbia** (f)	['rabbia]
rage (fury)	**rabbia** (f)	['rabbia]
depression	**depressione** (f)	[depres'sjone]
discomfort (unease)	**disagio** (m)	[di'zadʒo]
comfort	**conforto** (m)	[kon'forto]
to regret (be sorry)	**rincrescere** (vi)	[rin'kreʃere]
regret	**rincrescimento** (m)	[rinkreʃi'mento]
bad luck	**sfortuna** (f)	[sfor'tuna]
sadness	**tristezza** (f)	[tri'stettsa]
shame (remorse)	**vergogna** (f)	[ver'goɲa]
gladness	**allegria** (f)	[alle'gria]
enthusiasm, zeal	**entusiasmo** (m)	[entu'zjazmo]
enthusiast	**entusiasta** (m)	[entu'zjasta]
to show enthusiasm	**mostrare entusiasmo**	[mo'strare entu'zjazmo]

62. Character. Personality

character	**carattere** (m)	[ka'rattere]
character flaw	**difetto** (m)	[di'fetto]
mind	**mente** (f)	['mente]
reason	**intelletto** (m)	[intel'letto]
conscience	**coscienza** (f)	[ko'ʃentsa]
habit (custom)	**abitudine** (f)	[abi'tudine]
ability (talent)	**capacità** (f)	[kapatʃi'ta]
can (e.g., ~ swim)	**sapere** (vt)	[sa'pere]
patient (adj)	**paziente**	[pa'tsjente]
impatient (adj)	**impaziente**	[impa'tsjente]
curious (inquisitive)	**curioso**	[ku'rjozo]
curiosity	**curiosità** (f)	[kuriozi'ta]
modesty	**modestia** (f)	[mo'destia]
modest (adj)	**modesto**	[mo'desto]
immodest (adj)	**immodesto**	[immo'desto]
laziness	**pigrizia** (f)	[pi'gritsia]
lazy (adj)	**pigro**	['pigro]
lazy person (masc.)	**poltrone** (m)	[pol'trone]
cunning (n)	**furberia** (f)	[furbe'ria]
cunning (as adj)	**furbo**	['furbo]
distrust	**diffidenza** (f)	[diffi'dentsa]
distrustful (adj)	**diffidente**	[diffi'dente]
generosity	**generosità** (f)	[dʒenerozi'ta]
generous (adj)	**generoso**	[dʒene'rozo]
talented (adj)	**di talento**	[di ta'lento]

talent	**talento** (m)	[ta'lento]
courageous (adj)	**coraggioso**	[kora'dʒozo]
courage	**coraggio** (m)	[ko'radʒo]
honest (adj)	**onesto**	[o'nesto]
honesty	**onestà** (f)	[one'sta]
careful (cautious)	**prudente**	[pru'dente]
brave (courageous)	**valoroso**	[valo'rozo]
serious (adj)	**serio**	['serio]
strict (severe, stern)	**severo**	[se'vero]
decisive (adj)	**deciso**	[de'tʃizo]
indecisive (adj)	**indeciso**	[inde'tʃizo]
shy, timid (adj)	**timido**	['timido]
shyness, timidity	**timidezza** (f)	[timi'dettsa]
confidence (trust)	**fiducia** (f)	[fi'dutʃa]
to believe (trust)	**fidarsi** (vr)	[fi'darsi]
trusting (credulous)	**fiducioso**	[fidu'tʃozo]
sincerely (adv)	**sinceramente**	[sintʃera'mente]
sincere (adj)	**sincero**	[sin'tʃero]
sincerity	**sincerità** (f)	[sintʃeri'ta]
open (person)	**aperto**	[a'perto]
calm (adj)	**tranquillo**	[tran'kwillo]
frank (sincere)	**sincero**	[sin'tʃero]
naïve (adj)	**ingenuo**	[in'dʒenuo]
absent-minded (adj)	**distratto**	[di'stratto]
funny (odd)	**buffo**	['buffo]
greed, stinginess	**avidità** (f)	[avidi'ta]
greedy, stingy (adj)	**avido**	['avido]
stingy (adj)	**avaro**	[a'varo]
evil (adj)	**cattivo**	[kat'tivo]
stubborn (adj)	**testardo**	[te'stardo]
unpleasant (adj)	**antipatico**	[anti'patiko]
selfish person (masc.)	**egoista** (m)	[ego'ista]
selfish (adj)	**egoistico**	[ego'istiko]
coward	**codardo** (m)	[ko'dardo]
cowardly (adj)	**codardo**	[ko'dardo]

63. Sleep. Dreams

to sleep (vi)	**dormire** (vi)	[dor'mire]
sleep, sleeping	**sonno** (m)	['sonno]
dream	**sogno** (m)	['soɲo]
to dream (in sleep)	**sognare** (vi)	[so'ɲare]
sleepy (adj)	**sonnolento**	[sonno'lento]

bed	**letto** (m)	['letto]
mattress	**materasso** (m)	[mate'rasso]
blanket (comforter)	**coperta** (f)	[ko'perta]
pillow	**cuscino** (m)	[ku'ʃino]
sheet	**lenzuolo** (m)	[lentsu'olo]
insomnia	**insonnia** (f)	[in'sonnia]
sleepless (adj)	**insonne**	[in'sonne]
sleeping pill	**sonnifero** (m)	[son'nifero]
to take a sleeping pill	**prendere il sonnifero**	['prendere il son'nifero]
to feel sleepy	**avere sonno**	[a'vere 'sonno]
to yawn (vi)	**sbadigliare** (vi)	[zbadiʎ'ʎare]
to go to bed	**andare a letto**	[an'dare a 'letto]
to make up the bed	**fare il letto**	['fare il 'letto]
to fall asleep	**addormentarsi** (vr)	[addormen'tarsi]
nightmare	**incubo** (m)	['inkubo]
snore, snoring	**russare** (m)	[rus'sare]
to snore (vi)	**russare** (vi)	[rus'sare]
alarm clock	**sveglia** (f)	['zveʎʎa]
to wake (vt)	**svegliare** (vt)	[zveʎ'ʎare]
to wake up	**svegliarsi** (vr)	[zveʎ'ʎarsi]
to get up (vi)	**alzarsi** (vr)	[al'tsarsi]
to wash up (wash face)	**lavarsi** (vr)	[la'varsi]

64. Humour. Laughter. Gladness

humor (wit, fun)	**umorismo** (m)	[umo'rizmo]
sense of humor	**senso** (m) **dello humour**	['senso 'dello u'mur]
to enjoy oneself	**divertirsi** (vr)	[diver'tirsi]
cheerful (merry)	**allegro**	[al'legro]
merriment (gaiety)	**allegria** (f)	[alle'gria]
smile	**sorriso** (m)	[sor'rizo]
to smile (vi)	**sorridere** (vi)	[sor'ridere]
to start laughing	**mettersi a ridere**	['mettersi a 'ridere]
to laugh (vi)	**ridere** (vi)	['ridere]
laugh, laughter	**riso** (m)	['rizo]
anecdote	**aneddoto** (m)	[a'neddoto]
funny (anecdote, etc.)	**divertente**	[diver'tente]
funny (odd)	**ridicolo**	[ri'dikolo]
to joke (vi)	**scherzare** (vi)	[sker'tsare]
joke (verbal)	**scherzo** (m)	['skertso]
joy (emotion)	**gioia** (f)	['ʤoja]
to rejoice (vi)	**rallegrarsi** (vr)	[ralle'grarsi]
joyful (adj)	**allegro**	[al'legro]

65. Discussion, conversation. Part 1

communication	**comunicazione** (f)	[komunika'tsjone]
to communicate	**comunicare** (vi)	[komuni'kare]
conversation	**conversazione** (f)	[konversa'tsjone]
dialog	**dialogo** (m)	[di'alogo]
discussion (discourse)	**discussione** (f)	[diskus'sjone]
dispute (debate)	**dibattito** (m)	[di'battito]
to dispute	**discutere** (vi)	[di'skutere]
interlocutor	**interlocutore** (m)	[interloku'tore]
topic (theme)	**tema** (m)	['tema]
point of view	**punto** (m) **di vista**	['punto di 'vista]
opinion (point of view)	**opinione** (f)	[opi'njone]
speech (talk)	**discorso** (m)	[di'skorso]
discussion (of report, etc.)	**discussione** (f)	[diskus'sjone]
to discuss (vt)	**discutere** (vt)	[di'skutere]
talk (conversation)	**conversazione** (f)	[konversa'tsjone]
to talk (to chat)	**conversare** (vi)	[konver'sare]
meeting (encounter)	**incontro** (m)	[in'kontro]
to meet (vi, vt)	**incontrarsi** (vr)	[inkon'trarsi]
proverb	**proverbio** (m)	[pro'verbio]
saying	**detto** (m)	['detto]
riddle (poser)	**indovinello** (m)	[indovi'nello]
to pose a riddle	**fare un indovinello**	['fare un indovi'nello]
password	**parola** (f) **d'ordine**	[pa'rola 'dordine]
secret	**segreto** (m)	[se'greto]
oath (vow)	**giuramento** (m)	[dʒura'mento]
to swear (an oath)	**giurare** (vi)	[dʒu'rare]
promise	**promessa** (f)	[pro'messa]
to promise (vt)	**promettere** (vt)	[pro'mettere]
advice (counsel)	**consiglio** (m)	[kon'siʎʎo]
to advise (vt)	**consigliare** (vt)	[konsiʎ'ʎare]
to listen to ... (obey)	**ubbidire** (vi)	[ubi'dire]
news	**notizia** (f)	[no'titsia]
sensation (news)	**sensazione** (f)	[sensa'tsjone]
information (report)	**informazioni** (f pl)	[informa'tsjoni]
conclusion (decision)	**conclusione** (f)	[konklu'zjone]
voice	**voce** (f)	['votʃe]
compliment	**complimento** (m)	[kompli'mento]
kind (nice)	**gentile**	[dʒen'tile]
word	**parola** (f)	[pa'rola]
phrase	**frase** (f)	['fraze]
answer	**risposta** (f)	[ris'posta]

truth	**verità** (f)	[veri'ta]
lie	**menzogna** (f)	[men'tsoɲa]
thought	**pensiero** (m)	[pen'sjero]
idea (inspiration)	**idea** (f), **pensiero** (m)	[i'dea], [pen'sjero]
fantasy	**fantasia** (f)	[fanta'zia]

66. Discussion, conversation. Part 2

respected (adj)	**rispettato**	[rispet'tato]
to respect (vt)	**rispettare** (vt)	[rispet'tare]
respect	**rispetto** (m)	[ris'petto]
Dear ... (letter)	**Egregio ...**	[e'gredʒo]
to introduce (sb to sb)	**presentare** (vt)	[prezen'tare]
intention	**intenzione** (f)	[inten'tsjone]
to intend (have in mind)	**avere intenzione**	[a'vere inten'tsjone]
wish	**augurio** (m)	[au'gurio]
to wish (~ good luck)	**augurare** (vt)	[augu'rare]
surprise (astonishment)	**sorpresa** (f)	[sor'preza]
to surprise (amaze)	**sorprendere** (vt)	[sor'prendere]
to be surprised	**stupirsi** (vr)	[stu'pirsi]
to give (vt)	**dare** (vt)	['dare]
to take (get hold of)	**prendere** (vt)	['prendere]
to give back	**rendere** (vt)	['rendere]
to return (give back)	**restituire** (vt)	[restitu'ire]
to apologize (vi)	**scusarsi** (vr)	[sku'zarsi]
apology	**scusa** (f)	['skuza]
to forgive (vt)	**perdonare** (vt)	[perdo'nare]
to talk (speak)	**parlare** (vi, vt)	[par'lare]
to listen (vi)	**ascoltare** (vi)	[askol'tare]
to hear out	**ascoltare fino in fondo**	[askol'tare 'fino in 'fondo]
to understand (vt)	**capire** (vt)	[ka'pire]
to show (to display)	**mostrare** (vt)	[mo'strare]
to look at ...	**guardare** (vt)	[gwar'dare]
to call (yell for sb)	**chiamare** (vt)	[kja'mare]
to disturb (vt)	**disturbare** (vt)	[distur'bare]
to pass (to hand sth)	**consegnare** (vt)	[konse'ɲare]
demand (request)	**richiesta** (f)	[ri'kjesta]
to request (ask)	**chiedere** (vt)	['kjedere]
demand (firm request)	**esigenza** (f)	[ezi'dʒentsa]
to demand (request firmly)	**esigere** (vt)	[e'zidʒere]
to tease (call names)	**stuzzicare** (vt)	[stuttsi'kare]
to mock (make fun of)	**canzonare** (vt)	[kantso'nare]

mockery, derision	**burla** (f), **beffa** (f)	['burla], ['beffa]
nickname	**soprannome** (m)	[sopran'nome]
insinuation	**allusione** (f)	[allu'zjone]
to insinuate (imply)	**alludere** (vi)	[al'ludere]
to mean (vt)	**intendere** (vt)	[in'tendere]
description	**descrizione** (f)	[deskri'tsjone]
to describe (vt)	**descrivere** (vt)	[de'skrivere]
praise (compliments)	**lode** (f)	['lode]
to praise (vt)	**lodare** (vt)	[lo'dare]
disappointment	**delusione** (f)	[delu'zjone]
to disappoint (vt)	**deludere** (vt)	[de'ludere]
to be disappointed	**rimanere deluso**	[rima'nere de'luzo]
supposition	**supposizione** (f)	[suppozi'tsjone]
to suppose (assume)	**supporre** (vt)	[sup'porre]
warning (caution)	**avvertimento** (m)	[avverti'mento]
to warn (vt)	**avvertire** (vt)	[avver'tire]

67. Discussion, conversation. Part 3

to talk into (convince)	**persuadere** (vt)	[persua'dere]
to calm down (vt)	**tranquillizzare** (vt)	[trankwillid'dzare]
silence (~ is golden)	**silenzio** (m)	[si'lentsio]
to be silent (not speaking)	**tacere** (vi)	[ta'tʃere]
to whisper (vi, vt)	**sussurrare** (vt)	[sussur'rare]
whisper	**sussurro** (m)	[sus'surro]
frankly, sincerely (adv)	**francamente**	[franka'mente]
in my opinion ...	**secondo me ...**	[se'kondo me]
detail (of the story)	**dettaglio** (m)	[det'taʎʎo]
detailed (adj)	**dettagliato**	[dettaʎ'ʎato]
in detail (adv)	**dettagliatamente**	[dettaʎʎata'mente]
hint, clue	**suggerimento** (m)	[sudʒeri'mento]
to give a hint	**suggerire** (vt)	[sudʒe'rire]
look (glance)	**sguardo** (m)	['zgwardo]
to have a look	**gettare uno sguardo**	[dʒet'tare 'uno 'zgwardo]
fixed (look)	**fisso**	['fisso]
to blink (vi)	**battere le palpebre**	['battere le 'palpebre]
to wink (vi)	**ammiccare** (vi)	[ammik'kare]
to nod (in assent)	**accennare col capo**	[atʃen'nare kol 'kapo]
sigh	**sospiro** (m)	[sos'piro]
to sigh (vi)	**sospirare** (vi)	[sospi'rare]

to shudder (vi)	**sussultare** (vi)	[sussul'tare]
gesture	**gesto** (m)	['dʒesto]
to touch (one's arm, etc.)	**toccare** (vt)	[tok'kare]
to seize (e.g., ~ by the arm)	**afferrare** (vt)	[affer'rare]
to tap (on the shoulder)	**picchiettare** (vt)	[pikjet'tare]
Look out!	**Attenzione!**	[atten'tsjone]
Really?	**Davvero?**	[dav'vero]
Are you sure?	**Sei sicuro?**	[sej si'kuro]
Good luck!	**Buona fortuna!**	[bu'ona for'tuna]
I see!	**Capito!**	[ka'pito]
What a pity!	**Peccato!**	[pek'kato]

68. Agreement. Refusal

consent	**accordo** (m)	[ak'kordo]
to consent (vi)	**essere d'accordo**	['essere dak'kordo]
approval	**approvazione** (f)	[approva'tsjone]
to approve (vt)	**approvare** (vt)	[appro'vare]
refusal	**rifiuto** (m)	[ri'fjuto]
to refuse (vi, vt)	**rifiutarsi** (vr)	[rifju'tarsi]
Great!	**Perfetto!**	[per'fetto]
All right!	**Va bene!**	[va 'bene]
Okay! (I agree)	**D'accordo!**	[dak'kordo]
forbidden (adj)	**vietato, proibito**	[vje'tato], [proi'bito]
it's forbidden	**è proibito**	[e proi'bito]
it's impossible	**è impossibile**	[e impos'sibile]
incorrect (adj)	**sbagliato**	[zbaʎ'ʎato]
to reject (~ a demand)	**respingere** (vt)	[re'spindʒere]
to support (cause, idea)	**sostenere** (vt)	[soste'nere]
to accept (~ an apology)	**accettare** (vt)	[atʧet'tare]
to confirm (vt)	**confermare** (vt)	[konfer'mare]
confirmation	**conferma** (f)	[kon'ferma]
permission	**permesso** (m)	[per'messo]
to permit (vt)	**permettere** (vt)	[per'mettere]
decision	**decisione** (f)	[deʧi'zjone]
to say nothing (hold one's tongue)	**non dire niente**	[non 'dire 'njente]
condition (term)	**condizione** (f)	[kondi'tsjone]
excuse (pretext)	**pretesto** (m)	[pre'testo]
praise (compliments)	**lode** (f)	['lode]
to praise (vt)	**lodare** (vt)	[lo'dare]

69. Success. Good luck. Failure

success	**successo** (m)	[su'tʃesso]
successfully (adv)	**con successo**	[kon su'tʃesso]
successful (adj)	**ben riuscito**	[ben riu'ʃito]
luck (good luck)	**fortuna** (f)	[for'tuna]
Good luck!	**Buona fortuna!**	[bu'ona for'tuna]
lucky (e.g., ~ day)	**felice, fortunato**	[fe'litʃe], [fortu'nato]
lucky (fortunate)	**fortunato**	[fortu'nato]
failure	**fiasco** (m)	[fi'asko]
misfortune	**disdetta** (f)	[diz'detta]
bad luck	**sfortuna** (f)	[sfor'tuna]
unsuccessful (adj)	**fallito**	[fal'lito]
catastrophe	**disastro** (m)	[di'zastro]
pride	**orgoglio** (m)	[or'goʎʎo]
proud (adj)	**orgoglioso**	[orgoʎ'ʎozo]
to be proud	**essere fiero di ...**	['essere 'fjero di]
winner	**vincitore** (m)	[vintʃi'tore]
to win (vi)	**vincere** (vi)	['vintʃere]
to lose (not win)	**perdere** (vi)	['perdere]
try	**tentativo** (m)	[tenta'tivo]
to try (vi)	**tentare** (vi)	[ten'tare]
chance (opportunity)	**chance** (f)	[ʃans]

70. Quarrels. Negative emotions

shout (scream)	**grido** (m)	['grido]
to shout (vi)	**gridare** (vi)	[gri'dare]
to start to cry out	**mettersi a gridare**	['mettersi a gri'dare]
quarrel	**litigio** (m)	[li'tidʒo]
to quarrel (vi)	**litigare** (vi)	[liti'gare]
fight (squabble)	**lite** (f)	['lite]
to make a scene	**litigare** (vi)	[liti'gare]
conflict	**conflitto** (m)	[kon'flitto]
misunderstanding	**fraintendimento** (m)	[fraintendi'mento]
insult	**insulto** (m)	[in'sulto]
to insult (vt)	**insultare** (vt)	[insul'tare]
insulted (adj)	**offeso**	[of'fezo]
resentment	**offesa** (f)	[of'feza]
to offend (vt)	**offendere** (vt)	[of'fendere]
to take offense	**offendersi** (vr)	[of'fendersi]
indignation	**indignazione** (f)	[indiɲa'tsjone]
to be indignant	**indignarsi** (vr)	[indi'ɲarsi]

complaint	**lamentela** (f)	[lamen'tela]
to complain (vi, vt)	**lamentarsi** (vr)	[lamen'tarsi]
apology	**scusa** (f)	['skuza]
to apologize (vi)	**scusarsi** (vr)	[sku'zarsi]
to beg pardon	**chiedere scusa**	['kjedere 'skuza]
criticism	**critica** (f)	['kritika]
to criticize (vt)	**criticare** (vt)	[kriti'kare]
accusation (charge)	**accusa** (f)	[ak'kuza]
to accuse (vt)	**accusare** (vt)	[akku'zare]
revenge	**vendetta** (f)	[ven'detta]
to avenge (get revenge)	**vendicare** (vt)	[vendi'kare]
to pay back	**vendicarsi** (vr)	[vendi'karsi]
disdain	**disprezzo** (m)	[dis'prettso]
to despise (vt)	**disprezzare** (vt)	[dispret'tsare]
hatred, hate	**odio** (m)	['odio]
to hate (vt)	**odiare** (vt)	[odi'are]
nervous (adj)	**nervoso**	[ner'vozo]
to be nervous	**essere nervoso**	['essere ner'vozo]
angry (mad)	**arrabbiato**	[arrab'bjato]
to make angry	**fare arrabbiare**	['fare arrab'bjare]
humiliation	**umiliazione** (f)	[umilja'tsjone]
to humiliate (vt)	**umiliare** (vt)	[umi'ljare]
to humiliate oneself	**umiliarsi** (vr)	[umi'ljarsi]
shock	**shock** (m)	[ʃok]
to shock (vt)	**scandalizzare** (vt)	[skandalid'dzare]
trouble (e.g., serious ~)	**problema** (m)	[pro'blema]
unpleasant (adj)	**spiacevole**	[spja'tʃevole]
fear (dread)	**spavento** (m), **paura** (f)	[spa'vento], [pa'ura]
terrible (storm, heat)	**terribile**	[ter'ribile]
scary (e.g., ~ story)	**spaventoso**	[spaven'toso]
horror	**orrore** (m)	[or'rore]
awful (crime, news)	**orrendo**	[orrendo]
to begin to tremble	**cominciare a tremare**	[komin'tʃare a tre'mare]
to cry (weep)	**piangere** (vi)	['pjandʒere]
to start crying	**mettersi a piangere**	['mettersi a 'pjandʒere]
tear	**lacrima** (f)	['lakrima]
fault	**colpa** (f)	['kolpa]
guilt (feeling)	**senso** (m) **di colpa**	['senso di 'kolpa]
dishonor (disgrace)	**vergogna** (f)	[ver'goɲa]
protest	**protesta** (f)	[pro'testa]
stress	**stress** (m)	['stress]

to disturb (vt)	**disturbare** (vt)	[distur'bare]
to be furious	**essere arrabbiato**	['essere arrab'bjato]
mad, angry (adj)	**arrabbiato**	[arrab'bjato]
to end (~ a relationship)	**porre fine a ...**	['porre 'fine a]
to swear (at sb)	**rimproverare** (vt)	[rimprove'rare]
to scare (become afraid)	**spaventarsi** (vr)	[spaven'tarsi]
to hit (strike with hand)	**colpire** (vt)	[kol'pire]
to fight (street fight, etc.)	**picchiarsi** (vr)	[pik'kjarsi]
to settle (a conflict)	**regolare** (vt)	[rego'lare]
discontented (adj)	**scontento**	[skon'tento]
furious (adj)	**furioso**	[fu'rjozo]
It's not good!	**Non sta bene!**	[non sta 'bene]
It's bad!	**Fa male!**	[fa 'male]

Medicine

71. Diseases

sickness	**malattia** (f)	[malat'tia]
to be sick	**essere malato**	['essere ma'lato]
health	**salute** (f)	[sa'lute]
runny nose (coryza)	**raffreddore** (m)	[raffred'dore]
tonsillitis	**tonsillite** (f)	[tonsil'lite]
cold (illness)	**raffreddore** (m)	[raffred'dore]
to catch a cold	**raffreddarsi** (vr)	[raffred'darsi]
bronchitis	**bronchite** (f)	[bron'kite]
pneumonia	**polmonite** (f)	[polmo'nite]
flu, influenza	**influenza** (f)	[influ'entsa]
nearsighted (adj)	**miope**	['miope]
farsighted (adj)	**presbite**	['prezbite]
strabismus (crossed eyes)	**strabismo** (m)	[stra'bizmo]
cross-eyed (adj)	**strabico**	['strabiko]
cataract	**cateratta** (f)	[kate'ratta]
glaucoma	**glaucoma** (m)	[glau'koma]
stroke	**ictus** (m) **cerebrale**	['iktus tʃere'brale]
heart attack	**attacco** (m) **di cuore**	[at'tako di ku'ore]
myocardial infarction	**infarto** (m) **miocardico**	[in'farto miokar'diko]
paralysis	**paralisi** (f)	[pa'ralizi]
to paralyze (vt)	**paralizzare** (vt)	[paralid'dzare]
allergy	**allergia** (f)	[aller'dʒia]
asthma	**asma** (f)	['azma]
diabetes	**diabete** (m)	[dia'bete]
toothache	**mal** (m) **di denti**	[mal di 'denti]
caries	**carie** (f)	['karie]
diarrhea	**diarrea** (f)	[diar'rea]
constipation	**stitichezza** (f)	[stiti'kettsa]
stomach upset	**disturbo** (m) **gastrico**	[di'sturbo 'gastriko]
food poisoning	**intossicazione** (f) **alimentare**	[intossika'tsjone alimen'tare]
to get food poisoning	**intossicarsi** (vr)	[intossi'karsi]
arthritis	**artrite** (f)	[ar'trite]
rickets	**rachitide** (f)	[ra'kitide]

rheumatism	**reumatismo** (m)	[reuma'tizmo]
atherosclerosis	**aterosclerosi** (f)	[ateroskle'rozi]
gastritis	**gastrite** (f)	[ga'strite]
appendicitis	**appendicite** (f)	[appendi'ʧite]
cholecystitis	**colecistite** (f)	[koleʧi'stite]
ulcer	**ulcera** (f)	['ulʧera]
measles	**morbillo** (m)	[mor'billo]
rubella (German measles)	**rosolia** (f)	[rozo'lia]
jaundice	**itterizia** (f)	[itte'ritsia]
hepatitis	**epatite** (f)	[epa'tite]
schizophrenia	**schizofrenia** (f)	[skidzofre'nia]
rabies (hydrophobia)	**rabbia** (f)	['rabbia]
neurosis	**nevrosi** (f)	[ne'vrozi]
concussion	**commozione** (f) **cerebrale**	[kommo'tsjone ʧere'brale]
cancer	**cancro** (m)	['kankro]
sclerosis	**sclerosi** (f)	[skle'rozi]
multiple sclerosis	**sclerosi** (f) **multipla**	[skle'rozi 'multipla]
alcoholism	**alcolismo** (m)	[alko'lizmo]
alcoholic (n)	**alcolizzato** (m)	[alkolid'dzato]
syphilis	**sifilide** (f)	[si'filide]
AIDS	**AIDS** (m)	['aids]
tumor	**tumore** (m)	[tu'more]
malignant (adj)	**maligno**	[ma'liɲo]
benign (adj)	**benigno**	[be'niɲo]
fever	**febbre** (f)	['febbre]
malaria	**malaria** (f)	[ma'laria]
gangrene	**cancrena** (f)	[kan'krena]
seasickness	**mal** (m) **di mare**	[mal di 'mare]
epilepsy	**epilessia** (f)	[epiles'sia]
epidemic	**epidemia** (f)	[epide'mia]
typhus	**tifo** (m)	['tifo]
tuberculosis	**tubercolosi** (f)	[tuberko'lozi]
cholera	**colera** (m)	[ko'lera]
plague (bubonic ~)	**peste** (f)	['peste]

72. Symptoms. Treatments. Part 1

symptom	**sintomo** (m)	['sintomo]
temperature	**temperatura** (f)	[tempera'tura]
high temperature (fever)	**febbre** (f) **alta**	['febbre 'alta]
pulse (heartbeat)	**polso** (m)	['polso]
dizziness (vertigo)	**capogiro** (m)	[kapo'dʒiro]
hot (adj)	**caldo**	['kaldo]

shivering	**brivido** (m)	['brivido]
pale (e.g., ~ face)	**pallido**	['pallido]
cough	**tosse** (f)	['tosse]
to cough (vi)	**tossire** (vi)	[tos'sire]
to sneeze (vi)	**starnutire** (vi)	[starnu'tire]
faint	**svenimento** (m)	[zveni'mento]
to faint (vi)	**svenire** (vi)	[zve'nire]
bruise (hématome)	**livido** (m)	['livido]
bump (lump)	**bernoccolo** (m)	[ber'nokkolo]
to bang (bump)	**farsi un livido**	['farsi un 'livido]
contusion (bruise)	**contusione** (f)	[kontu'zjone]
to get a bruise	**farsi male**	['farsi 'male]
to limp (vi)	**zoppicare** (vi)	[dzoppi'kare]
dislocation	**slogatura** (f)	[zloga'tura]
to dislocate (vt)	**slogarsi** (vr)	[zlo'garsi]
fracture	**frattura** (f)	[frat'tura]
to have a fracture	**fratturarsi** (vr)	[frattu'rarsi]
cut (e.g., paper ~)	**taglio** (m)	['taʎʎo]
to cut oneself	**tagliarsi** (vr)	[taʎ'ʎarsi]
bleeding	**emorragia** (f)	[emorra'dʒia]
burn (injury)	**scottatura** (f)	[skotta'tura]
to get burned	**scottarsi** (vr)	[skot'tarsi]
to prick (vt)	**pungere** (vt)	['pundʒere]
to prick oneself	**pungersi** (vr)	['pundʒersi]
to injure (vt)	**ferire** (vt)	[fe'rire]
injury	**ferita** (f)	[fe'rita]
wound	**lesione** (f)	[le'zjone]
trauma	**trauma** (m)	['trauma]
to be delirious	**delirare** (vi)	[deli'rare]
to stutter (vi)	**tartagliare** (vi)	[tartaʎ'ʎare]
sunstroke	**colpo** (m) **di sole**	['kolpo di 'sole]

73. Symptoms. Treatments. Part 2

pain, ache	**dolore** (m), **male** (m)	[do'lore], ['male]
splinter (in foot, etc.)	**scheggia** (f)	['skedʒa]
sweat (perspiration)	**sudore** (m)	[su'dore]
to sweat (perspire)	**sudare** (vi)	[su'dare]
vomiting	**vomito** (m)	['vomito]
convulsions	**convulsioni** (f pl)	[konvul'sjoni]
pregnant (adj)	**incinta**	[in'tʃinta]
to be born	**nascere** (vi)	['naʃere]

delivery, labor	**parto** (m)	['parto]
to deliver (~ a baby)	**essere in travaglio**	['essere in tra'vaʎʎo]
abortion	**aborto** (m)	[a'borto]
breathing, respiration	**respirazione** (f)	[respira'tsjone]
in-breath (inhalation)	**inspirazione** (f)	[inspira'tsjone]
out-breath (exhalation)	**espirazione** (f)	[espira'tsjone]
to exhale (breathe out)	**espirare** (vi)	[espi'rare]
to inhale (vi)	**inspirare** (vi)	[inspi'rare]
disabled person	**invalido** (m)	[in'valido]
cripple	**storpio** (m)	['storpjo]
drug addict	**battaglia** (f)	[bat'taʎʎa]
deaf (adj)	**sordo**	['sordo]
mute (adj)	**muto**	['muto]
deaf mute (adj)	**sordomuto**	[sordo'muto]
mad, insane (adj)	**matto**	['matto]
madman (demented person)	**matto** (m)	['matto]
madwoman	**matta** (f)	['matta]
to go insane	**impazzire** (vi)	[impat'tsire]
gene	**gene** (m)	['ʤene]
immunity	**immunità** (f)	[immuni'ta]
hereditary (adj)	**ereditario**	[eredi'tario]
congenital (adj)	**innato**	[in'nato]
virus	**virus** (m)	['virus]
microbe	**microbo** (m)	['mikrobo]
bacterium	**batterio** (m)	[bat'terio]
infection	**infezione** (f)	[infe'tsjone]

74. Symptoms. Treatments. Part 3

hospital	**ospedale** (m)	[ospe'dale]
patient	**paziente** (m)	[pa'tsjente]
diagnosis	**diagnosi** (f)	[di'aɲozi]
cure	**cura** (f)	['kura]
medical treatment	**trattamento** (m)	[tratta'mento]
to get treatment	**curarsi** (vr)	[ku'rarsi]
to treat (~ a patient)	**curare** (vt)	[ku'rare]
to nurse (look after)	**accudire**	[akku'dire]
care (nursing ~)	**assistenza** (f)	[assi'stentsa]
operation, surgery	**operazione** (f)	[opera'tsjone]
to bandage (head, limb)	**bendare** (vt)	[ben'dare]
bandaging	**fasciatura** (f)	[faʃa'tura]

vaccination	**vaccinazione** (f)	[vatʃina'tsjone]
to vaccinate (vt)	**vaccinare** (vt)	[vatʃi'nare]
injection, shot	**iniezione** (f)	[inje'tsjone]
to give an injection	**fare una puntura**	['fare 'una pun'tura]
attack	**attacco** (m)	[at'takko]
amputation	**amputazione** (f)	[amputa'tsjone]
to amputate (vt)	**amputare** (vt)	[ampu'tare]
coma	**coma** (m)	['koma]
to be in a coma	**essere in coma**	['essere in 'koma]
intensive care	**rianimazione** (f)	[rianima'tsjone]
to recover (~ from flu)	**guarire** (vi)	[gwa'rire]
condition (patient's ~)	**stato** (f)	['stato]
consciousness	**conoscenza** (f)	[kono'ʃentsa]
memory (faculty)	**memoria** (f)	[me'moria]
to pull out (tooth)	**estrarre** (vt)	[e'strarre]
filling	**otturazione** (f)	[ottura'tsjone]
to fill (a tooth)	**otturare** (vt)	[ottu'rare]
hypnosis	**ipnosi** (f)	[ip'nozi]
to hypnotize (vt)	**ipnotizzare** (vt)	[ipnotid'dzare]

75. Doctors

doctor	**medico** (m)	['mediko]
nurse	**infermiera** (f)	[infer'mjera]
personal doctor	**medico** (m) **personale**	['mediko perso'nale]
dentist	**dentista** (m)	[den'tista]
eye doctor	**oculista** (m)	[oku'lista]
internist	**internista** (m)	[inter'nista]
surgeon	**chirurgo** (m)	[ki'rurgo]
psychiatrist	**psichiatra** (m)	[psiki'atra]
pediatrician	**pediatra** (m)	[pedi'atra]
psychologist	**psicologo** (m)	[psi'kologo]
gynecologist	**ginecologo** (m)	[dʒine'kologo]
cardiologist	**cardiologo** (m)	[kar'djologo]

76. Medicine. Drugs. Accessories

medicine, drug	**medicina** (f)	[medi'tʃina]
remedy	**rimedio** (m)	[ri'medio]
to prescribe (vt)	**prescrivere** (vt)	[pres'krivere]
prescription	**prescrizione** (f)	[preskri'tsjone]
tablet, pill	**compressa** (f)	[kom'pressa]

ointment	**unguento** (m)	[un'gwento]
ampule	**fiala** (f)	[fi'ala]
mixture, solution	**pozione** (f)	[po'tsjone]
syrup	**sciroppo** (m)	[ʃi'roppo]
capsule	**pillola** (f)	['pillola]
powder	**polverina** (f)	[polve'rina]
gauze bandage	**benda** (f)	['benda]
cotton wool	**ovatta** (f)	[o'vatta]
iodine	**iodio** (m)	[i'odio]
Band-Aid	**cerotto** (m)	[ʧe'rotto]
eyedropper	**contagocce** (m)	[konta'goʧe]
thermometer	**termometro** (m)	[ter'mometro]
syringe	**siringa** (f)	[si'ringa]
wheelchair	**sedia** (f) **a rotelle**	['sedia a ro'telle]
crutches	**stampelle** (f pl)	[stam'pelle]
painkiller	**analgesico** (m)	[anal'ʤeziko]
laxative	**lassativo** (m)	[lassa'tivo]
spirits (ethanol)	**alcol** (m)	[al'kol]
medicinal herbs	**erba** (f) **officinale**	['erba offiʧi'nale]
herbal (~ tea)	**d'erbe**	['derbe]

77. Smoking. Tobacco products

tobacco	**tabacco** (m)	[ta'bakko]
cigarette	**sigaretta** (f)	[siga'retta]
cigar	**sigaro** (m)	['sigaro]
pipe	**pipa** (f)	['pipa]
pack (of cigarettes)	**pacchetto** (m)	[pak'ketto]
matches	**fiammiferi** (m pl)	[fjam'miferi]
matchbox	**scatola** (f) **di fiammiferi**	['skatola di fjam'miferi]
lighter	**accendino** (m)	[aʧen'dino]
ashtray	**portacenere** (m)	[porta·'ʧenere]
cigarette case	**portasigarette** (m)	[porta·siga'rette]
cigarette holder	**bocchino** (m)	[bok'kino]
filter (cigarette tip)	**filtro** (m)	['filtro]
to smoke (vi, vt)	**fumare** (vi, vt)	[fu'mare]
to light a cigarette	**accendere una sigaretta**	[a'ʧendere 'una siga'retta]
smoking	**fumo** (m)	['fumo]
smoker	**fumatore** (m)	[fuma'tore]
stub, butt (of cigarette)	**cicca** (f)	['ʧikka]
smoke, fumes	**fumo** (m)	['fumo]
ash	**cenere** (f)	['ʧenere]

HUMAN HABITAT

City

78. City. Life in the city

city, town	**città** (f)	[tʃit'ta]
capital city	**capitale** (f)	[kapi'tale]
village	**villaggio** (m)	[vil'ladʒo]
city map	**mappa** (f) **della città**	['mappa 'della tʃit'ta]
downtown	**centro** (m) **della città**	['tʃentro 'della tʃit'ta]
suburb	**sobborgo** (m)	[sob'borgo]
suburban (adj)	**suburbano**	[subur'bano]
outskirts	**periferia** (f)	[perife'ria]
environs (suburbs)	**dintorni** (m pl)	[din'torni]
city block	**isolato** (m)	[izo'lato]
residential block (area)	**quartiere** (m) **residenziale**	[kwar'tjere reziden'tsjale]
traffic	**traffico** (m)	['traffiko]
traffic lights	**semaforo** (m)	[se'maforo]
public transportation	**trasporti** (m pl) **urbani**	[tras'porti ur'bani]
intersection	**incrocio** (m)	[in'krotʃo]
crosswalk	**passaggio** (m) **pedonale**	[pas'sadʒo pedo'nale]
pedestrian underpass	**sottopassaggio** (m)	[sotto·pas'sadʒo]
to cross (~ the street)	**attraversare** (vt)	[attraver'sare]
pedestrian	**pedone** (m)	[pe'done]
sidewalk	**marciapiede** (m)	[martʃa'pjede]
bridge	**ponte** (m)	['ponte]
embankment (river walk)	**banchina** (f)	[baŋ'kina]
fountain	**fontana** (f)	[fon'tana]
allée (garden walkway)	**vialetto** (m)	[via'letto]
park	**parco** (m)	['parko]
boulevard	**boulevard** (m)	[bul'var]
square	**piazza** (f)	['pjattsa]
avenue (wide street)	**viale** (m), **corso** (m)	[vi'ale], ['korso]
street	**via** (f), **strada** (f)	['via], ['strada]
side street	**vicolo** (m)	['vikolo]
dead end	**vicolo** (m) **cieco**	['vikolo 'tʃjeko]
house	**casa** (f)	['kaza]

building	**edificio** (m)	[edi'fitʃo]
skyscraper	**grattacielo** (m)	[gratta'tʃelo]
facade	**facciata** (f)	[fa'tʃata]
roof	**tetto** (m)	['tetto]
window	**finestra** (f)	[fi'nestra]
arch	**arco** (m)	['arko]
column	**colonna** (f)	[ko'lonna]
corner	**angolo** (m)	['angolo]
store window	**vetrina** (f)	[ve'trina]
signboard (store sign, etc.)	**insegna** (f)	[in'seɲa]
poster (e.g., playbill)	**cartellone** (m)	[kartel'lone]
advertising poster	**cartellone** (m) **pubblicitario**	[kartel'lone pubbliʧi'tario]
billboard	**tabellone** (m) **pubblicitario**	[tabel'lone pubbliʧi'tario]
garbage, trash	**pattume** (m), **spazzatura** (f)	[pat'tume], [spattsa'tura]
trash can (public ~)	**pattumiera** (f)	[pattu'mjera]
to litter (vi)	**sporcare** (vi)	[spor'kare]
garbage dump	**discarica** (f) **di rifiuti**	[dis'karika di ri'fjuti]
phone booth	**cabina** (f) **telefonica**	[ka'bina tele'fonika]
lamppost	**lampione** (m)	[lam'pjone]
bench (park ~)	**panchina** (f)	[paŋ'kina]
police officer	**poliziotto** (m)	[poli'tsjotto]
police	**polizia** (f)	[poli'tsia]
beggar	**mendicante** (m)	[mendi'kante]
homeless (n)	**barbone** (m)	[bar'bone]

79. Urban institutions

store	**negozio** (m)	[ne'gotsio]
drugstore, pharmacy	**farmacia** (f)	[farma'tʃia]
eyeglass store	**ottica** (f)	['ottika]
shopping mall	**centro** (m) **commerciale**	['tʃentro kommer'tʃale]
supermarket	**supermercato** (m)	[supermer'kato]
bakery	**panetteria** (f)	[panette'ria]
baker	**fornaio** (m)	[for'najo]
pastry shop	**pasticceria** (f)	[pastitʃe'ria]
grocery store	**drogheria** (f)	[droge'ria]
butcher shop	**macelleria** (f)	[matʃelle'ria]
produce store	**fruttivendolo** (m)	[frutti'vendolo]
market	**mercato** (m)	[mer'kato]
coffee house	**caffè** (m)	[kaf'fe]
restaurant	**ristorante** (m)	[risto'rante]

pub, bar	**birreria** (f), **pub** (m)	[birre'ria], [pab]
pizzeria	**pizzeria** (f)	[pittse'ria]
hair salon	**salone** (m) **di parrucchiere**	[sa'lone di parruk'kjere]
post office	**ufficio** (m) **postale**	[uf'fitʃo po'stale]
dry cleaners	**lavanderia** (f) **a secco**	[lavande'ria a 'sekko]
photo studio	**studio** (m) **fotografico**	['studio foto'grafiko]
shoe store	**negozio** (m) **di scarpe**	[ne'gotsio di 'skarpe]
bookstore	**libreria** (f)	[libre'ria]
sporting goods store	**negozio** (m) **sportivo**	[ne'gotsio spor'tivo]
clothes repair shop	**riparazione** (f) **di abiti**	[ripara'tsjone di 'abiti]
formal wear rental	**noleggio** (m) **di abiti**	[no'ledʒo di 'abiti]
video rental store	**noleggio** (m) **di film**	[no'ledʒo di film]
circus	**circo** (m)	['tʃirko]
zoo	**zoo** (m)	['dzoo]
movie theater	**cinema** (m)	['tʃinema]
museum	**museo** (m)	[mu'zeo]
library	**biblioteca** (f)	[biblio'teka]
theater	**teatro** (m)	[te'atro]
opera (opera house)	**teatro** (m) **dell'opera**	[te'atro dell 'opera]
nightclub	**locale notturno** (m)	[lo'kale not'turno]
casino	**casinò** (m)	[kazi'no]
mosque	**moschea** (f)	[mos'kea]
synagogue	**sinagoga** (f)	[sina'goga]
cathedral	**cattedrale** (f)	[katte'drale]
temple	**tempio** (m)	['tempjo]
church	**chiesa** (f)	['kjeza]
college	**istituto** (m)	[isti'tuto]
university	**università** (f)	[universi'ta]
school	**scuola** (f)	['skwola]
prefecture	**prefettura** (f)	[prefet'tura]
city hall	**municipio** (m)	[muni'tʃipio]
hotel	**albergo** (m)	[al'bergo]
bank	**banca** (f)	['banka]
embassy	**ambasciata** (f)	[amba'ʃata]
travel agency	**agenzia** (f) **di viaggi**	[adʒen'tsia di 'vjadʒi]
information office	**ufficio** (m) **informazioni**	[uf'fitʃo informa'tsjoni]
currency exchange	**ufficio** (m) **dei cambi**	[uf'fitʃo dei 'kambi]
subway	**metropolitana** (f)	[metropoli'tana]
hospital	**ospedale** (m)	[ospe'dale]
gas station	**distributore** (m) **di benzina**	[distribu'tore di ben'dzina]
parking lot	**parcheggio** (m)	[par'kedʒo]

80. Signs

signboard (store sign, etc.)	**insegna** (f)	[in'seɲa]
notice (door sign, etc.)	**iscrizione** (f)	[iskri'tsjone]
poster	**cartellone** (m)	[kartel'lone]
direction sign	**segnale** (m) **di direzione**	[se'ɲale di dire'tsjone]
arrow (sign)	**freccia** (f)	['fretʃa]
caution	**avvertimento** (m)	[avverti'mento]
warning sign	**avvertimento** (m)	[avverti'mento]
to warn (vt)	**avvertire** (vt)	[avver'tire]
rest day (weekly ~)	**giorno** (m) **di riposo**	['dʒorno di ri'pozo]
timetable (schedule)	**orario** (m)	[o'rario]
opening hours	**orario** (m) **di apertura**	[o'rario di aper'tura]
WELCOME!	**BENVENUTI!**	[benve'nuti]
ENTRANCE	**ENTRATA**	[en'trata]
EXIT	**USCITA**	[u'ʃita]
PUSH	**SPINGERE**	['spindʒere]
PULL	**TIRARE**	[ti'rare]
OPEN	**APERTO**	[a'perto]
CLOSED	**CHIUSO**	['kjuzo]
WOMEN	**DONNE**	['donne]
MEN	**UOMINI**	[u'omini]
DISCOUNTS	**SCONTI**	['skonti]
SALE	**SALDI**	['saldi]
NEW!	**NOVITÀ!**	[novi'ta]
FREE	**GRATIS**	['gratis]
ATTENTION!	**ATTENZIONE!**	[atten'tsjone]
NO VACANCIES	**COMPLETO**	[kom'pleto]
RESERVED	**RISERVATO**	[rizer'vato]
ADMINISTRATION	**AMMINISTRAZIONE**	[amministra'tsjone]
STAFF ONLY	**RISERVATO AL PERSONALE**	[rizer'vato al perso'nale]
BEWARE OF THE DOG!	**ATTENTI AL CANE**	[at'tenti al 'kane]
NO SMOKING	**VIETATO FUMARE!**	[vje'tato fu'mare]
DO NOT TOUCH!	**NON TOCCARE**	[non tok'kare]
DANGEROUS	**PERICOLOSO**	[periko'lozo]
DANGER	**PERICOLO**	[pe'rikolo]
HIGH VOLTAGE	**ALTA TENSIONE**	['alta ten'sjone]
NO SWIMMING!	**DIVIETO DI BALNEAZIONE**	[di'vjeto di balnea'tsjone]
OUT OF ORDER	**GUASTO**	['gwasto]

FLAMMABLE	**INFIAMMABILE**	[infjam'mabile]
FORBIDDEN	**VIETATO**	[vje'tato]
NO TRESPASSING!	**VIETATO L'INGRESSO**	[vje'tato lin'greso]
WET PAINT	**VERNICE FRESCA**	[ver'nitʃe 'freska]

81. Urban transportation

bus	**autobus** (m)	['autobus]
streetcar	**tram** (m)	[tram]
trolley bus	**filobus** (m)	['filobus]
route (of bus, etc.)	**itinerario** (m)	[itine'rario]
number (e.g., bus ~)	**numero** (m)	['numero]
to go by ...	**andare in ...**	[an'dare in]
to get on (~ the bus)	**salire su ...**	[sa'lire su]
to get off ...	**scendere da ...**	['ʃendere da]
stop (e.g., bus ~)	**fermata** (f)	[fer'mata]
next stop	**prossima fermata** (f)	['prossima fer'mata]
terminus	**capolinea** (m)	[kapo'linea]
schedule	**orario** (m)	[o'rario]
to wait (vt)	**aspettare** (vt)	[aspet'tare]
ticket	**biglietto** (m)	[biʎ'ʎetto]
fare	**prezzo** (m) **del biglietto**	['prettso del biʎ'ʎetto]
cashier (ticket seller)	**cassiere** (m)	[kas'sjere]
ticket inspection	**controllo** (m) **dei biglietti**	[kon'trollo dei biʎ'ʎeti]
ticket inspector	**bigliettaio** (m)	[biʎʎet'tajo]
to be late (for ...)	**essere in ritardo**	['essere in ri'tardo]
to miss (~ the train, etc.)	**perdere** (vt)	['perdere]
to be in a hurry	**avere fretta**	[a'vere 'fretta]
taxi, cab	**taxi** (m)	['taksi]
taxi driver	**taxista** (m)	[ta'ksista]
by taxi	**in taxi**	[in 'taksi]
taxi stand	**parcheggio** (m) **di taxi**	[par'keʤo di 'taksi]
to call a taxi	**chiamare un taxi**	[kja'mare un 'taksi]
to take a taxi	**prendere un taxi**	['prendere un 'taksi]
traffic	**traffico** (m)	['traffiko]
traffic jam	**ingorgo** (m)	[in'gorgo]
rush hour	**ore** (f pl) **di punta**	['ore di 'punta]
to park (vi)	**parcheggiarsi** (vr)	[parke'ʤarsi]
to park (vt)	**parcheggiare** (vt)	[parke'ʤare]
parking lot	**parcheggio** (m)	[par'keʤo]
subway	**metropolitana** (f)	[metropoli'tana]
station	**stazione** (f)	[sta'tsjone]

to take the subway	**prendere la metropolitana**	['prendere la metropoli'tana]
train	**treno** (m)	['treno]
train station	**stazione** (f) **ferroviaria**	[sta'tsjone ferro'vjaria]

82. Sightseeing

monument	**monumento** (m)	[monu'mento]
fortress	**fortezza** (f)	[for'tettsa]
palace	**palazzo** (m)	[pa'lattso]
castle	**castello** (m)	[ka'stello]
tower	**torre** (f)	['torre]
mausoleum	**mausoleo** (m)	[mauzo'leo]
architecture	**architettura** (f)	[arkitet'tura]
medieval (adj)	**medievale**	[medje'vale]
ancient (adj)	**antico**	[an'tiko]
national (adj)	**nazionale**	[natsio'nale]
famous (monument, etc.)	**famoso**	[fa'mozo]
tourist	**turista** (m)	[tu'rista]
guide (person)	**guida** (f)	['gwida]
excursion, sightseeing tour	**escursione** (f)	[eskur'sjone]
to show (vt)	**fare vedere**	['fare ve'dere]
to tell (vt)	**raccontare** (vt)	[rakkon'tare]
to find (vt)	**trovare** (vt)	[tro'vare]
to get lost (lose one's way)	**perdersi** (vr)	['perdersi]
map (e.g., subway ~)	**mappa** (f)	['mappa]
map (e.g., city ~)	**piantina** (f)	[pjan'tina]
souvenir, gift	**souvenir** (m)	[suve'nir]
gift shop	**negozio** (m) **di articoli da regalo**	[ne'gotsio di ar'tikoli da re'galo]
to take pictures	**fare foto**	['fare 'foto]
to have one's picture taken	**fotografarsi**	[fotogra'farsi]

83. Shopping

to buy (purchase)	**comprare** (vt)	[kom'prare]
purchase	**acquisto** (m)	[a'kwisto]
to go shopping	**fare acquisti**	['fare a'kwisti]
shopping	**shopping** (m)	['ʃopping]
to be open (ab. store)	**essere aperto**	['essere a'perto]
to be closed	**essere chiuso**	['essere 'kjuzo]
footwear, shoes	**calzature** (f pl)	[kaltsa'ture]
clothes, clothing	**abbigliamento** (m)	[abbiʎʎa'mento]

cosmetics	**cosmetica** (f)	[ko'zmetika]
food products	**alimentari** (m pl)	[alimen'tari]
gift, present	**regalo** (m)	[re'galo]
salesman	**commesso** (m)	[kom'messo]
saleswoman	**commessa** (f)	[kom'messa]
check out, cash desk	**cassa** (f)	['kassa]
mirror	**specchio** (m)	['spekkio]
counter (store ~)	**banco** (m)	['banko]
fitting room	**camerino** (m)	[kame'rino]
to try on	**provare** (vt)	[pro'vare]
to fit (ab. dress, etc.)	**stare bene**	['stare 'bene]
to like (I like ...)	**piacere** (vi)	[pja'ʧere]
price	**prezzo** (m)	['prettso]
price tag	**etichetta** (f) **del prezzo**	[eti'ketta del 'prettso]
to cost (vt)	**costare** (vt)	[ko'stare]
How much?	**Quanto?**	['kwanto]
discount	**sconto** (m)	['skonto]
inexpensive (adj)	**no muy caro**	[no muj 'karo]
cheap (adj)	**a buon mercato**	[a bu'on mer'kato]
expensive (adj)	**caro**	['karo]
It's expensive	**È caro**	[e 'karo]
rental (n)	**noleggio** (m)	[no'leʤo]
to rent (~ a tuxedo)	**noleggiare** (vt)	[nole'ʤare]
credit (trade credit)	**credito** (m)	['kredito]
on credit (adv)	**a credito**	[a 'kredito]

84. Money

money	**soldi** (m pl)	['soldi]
currency exchange	**cambio** (m)	['kambio]
exchange rate	**corso** (m) **di cambio**	['korso di 'kambio]
ATM	**bancomat** (m)	['bankomat]
coin	**moneta** (f)	[mo'neta]
dollar	**dollaro** (m)	['dollaro]
euro	**euro** (m)	['euro]
lira	**lira** (f)	['lira]
Deutschmark	**marco** (m)	['marko]
franc	**franco** (m)	['franko]
pound sterling	**sterlina** (f)	[ster'lina]
yen	**yen** (m)	[jen]
debt	**debito** (m)	['debito]
debtor	**debitore** (m)	[debi'tore]

to lend (money)	**prestare** (vt)	[pre'stare]
to borrow (vi, vt)	**prendere in prestito**	['prendere in 'prestito]
bank	**banca** (f)	['banka]
account	**conto** (m)	['konto]
to deposit into the account	**versare sul conto**	[ver'sare sul 'konto]
to withdraw (vt)	**prelevare dal conto**	[prele'vare dal 'konto]
credit card	**carta** (f) **di credito**	['karta di 'kredito]
cash	**contanti** (m pl)	[kon'tanti]
check	**assegno** (m)	[as'seɲo]
to write a check	**emettere un assegno**	[e'mettere un as'seɲo]
checkbook	**libretto** (m) **di assegni**	[li'bretto di as'seɲi]
wallet	**portafoglio** (m)	[porta·'foʎʎo]
change purse	**borsellino** (m)	[borsel'lino]
safe	**cassaforte** (f)	[kassa'forte]
heir	**erede** (m)	[e'rede]
inheritance	**eredità** (f)	[eredi'ta]
fortune (wealth)	**fortuna** (f)	[for'tuna]
lease	**affitto** (m)	[af'fitto]
rent (money)	**affitto** (m)	[af'fitto]
to rent (sth from sb)	**affittare** (vt)	[affit'tare]
price	**prezzo** (m)	['prettso]
cost	**costo** (m), **prezzo** (m)	['kosto], ['prettso]
sum	**somma** (f)	['somma]
to spend (vt)	**spendere** (vt)	['spendere]
expenses	**spese** (f pl)	['speze]
to economize (vi, vt)	**economizzare** (vi, vt)	[ekonomid'dzare]
economical	**economico**	[eko'nomiko]
to pay (vi, vt)	**pagare** (vi, vt)	[pa'gare]
payment	**pagamento** (m)	[paga'mento]
change (give the ~)	**resto** (m)	['resto]
tax	**imposta** (f)	[im'posta]
fine	**multa** (f), **ammenda** (f)	['multa], [am'menda]
to fine (vt)	**multare** (vt)	[mul'tare]

85. Post. Postal service

post office	**posta** (f), **ufficio** (m) **postale**	['posta], [uf'fitʃo po'stale]
mail (letters, etc.)	**posta** (f)	['posta]
mailman	**postino** (m)	[po'stino]
opening hours	**orario** (m) **di apertura**	[o'rario di aper'tura]

letter	**lettera** (f)	['lettera]
registered letter	**raccomandata** (f)	[rakkoman'data]
postcard	**cartolina** (f)	[karto'lina]
telegram	**telegramma** (m)	[tele'gramma]
package (parcel)	**pacco** (m) **postale**	['pakko po'stale]
money transfer	**vaglia** (m) **postale**	['vaʎʎa po'stale]
to receive (vt)	**ricevere** (vt)	[ri'ʧevere]
to send (vt)	**spedire** (vt)	[spe'dire]
sending	**invio** (m)	[in'vio]
address	**indirizzo** (m)	[indi'rittso]
ZIP code	**codice** (m) **postale**	['koditʃe po'stale]
sender	**mittente** (m)	[mit'tente]
receiver	**destinatario** (m)	[destina'tario]
name (first name)	**nome** (m)	['nome]
surname (last name)	**cognome** (m)	[ko'ɲome]
postage rate	**tariffa** (f)	[ta'riffa]
standard (adj)	**ordinario**	[ordi'nario]
economical (adj)	**standard**	['standar]
weight	**peso** (m)	['pezo]
to weigh (~ letters)	**pesare** (vt)	[pe'zare]
envelope	**busta** (f)	['busta]
postage stamp	**francobollo** (m)	[franko'bollo]

Dwelling. House. Home

86. House. Dwelling

house	**casa** (f)	['kaza]
at home (adv)	**a casa**	[a 'kaza]
yard	**cortile** (m)	[kor'tile]
fence (iron ~)	**recinto** (m)	[re'ʧinto]
brick (n)	**mattone** (m)	[mat'tone]
brick (as adj)	**di mattoni**	[di mat'toni]
stone (n)	**pietra** (f)	['pjetra]
stone (as adj)	**di pietra**	[di 'pjetra]
concrete (n)	**beton** (m)	[be'ton]
concrete (as adj)	**di beton**	[di be'ton]
new (new-built)	**nuovo**	[nu'ovo]
old (adj)	**vecchio**	['vekkio]
decrepit (house)	**fatiscente**	[fati'ʃente]
modern (adj)	**moderno**	[mo'derno]
multistory (adj)	**a molti piani**	[a 'molti 'pjani]
tall (~ building)	**alto**	['alto]
floor, story	**piano** (m)	['pjano]
single-story (adj)	**di un piano**	[di un 'pjano]
1st floor	**pianoterra** (m)	[pjano'terra]
top floor	**ultimo piano** (m)	['ultimo 'pjano]
roof	**tetto** (m)	['tetto]
chimney	**ciminiera** (f)	[ʧimi'njera]
roof tiles	**tegola** (f)	['tegola]
tiled (adj)	**di tegole**	[di 'tegole]
attic (storage place)	**soffitta** (f)	[sof'fitta]
window	**finestra** (f)	[fi'nestra]
glass	**vetro** (m)	['vetro]
window ledge	**davanzale** (m)	[davan'tsale]
shutters	**imposte** (f pl)	[im'poste]
wall	**muro** (m)	['muro]
balcony	**balcone** (m)	[bal'kone]
downspout	**tubo** (m) **pluviale**	['tubo plu'vjale]
upstairs (to be ~)	**su, di sopra**	[su], [di 'sopra]
to go upstairs	**andare di sopra**	[an'dare di 'sopra]

to come down (the stairs)	**scendere** (vi)	['ʃendere]
to move (to new premises)	**trasferirsi** (vr)	[trasfe'rirsi]

87. House. Entrance. Lift

entrance	**entrata** (f)	[en'trata]
stairs (stairway)	**scala** (f)	['skala]
steps	**gradini** (m pl)	[gra'dini]
banister	**ringhiera** (f)	[rin'gjera]
lobby (hotel ~)	**hall** (f)	[oll]
mailbox	**cassetta** (f) **della posta**	[kas'setta 'della 'posta]
garbage can	**secchio** (m) **della spazzatura**	['sekkio 'della spattsa'tura]
trash chute	**scivolo** (m) **per la spazzatura**	['ʃivolo per la spattsa'tura]
elevator	**ascensore** (m)	[aʃen'sore]
freight elevator	**montacarichi** (m)	[monta'kariki]
elevator cage	**cabina** (f) **di ascensore**	[ka'bina de aʃen'sore]
to take the elevator	**prendere l'ascensore**	['prendere laʃen'sore]
apartment	**appartamento** (m)	[apparta'mento]
residents (~ of a building)	**inquilini** (m pl)	[inkwi'lini]
neighbor (masc.)	**vicino** (m)	[vi'ʧino]
neighbor (fem.)	**vicina** (f)	[vi'ʧina]
neighbors	**vicini** (m pl)	[vi'ʧini]

88. House. Electricity

electricity	**elettricità** (f)	[elettriʧi'ta]
light bulb	**lampadina** (f)	[lampa'dina]
switch	**interruttore** (m)	[interrut'tore]
fuse (plug fuse)	**fusibile** (m)	[fu'zibile]
cable, wire (electric ~)	**filo** (m)	['filo]
wiring	**impianto** (m) **elettrico**	[im'pjanto e'lettriko]
electricity meter	**contatore** (m) **dell'elettricità**	[konta'tore dell elettriʧi'ta]
readings	**lettura, indicazione** (f)	[let'tura], [indika'tsjone]

89. House. Doors. Locks

door	**porta** (f)	['porta]
gate (vehicle ~)	**cancello** (m)	[kan'ʧello]
handle, doorknob	**maniglia** (f)	[ma'niʎʎa]

to unlock (unbolt)	**togliere il catenaccio**	['toʎʎere il kate'natʧo]
to open (vt)	**aprire** (vt)	[a'prire]
to close (vt)	**chiudere** (vt)	['kjudere]
key	**chiave** (f)	['kjave]
bunch (of keys)	**mazzo** (m)	['mattso]
to creak (door, etc.)	**cigolare** (vi)	[ʧigo'lare]
creak	**cigolio** (m)	[ʧigo'lio]
hinge (door ~)	**cardine** (m)	['kardine]
doormat	**zerbino** (m)	[ʤer'bino]
door lock	**serratura** (f)	[serra'tura]
keyhole	**buco** (m) **della serratura**	['buko 'della serra'tura]
crossbar (sliding bar)	**chiavistello** (m)	[kjavi'stello]
door latch	**catenaccio** (m)	[kate'natʧo]
padlock	**lucchetto** (m)	[luk'ketto]
to ring (~ the door bell)	**suonare** (vt)	[suo'nare]
ringing (sound)	**suono** (m)	[su'ono]
doorbell	**campanello** (m)	[kampa'nello]
doorbell button	**pulsante** (m)	[pul'sante]
knock (at the door)	**bussata** (f)	[bus'sata]
to knock (vi)	**bussare** (vi)	[bus'sare]
code	**codice** (m)	['koditʃe]
combination lock	**serratura** (f) **a codice**	[serra'tura a 'koditʃe]
intercom	**citofono** (m)	[ʧi'tofono]
number (on the door)	**numero** (m)	['numero]
doorplate	**targhetta** (f)	[tar'getta]
peephole	**spioncino** (m)	[spion'ʧino]

90. Country house

village	**villaggio** (m)	[vil'laʤo]
vegetable garden	**orto** (m)	['orto]
fence	**recinto** (m)	[re'ʧinto]
picket fence	**steccato** (m)	[stek'kato]
wicket gate	**cancelletto** (m)	[kanʧel'letto]
granary	**granaio** (m)	[gra'najo]
root cellar	**cantina** (f), **scantinato** (m)	[kan'tina], [skanti'nato]
shed (garden ~)	**capanno** (m)	[ka'panno]
water well	**pozzo** (m)	['pottso]
stove (wood-fired ~)	**stufa** (f)	['stufa]
to stoke the stove	**attizzare** (vt)	[attid'ʤare]
firewood	**legna** (f) **da ardere**	['leɲa da 'ardere]
log (firewood)	**ciocco** (m)	['ʧokko]
veranda	**veranda** (f)	[ve'randa]
deck (terrace)	**terrazza** (f)	[ter'rattsa]

stoop (front steps)	**scala** (f) **d'ingresso**	['skala din'gresso]
swing (hanging seat)	**altalena** (f)	[alta'lena]

91. Villa. Mansion

country house	**casa** (f) **di campagna**	['kaza di kam'paɲa]
villa (seaside ~)	**villa** (f)	['villa]
wing (~ of a building)	**ala** (f)	['ala]
garden	**giardino** (m)	[ʤar'dino]
park	**parco** (m)	['parko]
conservatory (greenhouse)	**serra** (f)	['serra]
to look after (garden, etc.)	**prendersi cura di**	['prendersi 'kura di]
swimming pool	**piscina** (f)	[pi'ʃina]
gym (home gym)	**palestra** (f)	[pa'lestra]
tennis court	**campo** (m) **da tennis**	['kampo da 'tennis]
home theater (room)	**home cinema** (m)	['om 'ʧinema]
garage	**garage** (m)	[ga'raʒ]
private property	**proprietà** (f) **privata**	[proprie'ta pri'vata]
private land	**terreno** (m) **privato**	[ter'reno pri'vato]
warning (caution)	**avvertimento** (m)	[avverti'mento]
warning sign	**cartello** (m) **di avvertimento**	['kartello di avverti'mento]
security	**sicurezza** (f)	[siku'rettsa]
security guard	**guardia** (f) **giurata**	['gwardia ʤu'rata]
burglar alarm	**allarme** (f) **antifurto**	[al'larme anti'furto]

92. Castle. Palace

castle	**castello** (m)	[ka'stello]
palace	**palazzo** (m)	[pa'lattso]
fortress	**fortezza** (f)	[for'tettsa]
wall (round castle)	**muro** (m)	['muro]
tower	**torre** (f)	['torre]
keep, donjon	**torre** (f) **principale**	['torre prinʧi'pale]
portcullis	**saracinesca** (f)	[saraʧi'neska]
underground passage	**tunnel** (m)	['tunnel]
moat	**fossato** (m)	[fos'sato]
chain	**catena** (f)	[ka'tena]
arrow loop	**feritoia** (f)	[feri'toja]
magnificent (adj)	**magnifico**	[ma'ɲifiko]
majestic (adj)	**maestoso**	[mae'stozo]

impregnable (adj)	**inespugnabile**	[inespu'ɲabile]
medieval (adj)	**medievale**	[medje'vale]

93. Apartment

apartment	**appartamento** (m)	[apparta'mento]
room	**camera** (f), **stanza** (f)	['kamera], ['stantsa]
bedroom	**camera** (f) **da letto**	['kamera da 'letto]
dining room	**sala** (f) **da pranzo**	['sala da 'prantso]
living room	**salotto** (m)	[sa'lotto]
study (home office)	**studio** (m)	['studio]
entry room	**ingresso** (m)	[in'gresso]
bathroom (room with a bath or shower)	**bagno** (m)	['baɲo]
half bath	**gabinetto** (m)	[gabi'netto]
ceiling	**soffitto** (m)	[sof'fitto]
floor	**pavimento** (m)	[pavi'mento]
corner	**angolo** (m)	['angolo]

94. Apartment. Cleaning

to clean (vi, vt)	**pulire** (vt)	[pu'lire]
to put away (to stow)	**mettere via**	['mettere 'via]
dust	**polvere** (f)	['polvere]
dusty (adj)	**impolverato**	[impolve'rato]
to dust (vt)	**spolverare** (vt)	[spolve'rare]
vacuum cleaner	**aspirapolvere** (m)	[aspira·'polvere]
to vacuum (vt)	**passare l'aspirapolvere**	[pas'sare laspira·'polvere]
to sweep (vi, vt)	**spazzare** (vi, vt)	[spat'tsare]
sweepings	**spazzatura** (f)	[spattsa'tura]
order	**ordine** (m)	['ordine]
disorder, mess	**disordine** (m)	[di'sordine]
mop	**frettazzo** (m)	[fret'tattso]
dust cloth	**strofinaccio** (m)	[strofi'natʃo]
short broom	**scopa** (f)	['skopa]
dustpan	**paletta** (f)	[pa'letta]

95. Furniture. Interior

furniture	**mobili** (m pl)	['mobili]
table	**tavolo** (m)	['tavolo]
chair	**sedia** (f)	['sedia]

bed	**letto** (m)	['letto]
couch, sofa	**divano** (m)	[di'vano]
armchair	**poltrona** (f)	[pol'trona]
bookcase	**libreria** (f)	[libre'ria]
shelf	**ripiano** (m)	[ri'pjano]
wardrobe	**armadio** (m)	[ar'madio]
coat rack (wall-mounted ~)	**attaccapanni** (m) **da parete**	[attakka'panni da pa'rete]
coat stand	**appendiabiti** (m) **da terra**	[apen'djabiti da terra]
bureau, dresser	**comò** (m)	[ko'mo]
coffee table	**tavolino** (m) **da salotto**	[tavo'lina da sa'lotto]
mirror	**specchio** (m)	['spekkio]
carpet	**tappeto** (m)	[tap'peto]
rug, small carpet	**tappetino** (m)	[tappe'tino]
fireplace	**camino** (m)	[ka'mino]
candle	**candela** (f)	[kan'dela]
candlestick	**candeliere** (m)	[kande'ljere]
drapes	**tende** (f pl)	['tende]
wallpaper	**carta** (f) **da parati**	['karta da pa'rati]
blinds (jalousie)	**tende** (f pl) **alla veneziana**	['tende alla vene'tsjana]
table lamp	**lampada** (f) **da tavolo**	['lampada da 'tavolo]
wall lamp (sconce)	**lampada** (f) **da parete**	['lampada da pa'rete]
floor lamp	**lampada** (f) **a stelo**	['lampada a 'stelo]
chandelier	**lampadario** (m)	[lampa'dario]
leg (of chair, table)	**gamba** (f)	['gamba]
armrest	**bracciolo** (m)	['bratʃolo]
back (backrest)	**spalliera** (f)	[spal'ljera]
drawer	**cassetto** (m)	[kas'setto]

96. Bedding

bedclothes	**biancheria** (f) **da letto**	[bjanke'ria da 'letto]
pillow	**cuscino** (m)	[ku'ʃino]
pillowcase	**federa** (f)	['federa]
duvet, comforter	**coperta** (f)	[ko'perta]
sheet	**lenzuolo** (m)	[lentsu'olo]
bedspread	**copriletto** (m)	[kopri'letto]

97. Kitchen

kitchen	**cucina** (f)	[ku'tʃina]
gas	**gas** (m)	[gas]

gas stove (range)	**fornello** (m) **a gas**	[for'nello a gas]
electric stove	**fornello** (m) **elettrico**	[for'nello e'lettriko]
oven	**forno** (m)	['forno]
microwave oven	**forno** (m) **a microonde**	['forno a mikro'onde]
refrigerator	**frigorifero** (m)	[frigo'rifero]
freezer	**congelatore** (m)	[kondʒela'tore]
dishwasher	**lavastoviglie** (f)	[lavasto'viʎʎe]
meat grinder	**tritacarne** (m)	[trita'karne]
juicer	**spremifrutta** (m)	[spremi'frutta]
toaster	**tostapane** (m)	[tosta'pane]
mixer	**mixer** (m)	['mikser]
coffee machine	**macchina** (f) **da caffè**	['makkina da kaf'fe]
coffee pot	**caffettiera** (f)	[kaffet'tjera]
coffee grinder	**macinacaffè** (m)	[matʃinakaf'fe]
kettle	**bollitore** (m)	[bolli'tore]
teapot	**teiera** (f)	[te'jera]
lid	**coperchio** (m)	[ko'perkio]
tea strainer	**colino** (m) **da tè**	[ko'lino da te]
spoon	**cucchiaio** (m)	[kuk'kjajo]
teaspoon	**cucchiaino** (m) **da tè**	[kuk'kjajno da 'te]
soup spoon	**cucchiaio** (m)	[kuk'kjajo]
fork	**forchetta** (f)	[for'ketta]
knife	**coltello** (m)	[kol'tello]
tableware (dishes)	**stoviglie** (f pl)	[sto'viʎʎe]
plate (dinner ~)	**piatto** (m)	['pjatto]
saucer	**piattino** (m)	[pjat'tino]
shot glass	**cicchetto** (m)	[tʃik'ketto]
glass (tumbler)	**bicchiere** (m)	[bik'kjere]
cup	**tazzina** (f)	[tat'tsina]
sugar bowl	**zuccheriera** (f)	[dzukke'rjera]
salt shaker	**saliera** (f)	[sa'ljera]
pepper shaker	**pepiera** (f)	[pe'pjera]
butter dish	**burriera** (f)	[bur'rjera]
stock pot (soup pot)	**pentola** (f)	['pentola]
frying pan (skillet)	**padella** (f)	[pa'della]
ladle	**mestolo** (m)	['mestolo]
colander	**colapasta** (m)	[kola'pasta]
tray (serving ~)	**vassoio** (m)	[vas'sojo]
bottle	**bottiglia** (f)	[bot'tiʎʎa]
jar (glass)	**barattolo** (m) **di vetro**	[ba'rattolo di 'vetro]

can	**latta** (f), **lattina** (f)	['latta], [lat'tina]
bottle opener	**apribottiglie** (m)	[apribot'tiʎʎe]
can opener	**apriscatole** (m)	[apri'skatole]
corkscrew	**cavatappi** (m)	[kava'tappi]
filter	**filtro** (m)	['filtro]
to filter (vt)	**filtrare** (vt)	[fil'trare]
trash, garbage (food waste, etc.)	**spazzatura** (f)	[spattsa'tura]
trash can (kitchen ~)	**pattumiera** (f)	[pattu'mjera]

98. Bathroom

bathroom	**bagno** (m)	['baɲo]
water	**acqua** (f)	['akwa]
faucet	**rubinetto** (m)	[rubi'netto]
hot water	**acqua** (f) **calda**	['akwa 'kalda]
cold water	**acqua** (f) **fredda**	['akwa 'fredda]
toothpaste	**dentifricio** (m)	[denti'fritʃo]
to brush one's teeth	**lavarsi i denti**	[la'varsi i 'denti]
toothbrush	**spazzolino** (m) **da denti**	[spatso'lino da 'denti]
to shave (vi)	**rasarsi** (vr)	[ra'zarsi]
shaving foam	**schiuma** (f) **da barba**	['skjuma da 'barba]
razor	**rasoio** (m)	[ra'zojo]
to wash (one's hands, etc.)	**lavare** (vt)	[la'vare]
to take a bath	**fare un bagno**	['fare un 'baɲo]
shower	**doccia** (f)	['dotʃa]
to take a shower	**fare una doccia**	['fare 'una 'dotʃa]
bathtub	**vasca** (f) **da bagno**	['vaska da 'baɲo]
toilet (toilet bowl)	**water** (m)	['vater]
sink (washbasin)	**lavandino** (m)	[lavan'dino]
soap	**sapone** (m)	[sa'pone]
soap dish	**porta** (m) **sapone**	['porta sa'pone]
sponge	**spugna** (f)	['spuɲa]
shampoo	**shampoo** (m)	['ʃampo]
towel	**asciugamano** (m)	[aʃuga'mano]
bathrobe	**accappatoio** (m)	[akkappa'tojo]
laundry (laundering)	**bucato** (m)	[bu'kato]
washing machine	**lavatrice** (f)	[lava'tritʃe]
to do the laundry	**fare il bucato**	['fare il bu'kato]
laundry detergent	**detersivo** (m) **per il bucato**	[deter'sivo per il bu'kato]

99. Household appliances

TV set	**televisore** (m)	[televi'zore]
tape recorder	**registratore** (m) **a nastro**	[redʒistra'tore a 'nastro]
VCR (video recorder)	**videoregistratore** (m)	[video·redʒistra'tore]
radio	**radio** (f)	['radio]
player (CD, MP3, etc.)	**lettore** (m)	[let'tore]
video projector	**videoproiettore** (m)	[video·projet'tore]
home movie theater	**home cinema** (m)	['om 'ʧinema]
DVD player	**lettore** (m) **DVD**	[let'tore divu'di]
amplifier	**amplificatore** (m)	[amplifika'tore]
video game console	**console** (f) **video giochi**	['konsole 'video 'dʒoki]
video camera	**videocamera** (f)	[video·'kamera]
camera (photo)	**macchina** (f) **fotografica**	['makkina foto'grafika]
digital camera	**fotocamera** (f) **digitale**	[foto'kamera didʒi'tale]
vacuum cleaner	**aspirapolvere** (m)	[aspira·'polvere]
iron (e.g., steam ~)	**ferro** (m) **da stiro**	['ferro da 'stiro]
ironing board	**asse** (f) **da stiro**	['asse da 'stiro]
telephone	**telefono** (m)	[te'lefono]
cell phone	**telefonino** (m)	[telefo'nino]
typewriter	**macchina** (f) **da scrivere**	['makkina da 'skrivere]
sewing machine	**macchina** (f) **da cucire**	['makkina da ku'ʧire]
microphone	**microfono** (m)	[mi'krofono]
headphones	**cuffia** (f)	['kuffia]
remote control (TV)	**telecomando** (m)	[teleko'mando]
CD, compact disc	**CD** (m)	[ʧi'di]
cassette, tape	**cassetta** (f)	[kas'setta]
vinyl record	**disco** (m)	['disko]

100. Repairs. Renovation

renovations	**lavori** (m pl) **di restauro**	[la'vori di re'stauro]
to renovate (vt)	**rinnovare** (vt)	[rinno'vare]
to repair, to fix (vt)	**riparare** (vt)	[ripa'rare]
to put in order	**mettere in ordine**	['mettere in 'ordine]
to redo (do again)	**rifare** (vt)	[ri'fare]
paint	**vernice** (f), **pittura** (f)	[ver'niʧe], [pit'tura]
to paint (~ a wall)	**pitturare** (vt)	[pittu'rare]
house painter	**imbianchino** (m)	[imbjaŋ'kino]
paintbrush	**pennello** (m)	[pen'nello]
whitewash	**imbiancatura** (f)	[imbjanka'tura]
to whitewash (vt)	**imbiancare** (vt)	[imbjan'kare]

wallpaper	**carta** (f) **da parati**	['karta da pa'rati]
to wallpaper (vt)	**tappezzare** (vt)	[tappet'tsare]
varnish	**vernice** (f)	[ver'nitʃe]
to varnish (vt)	**verniciare** (vt)	[verni'tʃare]

101. Plumbing

water	**acqua** (f)	['akwa]
hot water	**acqua** (f) **calda**	['akwa 'kalda]
cold water	**acqua** (f) **fredda**	['akwa 'fredda]
faucet	**rubinetto** (m)	[rubi'netto]
drop (of water)	**goccia** (f)	['gotʃa]
to drip (vi)	**gocciolare** (vi)	[gotʃo'lare]
to leak (ab. pipe)	**perdere** (vi)	['perdere]
leak (pipe ~)	**perdita** (f)	['perdita]
puddle	**pozza** (f)	['pottsa]
pipe	**tubo** (m)	['tubo]
valve (e.g., ball ~)	**valvola** (f)	['valvola]
to be clogged up	**intasarsi** (vr)	[inta'zarsi]
tools	**strumenti** (m pl)	[stru'menti]
adjustable wrench	**chiave** (f) **inglese**	['kjave in'gleze]
to unscrew (lid, filter, etc.)	**svitare** (vt)	[zvi'tare]
to screw (tighten)	**avvitare** (vt)	[avvi'tare]
to unclog (vt)	**stasare** (vt)	[sta'zare]
plumber	**idraulico** (m)	[i'drauliko]
basement	**seminterrato** (m)	[seminter'rato]
sewerage (system)	**fognatura** (f)	[foɲa'tura]

102. Fire. Conflagration

fire (accident)	**fuoco** (m)	[fu'oko]
flame	**fiamma** (f)	['fjamma]
spark	**scintilla** (f)	[ʃin'tilla]
smoke (from fire)	**fumo** (m)	['fumo]
torch (flaming stick)	**fiaccola** (f)	['fjakkola]
campfire	**falò** (m)	[fa'lo]
gas, gasoline	**benzina** (f)	[ben'dzina]
kerosene (type of fuel)	**cherosene** (m)	[kero'zene]
flammable (adj)	**combustibile**	[kombu'stibile]
explosive (adj)	**esplosivo**	[esplo'zivo]
NO SMOKING	**VIETATO FUMARE!**	[vje'tato fu'mare]
safety	**sicurezza** (f)	[siku'rettsa]
danger	**pericolo** (m)	[pe'rikolo]

dangerous (adj)	**pericoloso**	[periko'lozo]
to catch fire	**prendere fuoco**	['prendere fu'oko]
explosion	**esplosione** (f)	[esplo'zjone]
to set fire	**incendiare** (vt)	[intʃen'djare]
arsonist	**incendiario** (m)	[intʃen'djario]
arson	**incendio** (m) **doloso**	[in'tʃendio do'lozo]
to blaze (vi)	**divampare** (vi)	[divam'pare]
to burn (be on fire)	**bruciare** (vi)	[bru'tʃare]
to burn down	**bruciarsi** (vr)	[bru'tʃarsi]
to call the fire department	**chiamare i pompieri**	[kja'mare i pom'pjeri]
firefighter, fireman	**pompiere** (m)	[pom'pjere]
fire truck	**autopompa** (f)	[auto'pompa]
fire department	**corpo** (m) **dei pompieri**	['korpo dei pom'pjeri]
fire truck ladder	**autoscala** (f) **da pompieri**	[auto'skala da pom'pjeri]
fire hose	**manichetta** (f)	[mani'ketta]
fire extinguisher	**estintore** (m)	[estin'tore]
helmet	**casco** (m)	['kasko]
siren	**sirena** (f)	[si'rena]
to cry (for help)	**gridare** (vi)	[gri'dare]
to call for help	**chiamare in aiuto**	[kja'mare in a'juto]
rescuer	**soccorritore** (m)	[sokkorri'tore]
to rescue (vt)	**salvare** (vt)	[sal'vare]
to arrive (vi)	**arrivare** (vi)	[arri'vare]
to extinguish (vt)	**spegnere** (vt)	['speɲere]
water	**acqua** (f)	['akwa]
sand	**sabbia** (f)	['sabbia]
ruins (destruction)	**rovine** (f pl)	[ro'vine]
to collapse (building, etc.)	**crollare** (vi)	[krol'lare]
to fall down (vi)	**cadere** (vi)	[ka'dere]
to cave in (ceiling, floor)	**collassare** (vi)	[kolla'sare]
piece of debris	**frammento** (m)	[fram'mento]
ash	**cenere** (f)	['tʃenere]
to suffocate (die)	**asfissiare** (vi)	[asfis'sjare]
to be killed (perish)	**morire, perire** (vi)	[mo'rire], [pe'rire]

HUMAN ACTIVITIES

Job. Business. Part 1

103. Office. Working in the office

office (company ~)	**ufficio** (m)	[uf'fitʃo]
office (of director, etc.)	**ufficio** (m)	[uf'fitʃo]
reception desk	**portineria** (f)	[portine'ria]
secretary	**segretario** (m)	[segre'tario]
secretary (fem.)	**segretaria** (f)	[segre'taria]
director	**direttore** (m)	[diret'tore]
manager	**manager** (m)	['menedʒer]
accountant	**contabile** (m)	[kon'tabile]
employee	**impiegato** (m)	[impje'gato]
furniture	**mobili** (m pl)	['mobili]
desk	**scrivania** (f)	[skriva'nia]
desk chair	**poltrona** (f)	[pol'trona]
drawer unit	**cassettiera** (f)	[kasset'tjera]
coat stand	**appendiabiti** (m) **da terra**	[apen'djabiti da terra]
computer	**computer** (m)	[kom'pjuter]
printer	**stampante** (f)	[stam'pante]
fax machine	**fax** (m)	[faks]
photocopier	**fotocopiatrice** (f)	[fotokopja'tritʃe]
paper	**carta** (f)	['karta]
office supplies	**cancelleria** (f)	[kantʃelle'ria]
mouse pad	**tappetino** (m) **del mouse**	[tappe'tino del 'maus]
sheet (of paper)	**foglio** (m)	['foʎʎo]
binder	**cartella** (f)	[kar'tella]
catalog	**catalogo** (m)	[ka'talogo]
phone directory	**elenco** (m) **del telefono**	[e'lenko del te'lefono]
documentation	**documentazione** (f)	[dokumenta'tsjone]
brochure (e.g., 12 pages ~)	**opuscolo** (m)	[o'puskolo]
leaflet (promotional ~)	**volantino** (m)	[volan'tino]
sample	**campione** (m)	[kam'pjone]
training meeting	**formazione** (f)	[forma'tsjone]
meeting (of managers)	**riunione** (f)	[riu'njone]
lunch time	**pausa** (f) **pranzo**	['pauza 'prantso]

to make a copy	**copiare** (vt)	[ko'pjare]
to make multiple copies	**fare copie**	['fare 'kopje]
to receive a fax	**ricevere un fax**	[ri'tʃevere un faks]
to send a fax	**spedire un fax**	[spe'dire un faks]
to call (by phone)	**telefonare** (vi, vt)	[telefo'nare]
to answer (vt)	**rispondere** (vi, vt)	[ris'pondere]
to put through	**passare** (vt)	[pas'sare]
to arrange, to set up	**fissare** (vt)	[fis'sare]
to demonstrate (vt)	**dimostrare** (vt)	[dimo'strare]
to be absent	**essere assente**	['essere as'sente]
absence	**assenza** (f)	[as'sentsa]

104. Business processes. Part 1

occupation	**occupazione** (f)	[okkupa'tsjone]
firm	**ditta** (f)	['ditta]
company	**compagnia** (f)	[kompa'ɲia]
corporation	**corporazione** (f)	[korpora'tsjone]
enterprise	**impresa** (f)	[im'preza]
agency	**agenzia** (f)	[adʒen'tsia]
agreement (contract)	**accordo** (m)	[ak'kordo]
contract	**contratto** (m)	[kon'tratto]
deal	**affare** (m)	[af'fare]
order (to place an ~)	**ordine** (m)	['ordine]
terms (of the contract)	**termine** (m) **dell'accordo**	['termine dell ak'kordo]
wholesale (adv)	**all'ingrosso**	[all in'grosso]
wholesale (adj)	**all'ingrosso**	[all in'grosso]
wholesale (n)	**vendita** (f) **all'ingrosso**	['vendita all in'grosso]
retail (adj)	**al dettaglio**	[al det'taʎʎo]
retail (n)	**vendita** (f) **al dettaglio**	['vendita al det'taʎʎo]
competitor	**concorrente** (m)	[konkor'rente]
competition	**concorrenza** (f)	[konkor'rentsa]
to compete (vi)	**competere** (vi)	[kom'petere]
partner (associate)	**socio** (m), **partner** (m)	['sotʃo], ['partner]
partnership	**partenariato** (m)	[partena'rjato]
crisis	**crisi** (f)	['krizi]
bankruptcy	**bancarotta** (f)	[banka'rotta]
to go bankrupt	**fallire** (vi)	[fal'lire]
difficulty	**difficoltà** (f)	[diffikol'ta]
problem	**problema** (m)	[pro'blema]
catastrophe	**disastro** (m)	[di'zastro]
economy	**economia** (f)	[ekono'mia]
economic (~ growth)	**economico**	[eko'nomiko]

economic recession	**recessione** (f) **economica**	[retʃes'sjone eko'nomika]
goal (aim)	**scopo** (m), **obiettivo** (m)	['skopo], [objet'tivo]
task	**incarico** (m)	[in'kariko]
to trade (vi)	**commerciare** (vi)	[kommer'tʃare]
network (distribution ~)	**rete** (f)	['rete]
inventory (stock)	**giacenza** (f)	[dʒia'tʃentsa]
range (assortment)	**assortimento** (m)	[assorti'mento]
leader (leading company)	**leader** (m), **capo** (m)	['lider], ['kapo]
large (~ company)	**grande**	['grande]
monopoly	**monopolio** (m)	[mono'polio]
theory	**teoria** (f)	[teo'ria]
practice	**pratica** (f)	['pratika]
experience (in my ~)	**esperienza** (f)	[espe'rjentsa]
trend (tendency)	**tendenza** (f)	[ten'dentsa]
development	**sviluppo** (m)	[zvi'luppo]

105. Business processes. Part 2

profit (foregone ~)	**profitto** (m)	[pro'fitto]
profitable (~ deal)	**profittevole**	[profit'tevole]
delegation (group)	**delegazione** (f)	[delega'tsjone]
salary	**stipendio** (m)	[sti'pendio]
to correct (an error)	**correggere** (vt)	[kor'redʒere]
business trip	**viaggio** (m) **d'affari**	['vjadʒo daf'fari]
commission	**commissione** (f)	[kommi'sjone]
to control (vt)	**controllare** (vt)	[kontrol'lare]
conference	**conferenza** (f)	[konfe'rentsa]
license	**licenza** (f)	[li'tʃentsa]
reliable (~ partner)	**affidabile**	[affi'dabile]
initiative (undertaking)	**iniziativa** (f)	[initsja'tiva]
norm (standard)	**norma** (f)	['norma]
circumstance	**circostanza** (f)	[tʃirko'stantsa]
duty (of employee)	**mansione** (f)	[man'sjone]
organization (company)	**impresa** (f)	[im'preza]
organization (process)	**organizzazione** (f)	[organiddza'tsjone]
organized (adj)	**organizzato**	[organid'dzato]
cancellation	**annullamento** (m)	[annulla'mento]
to cancel (call off)	**annullare** (vt)	[annul'lare]
report (official ~)	**rapporto** (m)	[rap'porto]
patent	**brevetto** (m)	[bre'vetto]
to patent (obtain patent)	**brevettare** (vt)	[brevet'tare]
to plan (vt)	**pianificare** (vt)	[pjanifi'kare]

bonus (money)	**premio** (m)	['premio]
professional (adj)	**professionale**	[professjo'nale]
procedure	**procedura** (f)	[protʃe'dura]
to examine (contract, etc.)	**esaminare** (vt)	[ezami'nare]
calculation	**calcolo** (m)	['kalkolo]
reputation	**reputazione** (f)	[reputa'tsjone]
risk	**rischio** (m)	['riskio]
to manage, to run	**dirigere** (vt)	[di'ridʒere]
information (report)	**informazioni** (f pl)	[informa'tsjoni]
property	**proprietà** (f)	[proprie'ta]
union	**unione** (f)	[uni'one]
life insurance	**assicurazione** (f) **sulla vita**	[assikura'tsjone 'sulla 'vita]
to insure (vt)	**assicurare** (vt)	[assiku'rare]
insurance	**assicurazione** (f)	[assikura'tsjone]
auction (~ sale)	**asta** (f)	['asta]
to notify (inform)	**avvisare** (vt)	[avvi'zare]
management (process)	**gestione** (f)	[dʒes'tjone]
service (~ industry)	**servizio** (m)	[ser'vitsio]
forum	**forum** (m)	['forum]
to function (vi)	**funzionare** (vi)	[funtsjo'nare]
stage (phase)	**stadio** (m)	['stadio]
legal (~ services)	**giuridico**	[dʒu'ridiko]
lawyer (legal advisor)	**esperto** (m) **legale**	[e'sperto le'gale]

106. Production. Works

plant	**stabilimento** (m)	[stabili'mento]
factory	**fabbrica** (f)	['fabbrika]
workshop	**officina** (f) **di produzione**	[offi'tʃina di produ'tsjone]
works, production site	**stabilimento** (m)	[stabili'mento]
industry (manufacturing)	**industria** (f)	[in'dustria]
industrial (adj)	**industriale**	[industri'ale]
heavy industry	**industria** (f) **pesante**	[in'dustria pe'zante]
light industry	**industria** (f) **leggera**	[in'dustria le'dʒera]
products	**prodotti** (m pl)	[pro'dotti]
to produce (vt)	**produrre** (vt)	[pro'durre]
raw materials	**materia** (f) **prima**	[ma'teria 'prima]
foreman (construction ~)	**caposquadra** (m)	[kapo'skwadra]
workers team (crew)	**squadra** (f)	['skwadra]
worker	**operaio** (m)	[ope'rajo]
working day	**giorno** (m) **lavorativo**	['dʒorno lavora'tivo]

pause (rest break)	**pausa** (f)	['pauza]
meeting	**riunione** (f)	[riu'njone]
to discuss (vt)	**discutere** (vt)	[di'skutere]
plan	**piano** (m)	['pjano]
to fulfill the plan	**eseguire il piano**	[eze'gwire il 'pjano]
rate of output	**tasso** (m) **di produzione**	['tasso di produ'tsjone]
quality	**qualità** (f)	[kwali'ta]
control (checking)	**controllo** (m)	[kon'trollo]
quality control	**controllo** (m) **di qualità**	[kon'trollo di kwali'ta]
workplace safety	**sicurezza** (f) **sul lavoro**	[siku'rettsa sul la'voro]
discipline	**disciplina** (f)	[diʃi'plina]
violation (of safety rules, etc.)	**infrazione** (f)	[infra'tsjone]
to violate (rules)	**violare** (vt)	[vio'lare]
strike	**sciopero** (m)	['ʃopero]
striker	**scioperante** (m)	[ʃope'rante]
to be on strike	**fare sciopero**	['fare 'ʃopero]
labor union	**sindacato** (m)	[sinda'kato]
to invent (machine, etc.)	**inventare** (vt)	[inven'tare]
invention	**invenzione** (f)	[inven'tsjone]
research	**ricerca** (f)	[ri'ʧerka]
to improve (make better)	**migliorare** (vt)	[miʎʎo'rare]
technology	**tecnologia** (f)	[teknolo'ʤia]
technical drawing	**disegno** (m) **tecnico**	[di'zeɲo 'tekniko]
load, cargo	**carico** (m)	['kariko]
loader (person)	**caricatore** (m)	[karika'tore]
to load (vehicle, etc.)	**caricare** (vt)	[kari'kare]
loading (process)	**caricamento** (m)	[karika'mento]
to unload (vi, vt)	**scaricare** (vt)	[skari'kare]
unloading	**scarico** (m)	['skariko]
transportation	**trasporto** (m)	[tras'porto]
transportation company	**società** (f) **di trasporti**	[soʧe'ta di tras'porti]
to transport (vt)	**trasportare** (vt)	[traspor'tare]
freight car	**vagone** (m) **merci**	[va'gone 'merʧi]
tank (e.g., oil ~)	**cisterna** (f)	[ʧi'sterna]
truck	**camion** (m)	['kamjon]
machine tool	**macchina** (f) **utensile**	['makkina u'tensile]
mechanism	**meccanismo** (m)	[mekka'nizmo]
industrial waste	**rifiuti** (m pl) **industriali**	[ri'fjuti industri'ali]
packing (process)	**imballaggio** (m)	[imbal'laʤo]
to pack (vt)	**imballare** (vt)	[imbal'lare]

107. Contract. Agreement

contract	**contratto** (m)	[kon'tratto]
agreement	**accordo** (m)	[ak'kordo]
addendum	**allegato** (m)	[alle'gato]
to sign a contract	**firmare un contratto**	[fir'mare un kon'tratto]
signature	**firma** (f)	['firma]
to sign (vt)	**firmare** (vt)	[fir'mare]
seal (stamp)	**timbro** (m)	['timbro]
subject of the contract	**oggetto** (m) **del contratto**	[o'dʒetto del kon'tratto]
clause	**clausola** (f)	['klauzola]
parties (in contract)	**parti** (f pl)	['parti]
legal address	**sede** (f) **legale**	['sede le'gale]
to violate the contract	**sciogliere un contratto**	['ʃoʎʎere un kon'tratto]
commitment (obligation)	**obbligo** (m)	['obbligo]
responsibility	**responsabilità** (f)	[responsabili'ta]
force majeure	**forza** (f) **maggiore**	['fortsa ma'dʒore]
dispute	**discussione** (f)	[diskus'sjone]
penalties	**sanzioni** (f pl)	[san'tsjoni]

108. Import & Export

import	**importazione** (f)	[importa'tsjone]
importer	**importatore** (m)	[importa'tore]
to import (vt)	**importare** (vt)	[impor'tare]
import (as adj.)	**d'importazione**	[dimporta'tsjone]
export (exportation)	**esportazione** (f)	[esporta'tsjone]
exporter	**esportatore** (m)	[esporta'tore]
to export (vi, vt)	**esportare** (vt)	[espor'tare]
export (as adj.)	**d'esportazione**	[desporta'tsjone]
goods (merchandise)	**merce** (f)	['mertʃe]
consignment, lot	**carico** (m)	['kariko]
weight	**peso** (m)	['pezo]
volume	**volume** (m)	[vo'lume]
cubic meter	**metro** (m) **cubo**	['metro 'kubo]
manufacturer	**produttore** (m)	[produt'tore]
transportation company	**società** (f) **di trasporti**	[sotʃe'ta di tras'porti]
container	**container** (m)	[kon'tejner]
border	**frontiera** (f)	[fron'tjera]
customs	**dogana** (f)	[do'gana]
customs duty	**dazio** (m) **doganale**	['datsio doga'nale]

customs officer	**doganiere** (m)	[doga'njere]
smuggling	**contrabbando** (m)	[kontrab'bando]
contraband (smuggled goods)	**merci** (f pl) **contrabbandate**	['mertʃi kontrabban'date]

109. Finances

stock (share)	**azione** (f)	[a'tsjone]
bond (certificate)	**obbligazione** (f)	[obbliga'tsjone]
promissory note	**cambiale** (f)	[kam'bjale]
stock exchange	**borsa** (f)	['borsa]
stock price	**quotazione** (f)	[kwota'tsjone]
to go down (become cheaper)	**diminuire di prezzo**	[diminu'ire di 'prettso]
to go up (become more expensive)	**aumentare di prezzo**	[aumen'tare di 'prettso]
share	**quota** (f)	['kwota]
controlling interest	**pacchetto** (m) **di maggioranza**	[pak'ketto di madʒo'rantsa]
investment	**investimento** (m)	[investi'mento]
to invest (vt)	**investire** (vt)	[inve'stire]
percent	**percento** (m)	[per'tʃento]
interest (on investment)	**interessi** (m pl)	[inte'ressi]
profit	**profitto** (m)	[pro'fitto]
profitable (adj)	**redditizio**	[redi'titsio]
tax	**imposta** (f)	[im'posta]
currency (foreign ~)	**valuta** (f)	[va'luta]
national (adj)	**nazionale**	[natsio'nale]
exchange (currency ~)	**cambio** (m)	['kambio]
accountant	**contabile** (m)	[kon'tabile]
accounting	**ufficio** (m) **contabilità**	[uf'fitʃo kontabili'ta]
bankruptcy	**bancarotta** (f)	[banka'rotta]
collapse, crash	**fallimento** (m)	[falli'mento]
ruin	**rovina** (f)	[ro'vina]
to be ruined (financially)	**andare in rovina**	[an'dare in ro'vina]
inflation	**inflazione** (f)	[infla'tsjone]
devaluation	**svalutazione** (f)	[zvaluta'tsjone]
capital	**capitale** (m)	[kapi'tale]
income	**reddito** (m)	['reddito]
turnover	**giro** (m) **di affari**	['dʒiro di af'fari]
resources	**risorse** (f pl)	[ri'sorse]

monetary resources	**mezzi** (m pl) **finanziari**	['meddzi finan'tsjari]
overhead	**spese** (f pl) **generali**	['speze dʒene'rali]
to reduce (expenses)	**ridurre** (vt)	[ri'durre]

110. Marketing

marketing	**marketing** (m)	['marketing]
market	**mercato** (m)	[mer'kato]
market segment	**segmento** (m) **di mercato**	[seg'mento di mer'kato]
product	**prodotto** (m)	[pro'dotto]
goods (merchandise)	**merce** (f)	['mertʃe]
brand	**brand** (m)	[brend]
trademark	**marchio** (m) **di fabbrica**	['markio di 'fabbrika]
logotype	**logotipo** (m)	[logo'tipo]
logo	**logo** (m)	[logo]
demand	**domanda** (f)	[do'manda]
supply	**offerta** (f)	[of'ferta]
need	**bisogno** (m)	[bi'zoɲo]
consumer	**consumatore** (m)	[konsuma'tore]
analysis	**analisi** (f)	[a'nalizi]
to analyze (vt)	**analizzare** (vt)	[analid'dzare]
positioning	**posizionamento** (m)	[pozitsjona'mento]
to position (vt)	**posizionare** (vt)	[pozitsjo'nare]
price	**prezzo** (m)	['prettso]
pricing policy	**politica** (f) **dei prezzi**	[po'litika 'dei 'prettsi]
price formation	**determinazione** (f) **dei prezzi**	[determina'tsjone del 'prettsi]

111. Advertising

advertising	**pubblicità** (f)	[pubblitʃi'ta]
to advertise (vt)	**pubblicizzare** (vt)	[pubblitʃid'dzare]
budget	**bilancio** (m)	[bi'lantʃo]
ad, advertisement	**annuncio** (m)	[an'nuntʃo]
TV advertising	**pubblicità** (f) **televisiva**	[pubblitʃi'ta televi'ziva]
radio advertising	**pubblicità** (f) **radiofonica**	[pubblitʃi'ta radio'fonika]
outdoor advertising	**pubblicità** (f) **esterna**	[pubblitʃi'ta es'terna]
mass media	**mass media** (m pl)	[mass 'media]
periodical (n)	**periodico** (m)	[pe'rjodiko]
image (public appearance)	**immagine** (f)	[im'madʒine]
slogan	**slogan** (m)	[zlogan]

motto (maxim)	**motto** (m)	['motto]
campaign	**campagna** (f)	[kam'paɲa]
advertising campaign	**campagna** (f) **pubblicitaria**	[kam'paɲa pubblitʃi'taria]
target group	**gruppo** (m) **di riferimento**	['gruppo de riferi'mento]
business card	**biglietto** (m) **da visita**	[biʎ'ʎetto da 'vizita]
leaflet (promotional ~)	**volantino** (m)	[volan'tino]
brochure (e.g., 12 pages ~)	**opuscolo** (m)	[o'puskolo]
pamphlet	**pieghevole** (m)	[pje'gevole]
newsletter	**bollettino** (m)	[bollet'tino]
signboard (store sign, etc.)	**insegna** (f)	[in'seɲa]
poster	**cartellone** (m)	[kartel'lone]
billboard	**tabellone** (m) **pubblicitario**	[tabel'lone pubblitʃi'tario]

112. Banking

bank	**banca** (f)	['banka]
branch (of bank, etc.)	**filiale** (f)	[fi'ljale]
bank clerk, consultant	**consulente** (m)	[konsu'lente]
manager (director)	**direttore** (m)	[diret'tore]
bank account	**conto** (m) **bancario**	['konto ban'kario]
account number	**numero** (m) **del conto**	['numero del 'konto]
checking account	**conto** (m) **corrente**	['konto kor'rente]
savings account	**conto** (m) **di risparmio**	['konto di ris'parmio]
to open an account	**aprire un conto**	[a'prire un 'konto]
to close the account	**chiudere il conto**	['kjudere il 'konto]
to deposit into the account	**versare sul conto**	[ver'sare sul 'konto]
to withdraw (vt)	**prelevare dal conto**	[prele'vare dal 'konto]
deposit	**deposito** (m)	[de'pozito]
to make a deposit	**depositare** (vt)	[depozi'tare]
wire transfer	**trasferimento** (m) **telegrafico**	[trasferi'mento tele'grafiko]
to wire, to transfer	**rimettere i soldi**	[ri'mettere i 'soldi]
sum	**somma** (f)	['somma]
How much?	**Quanto?**	['kwanto]
signature	**firma** (f)	['firma]
to sign (vt)	**firmare** (vt)	[fir'mare]
credit card	**carta** (f) **di credito**	['karta di 'kredito]
code (PIN code)	**codice** (m)	['koditʃe]

credit card number	**numero** (m) **della carta di credito**	['numero 'della 'karta di 'kredito]
ATM	**bancomat** (m)	['bankomat]
check	**assegno** (m)	[as'seɲo]
to write a check	**emettere un assegno**	[e'mettere un as'seɲo]
checkbook	**libretto** (m) **di assegni**	[li'bretto di as'seɲi]
loan (bank ~)	**prestito** (m)	['prestito]
to apply for a loan	**fare domanda per un prestito**	['fare do'manda per un 'prestito]
to get a loan	**ottenere un prestito**	[otte'nere un 'prestito]
to give a loan	**concedere un prestito**	[kon'ʧedere un 'prestito]
guarantee	**garanzia** (f)	[garan'tsia]

113. Telephone. Phone conversation

telephone	**telefono** (m)	[te'lefono]
cell phone	**telefonino** (m)	[telefo'nino]
answering machine	**segreteria** (f) **telefonica**	[segrete'ria tele'fonika]
to call (by phone)	**telefonare** (vi, vt)	[telefo'nare]
phone call	**chiamata** (f)	[kja'mata]
to dial a number	**comporre un numero**	[kom'porre un 'numero]
Hello!	**Pronto!**	['pronto]
to ask (vt)	**chiedere, domandare**	['kjedere], [doman'dare]
to answer (vi, vt)	**rispondere** (vi, vt)	[ris'pondere]
to hear (vt)	**udire, sentire** (vt)	[u'dire], [sen'tire]
well (adv)	**bene**	['bene]
not well (adv)	**male**	['male]
noises (interference)	**disturbi** (m pl)	[di'sturbi]
receiver	**cornetta** (f)	[kor'netta]
to pick up (~ the phone)	**alzare la cornetta**	[al'tsare la kor'netta]
to hang up (~ the phone)	**riattaccare la cornetta**	[riattak'kare la kor'netta]
busy (engaged)	**occupato**	[okku'pato]
to ring (ab. phone)	**squillare** (vi)	[skwil'lare]
telephone book	**elenco** (m) **telefonico**	[e'lenko tele'foniko]
local (adj)	**locale**	[lo'kale]
local call	**chiamata** (f) **locale**	[kja'mata lo'kale]
long distance (~ call)	**interurbano**	[interur'bano]
long-distance call	**chiamata** (f) **interurbana**	[kja'mata interur'bana]
international (adj)	**internazionale**	[internatsjo'nale]
international call	**chiamata** (f) **internazionale**	[kja'mata internatsjo'nale]

114. Cell phone

cell phone	**telefonino** (m)	[telefo'nino]
display	**schermo** (m)	['skermo]
button	**tasto** (m)	['tasto]
SIM card	**scheda SIM** (f)	['skeda 'sim]
battery	**pila** (f)	['pila]
to be dead (battery)	**essere scarico**	['essere 'skariko]
charger	**caricabatteria** (m)	[karika·batte'ria]
menu	**menù** (m)	[me'nu]
settings	**impostazioni** (f pl)	[imposta'tsjoni]
tune (melody)	**melodia** (f)	[melo'dia]
to select (vt)	**scegliere** (vt)	['ʃeʎʎere]
calculator	**calcolatrice** (f)	[kalkola'tritʃe]
voice mail	**segreteria** (f) **telefonica**	[segrete'ria tele'fonika]
alarm clock	**sveglia** (f)	['zveʎʎa]
contacts	**contatti** (m pl)	[kon'tatti]
SMS (text message)	**messaggio** (m) **SMS**	[mes'sadʒo ese'mese]
subscriber	**abbonato** (m)	[abbo'nato]

115. Stationery

ballpoint pen	**penna** (f) **a sfera**	[penna a 'sfera]
fountain pen	**penna** (f) **stilografica**	['penna stilo'grafika]
pencil	**matita** (f)	[ma'tita]
highlighter	**evidenziatore** (m)	[evidentsja'tore]
felt-tip pen	**pennarello** (m)	[penna'rello]
notepad	**taccuino** (m)	[tak'kwino]
agenda (diary)	**agenda** (f)	[a'dʒenda]
ruler	**righello** (m)	[ri'gello]
calculator	**calcolatrice** (f)	[kalkola'tritʃe]
eraser	**gomma** (f) **per cancellare**	['gomma per kantʃel'lare]
thumbtack	**puntina** (f)	[pun'tina]
paper clip	**graffetta** (f)	[graf'fetta]
glue	**colla** (f)	['kolla]
stapler	**pinzatrice** (f)	[pintsa'tritʃe]
hole punch	**perforatrice** (f)	[perfora'tritʃe]
pencil sharpener	**temperamatite** (m)	[temperama'tite]

116. Various kinds of documents

account (report)	**resoconto** (m)	[rezo'konto]
agreement	**accordo** (m)	[ak'kordo]
application form	**modulo** (m) **di richiesta**	['modulo di ri'kjesta]
authentic (adj)	**autentico**	[au'tentiko]
badge (identity tag)	**tesserino** (m)	[tesse'rino]
business card	**biglietto** (m) **da visita**	[biʎ'ʎetto da 'vizita]
certificate (~ of quality)	**certificato** (m)	[ʧertifi'kato]
check (e.g., draw a ~)	**assegno** (m)	[as'seɲo]
check (in restaurant)	**conto** (m)	['konto]
constitution	**costituzione** (f)	[kostitu'tsjone]
contract (agreement)	**contratto** (m)	[kon'tratto]
copy	**copia** (f)	['kopia]
copy (of contract, etc.)	**copia** (f)	['kopia]
customs declaration	**dichiarazione** (f)	[dikjara'tsjone]
document	**documento** (m)	[doku'mento]
driver's license	**patente** (f) **di guida**	[pa'tente di 'gwida]
addendum	**allegato** (m)	[alle'gato]
form	**modulo** (m)	['modulo]
ID card (e.g., FBI ~)	**carta** (f) **d'identità**	['karta didenti'ta]
inquiry (request)	**richiesta** (f) **di informazioni**	[ri'kjesta di informa'tsjoni]
invitation card	**biglietto** (m) **d'invito**	[biʎ'ʎetto din'vito]
invoice	**fattura** (f)	[fat'tura]
law	**legge** (f)	['leʤe]
letter (mail)	**lettera** (f)	['lettera]
letterhead	**carta** (f) **intestata**	['karta inte'stata]
list (of names, etc.)	**lista** (f)	['lista]
manuscript	**manoscritto** (m)	[mano'skritto]
newsletter	**bollettino** (m)	[bollet'tino]
note (short letter)	**appunto** (m), **nota** (f)	[ap'punto], ['nota]
pass (for worker, visitor)	**lasciapassare** (m)	[laʃapas'sare]
passport	**passaporto** (m)	[passa'porto]
permit	**permesso** (m)	[per'messo]
résumé	**curriculum vitae** (f)	[kur'rikulum 'vite]
debt note, IOU	**nota** (f) **di addebito**	['nota di ad'debito]
receipt (for purchase)	**ricevuta** (f)	[riʧe'vuta]
sales slip, receipt	**scontrino** (m)	[skon'trino]
report (mil.)	**rapporto** (m)	[rap'porto]
to show (ID, etc.)	**mostrare** (vt)	[mo'strare]
to sign (vt)	**firmare** (vt)	[fir'mare]
signature	**firma** (f)	['firma]
seal (stamp)	**timbro** (m)	['timbro]

text	**testo** (m)	['testo]
ticket (for entry)	**biglietto** (m)	[biʎ'ʎetto]
to cross out	**cancellare** (vt)	[kantʃel'lare]
to fill out (~ a form)	**riempire** (vt)	[riem'pire]
waybill (shipping invoice)	**bolla** (f) **di consegna**	['bolla di kon'seɲa]
will (testament)	**testamento** (m)	[testa'mento]

117. Kinds of business

accounting services	**servizi** (m pl) **di contabilità**	[ser'vitsi di kontabili'ta]
advertising	**pubblicità** (f)	[pubblitʃi'ta]
advertising agency	**agenzia** (f) **pubblicitaria**	[adʒen'tsia pubblitʃi'taria]
air-conditioners	**condizionatori** (m pl) **d'aria**	[konditsjona'tori 'daria]
airline	**compagnia** (f) **aerea**	[kompa'ɲia a'erea]
alcoholic beverages	**bevande** (f pl) **alcoliche**	[be'vande al'kolike]
antiques (antique dealers)	**antiquariato** (m)	[antikwa'rjato]
art gallery (contemporary ~)	**galleria** (f) **d'arte**	[galle'ria 'darte]
audit services	**società** (f) **di revisione contabile**	[sotʃe'ta di revi'zone kon'tabile]
banking industry	**imprese** (f pl) **bancarie**	[im'preze ban'karie]
bar	**bar** (m)	[bar]
beauty parlor	**salone** (m) **di bellezza**	[sa'lone di bel'lettsa]
bookstore	**libreria** (f)	[libre'ria]
brewery	**birreria** (f)	[birre'ria]
business center	**business centro** (m)	['biznes 'tʃentro]
business school	**scuola** (f) **di commercio**	['skwola di kom'mertʃo]
casino	**casinò** (m)	[kazi'no]
construction	**edilizia** (f)	[edi'litsia]
consulting	**consulenza** (f)	[konsu'lentsa]
dental clinic	**odontoiatria** (f)	[odontoja'tria]
design	**design** (m)	[di'zajn]
drugstore, pharmacy	**farmacia** (f)	[farma'tʃia]
dry cleaners	**lavanderia** (f) **a secco**	[lavande'ria a 'sekko]
employment agency	**agenzia** (f) **di collocamento**	[adʒen'tsia di kolloka'mento]
financial services	**servizi** (m pl) **finanziari**	[ser'vitsi finan'tsjari]
food products	**industria** (f) **alimentare**	[in'dustria alimen'tare]
funeral home	**agenzia** (f) **di pompe funebri**	[adʒen'tsia di 'pompe 'funebri]

furniture (e.g., house ~)	**mobili** (m pl)	['mobili]
clothing, garment	**abbigliamento** (m)	[abbiʎʎa'mento]
hotel	**albergo, hotel** (m)	[al'bergo], [o'tel]
ice-cream	**gelato** (m)	[ʤe'lato]
industry (manufacturing)	**industria** (f)	[in'dustria]
insurance	**assicurazione** (f)	[assikura'tsjone]
Internet	**internet** (f)	['internet]
investments (finance)	**investimenti** (m pl)	[investi'menti]
jeweler	**gioielliere** (m)	[ʤojel'ljere]
jewelry	**gioielli** (m pl)	[ʤo'jelli]
laundry (shop)	**lavanderia** (f)	[lavande'ria]
legal advisor	**consulente** (m) **legale**	[konsu'lente le'gale]
light industry	**industria** (f) **leggera**	[in'dustria le'ʤera]
magazine	**rivista** (f)	[ri'vista]
mail order selling	**vendite** (f pl) **per corrispondenza**	['vendite per korrispon'dentsa]
medicine	**medicina** (f)	[medi'ʧina]
movie theater	**cinema** (m)	['ʧinema]
museum	**museo** (m)	[mu'zeo]
news agency	**agenzia** (f) **di stampa**	[aʤen'tsia di 'stampa]
newspaper	**giornale** (m)	[ʤor'nale]
nightclub	**locale notturno** (m)	[lo'kale not'turno]
oil (petroleum)	**petrolio** (m)	[pe'trolio]
courier services	**corriere** (m) **espresso**	[kor'rjere e'spresso]
pharmaceutics	**farmaci** (m pl)	['farmaʧi]
printing (industry)	**stampa** (f)	['stampa]
publishing house	**casa** (f) **editrice**	['kaza edi'triʧe]
radio (~ station)	**radio** (f)	['radio]
real estate	**beni** (m pl) **immobili**	['beni im'mobili]
restaurant	**ristorante** (m)	[risto'rante]
security company	**agenzia** (f) **di sicurezza**	[aʤen'tsia di siku'rettsa]
sports	**sport** (m)	[sport]
stock exchange	**borsa** (f)	['borsa]
store	**negozio** (m)	[ne'gotsio]
supermarket	**supermercato** (m)	[supermer'kato]
swimming pool (public ~)	**piscina** (f)	[pi'ʃina]
tailor shop	**sartoria** (f)	[sarto'ria]
television	**televisione** (f)	[televi'zjone]
theater	**teatro** (m)	[te'atro]
trade (commerce)	**commercio** (m)	[kom'merʧo]
transportation	**mezzi** (m pl) **di trasporto**	['meddzi di tras'porto]
travel	**viaggio** (m)	['vjaʤo]
veterinarian	**veterinario** (m)	[veteri'nario]
warehouse	**deposito, magazzino** (m)	[de'pozito], [magad'dzino]
waste collection	**trattamento** (m) **dei rifiuti**	[tratta'mento dei ri'fjuti]

Job. Business. Part 2

118. Show. Exhibition

exhibition, show	**fiera** (f)	['fjera]
trade show	**fiera** (f) **campionaria**	['fjera kampjo'naria]
participation	**partecipazione** (f)	[partetʃipa'tsjone]
to participate (vi)	**partecipare** (vi)	[partetʃi'pare]
participant (exhibitor)	**partecipante** (m)	[partetʃi'pante]
director	**direttore** (m)	[diret'tore]
organizers' office	**ufficio** (m) **organizzativo**	[uf'fitʃo organiddza'tivo]
organizer	**organizzatore** (m)	[organiddza'tore]
to organize (vt)	**organizzare** (vt)	[organid'dzare]
participation form	**domanda** (f) **di partecipazione**	[do'manda di partetʃipa'tsjone]
to fill out (vt)	**riempire** (vt)	[riem'pire]
details	**dettagli** (m pl)	[det'taʎʎi]
information	**informazione** (f)	[informa'tsjone]
price (cost, rate)	**prezzo** (m)	['prettso]
including	**incluso**	[in'kluzo]
to include (vt)	**includere** (vt)	[in'kludere]
to pay (vi, vt)	**pagare** (vi, vt)	[pa'gare]
registration fee	**quota** (f) **d'iscrizione**	['kwota diskri'tsjone]
entrance	**entrata** (f)	[en'trata]
pavilion, hall	**padiglione** (m)	[padiʎ'ʎone]
to register (vt)	**registrare** (vt)	[redʒi'strare]
badge (identity tag)	**tesserino** (m)	[tesse'rino]
booth, stand	**stand** (m)	[stend]
to reserve, to book	**prenotare, riservare**	[preno'tare], [rizer'vare]
display case	**vetrina** (f)	[ve'trina]
spotlight	**faretto** (m)	[fa'retto]
design	**design** (m)	[di'zajn]
to place (put, set)	**collocare** (vt)	[kollo'kare]
to be placed	**collocarsi** (vr)	[kollo'karsi]
distributor	**distributore** (m)	[distribu'tore]
supplier	**fornitore** (m)	[forni'tore]
to supply (vt)	**fornire** (vt)	[for'nire]
country	**paese** (m)	[pa'eze]

foreign (adj)	**straniero**	[stra'njero]
product	**prodotto** (m)	[pro'dotto]
association	**associazione** (f)	[assotʃa'tsjone]
conference hall	**sala** (f) **conferenze**	['sala konfe'rentse]
congress	**congresso** (m)	[kon'gresso]
contest (competition)	**concorso** (m)	[kon'korso]
visitor (attendee)	**visitatore** (m)	[vizita'tore]
to visit (attend)	**visitare** (vt)	[vizi'tare]
customer	**cliente** (m)	[kli'ente]

119. Mass Media

newspaper	**giornale** (m)	[dʒor'nale]
magazine	**rivista** (f)	[ri'vista]
press (printed media)	**stampa** (f)	['stampa]
radio	**radio** (f)	['radio]
radio station	**stazione** (f) **radio**	[sta'tsjone 'radio]
television	**televisione** (f)	[televi'zjone]
presenter, host	**presentatore** (m)	[prezenta'tore]
newscaster	**annunciatore** (m)	[annuntʃa'tore]
commentator	**commentatore** (m)	[kommenta'tore]
journalist	**giornalista** (m)	[dʒorna'lista]
correspondent (reporter)	**corrispondente** (m)	[korrispon'dente]
press photographer	**fotocronista** (m)	[fotokro'nista]
reporter	**cronista** (m)	[kro'nista]
editor	**redattore** (m)	[redat'tore]
editor-in-chief	**redattore capo** (m)	[redat'tore 'kapo]
to subscribe (to ...)	**abbonarsi a ...**	[abbo'narsi]
subscription	**abbonamento** (m)	[abbona'mento]
subscriber	**abbonato** (m)	[abbo'nato]
to read (vi, vt)	**leggere** (vi, vt)	['ledʒere]
reader	**lettore** (m)	[let'tore]
circulation (of newspaper)	**tiratura** (f)	[tira'tura]
monthly (adj)	**mensile**	[men'sile]
weekly (adj)	**settimanale**	[settima'nale]
issue (edition)	**numero** (m)	['numero]
new (~ issue)	**fresco** (m)	['fresko]
headline	**testata** (f)	[te'stata]
short article	**trafiletto** (m)	[trafi'letto]
column (regular article)	**rubrica** (f)	[ru'brika]
article	**articolo** (m)	[ar'tikolo]
page	**pagina** (f)	['padʒina]

reportage, report	**servizio** (m)	[ser'vitsio]
event (happening)	**evento** (m)	[e'vento]
sensation (news)	**sensazione** (f)	[sensa'tsjone]
scandal	**scandalo** (m)	['skandalo]
scandalous (adj)	**scandaloso**	[skanda'lozo]
great (~ scandal)	**enorme, grande**	[e'norme], ['grande]
show (e.g., cooking ~)	**trasmissione** (f)	[trazmis'sjone]
interview	**intervista** (f)	[inter'vista]
live broadcast	**trasmissione** (f) **in diretta**	[trazmis'sjone in di'retta]
channel	**canale** (m)	[ka'nale]

120. Agriculture

agriculture	**agricoltura** (f)	[agrikol'tura]
peasant (masc.)	**contadino** (m)	[konta'dino]
peasant (fem.)	**contadina** (f)	[konta'dina]
farmer	**fattore** (m)	[fat'tore]
tractor (farm ~)	**trattore** (m)	[trat'tore]
combine, harvester	**mietitrebbia** (f)	[mjeti'trebbia]
plow	**aratro** (m)	[a'ratro]
to plow (vi, vt)	**arare** (vt)	[a'rare]
plowland	**terreno** (m) **coltivato**	[ter'reno kolti'vato]
furrow (in field)	**solco** (m)	['solko]
to sow (vi, vt)	**seminare** (vt)	[semi'nare]
seeder	**seminatrice** (f)	[semina'tritʃe]
sowing (process)	**semina** (f)	['semina]
scythe	**falce** (f)	['faltʃe]
to mow, to scythe	**falciare** (vt)	[fal'tʃare]
spade (tool)	**pala** (f)	['pala]
to till (vt)	**scavare** (vt)	[ska'vare]
hoe	**zappa** (f)	['tsappa]
to hoe, to weed	**zappare** (vt)	[tsap'pare]
weed (plant)	**erbaccia** (f)	[er'batʃa]
watering can	**innaffiatoio** (m)	[innaffja'tojo]
to water (plants)	**innaffiare** (vt)	[innaf'fjare]
watering (act)	**innaffiamento** (m)	[innaffja'mento]
pitchfork	**forca** (f)	['forka]
rake	**rastrello** (m)	[ra'strello]
fertilizer	**concime** (m)	[kon'tʃime]
to fertilize (vt)	**concimare** (vt)	[kontʃi'mare]

manure (fertilizer)	**letame** (m)	[le'tame]
field	**campo** (m)	['kampo]
meadow	**prato** (m)	['prato]
vegetable garden	**orto** (m)	['orto]
orchard (e.g., apple ~)	**frutteto** (m)	[frut'teto]
to graze (vt)	**pascolare** (vt)	[pasko'lare]
herder (herdsman)	**pastore** (m)	[pa'store]
pasture	**pascolo** (m)	['paskolo]
cattle breeding	**allevamento** (m) **di bestiame**	[alleva'mento di bes'tjame]
sheep farming	**allevamento** (m) **di pecore**	[alleva'mento di 'pekore]
plantation	**piantagione** (f)	[pjanta'ʤone]
row (garden bed ~s)	**filare** (m)	[fi'lare]
hothouse	**serra** (f) **da orto**	['serra da 'orto]
drought (lack of rain)	**siccità** (f)	[siʧʧi'ta]
dry (~ summer)	**secco, arido**	['sekko], ['arrido]
cereal crops	**cereali** (m pl)	[ʧere'ali]
to harvest, to gather	**raccogliere** (vt)	[rak'koʎʎere]
miller (person)	**mugnaio** (m)	[mu'ɲajo]
mill (e.g., gristmill)	**mulino** (m)	[mu'lino]
to grind (grain)	**macinare** (vt)	[maʧʧi'nare]
flour	**farina** (f)	[fa'rina]
straw	**paglia** (f)	['paʎʎa]

121. Building. Building process

construction site	**cantiere** (m) **edile**	[kan'tjere 'edile]
to build (vt)	**costruire** (vt)	[kostru'ire]
construction worker	**operaio** (m) **edile**	[ope'rajo e'dile]
project	**progetto** (m)	[pro'ʤetto]
architect	**architetto** (m)	[arki'tetto]
worker	**operaio** (m)	[ope'rajo]
foundation (of a building)	**fondamenta** (f pl)	[fonda'menta]
roof	**tetto** (m)	['tetto]
foundation pile	**palo** (m) **di fondazione**	['palo di fonda'tsjone]
wall	**muro** (m)	['muro]
reinforcing bars	**barre** (f pl) **di rinforzo**	['barre di rin'fortso]
scaffolding	**impalcatura** (f)	[impalka'tura]
concrete	**beton** (m)	[be'ton]
granite	**granito** (m)	[gra'nito]

stone	**pietra** (f)	['pjetra]
brick	**mattone** (m)	[mat'tone]
sand	**sabbia** (f)	['sabbia]
cement	**cemento** (m)	[tʃe'mento]
plaster (for walls)	**intonaco** (m)	[in'tonako]
to plaster (vt)	**intonacare** (vt)	[intona'kare]
paint	**pittura** (f)	[pit'tura]
to paint (~ a wall)	**pitturare** (vt)	[pittu'rare]
barrel	**botte** (f)	['botte]
crane	**gru** (f)	[gru]
to lift, to hoist (vt)	**sollevare** (vt)	[solle'vare]
to lower (vt)	**abbassare** (vt)	[abbas'sare]
bulldozer	**bulldozer** (m)	[bulldo'dzer]
excavator	**scavatrice** (f)	[skava'tritʃe]
scoop, bucket	**cucchiaia** (f)	[kuk'kjaja]
to dig (excavate)	**scavare** (vt)	[ska'vare]
hard hat	**casco** (m)	['kasko]

122. Science. Research. Scientists

science	**scienza** (f)	[ʃi'entsa]
scientific (adj)	**scientifico**	[ʃien'tifiko]
scientist	**scienziato** (m)	[ʃien'tsjato]
theory	**teoria** (f)	[teo'ria]
axiom	**assioma** (m)	[as'sjoma]
analysis	**analisi** (f)	[a'nalizi]
to analyze (vt)	**analizzare** (vt)	[analid'dzare]
argument (strong ~)	**argomento** (m)	[argo'mento]
substance (matter)	**sostanza** (f)	[so'stantsa]
hypothesis	**ipotesi** (f)	[i'potezi]
dilemma	**dilemma** (m)	[di'lemma]
dissertation	**tesi** (f)	['tezi]
dogma	**dogma** (m)	['dogma]
doctrine	**dottrina** (f)	[dot'trina]
research	**ricerca** (f)	[ri'tʃerka]
to research (vt)	**fare ricerche**	['fare ri'tʃerke]
tests (laboratory ~)	**prova** (f)	['prova]
laboratory	**laboratorio** (m)	[labora'torio]
method	**metodo** (m)	['metodo]
molecule	**molecola** (f)	[mo'lekola]
monitoring	**monitoraggio** (m)	[monito'radʒo]
discovery (act, event)	**scoperta** (f)	[sko'perta]

postulate	**postulato** (m)	[postu'lato]
principle	**principio** (m)	[prin'ʧipjo]
forecast	**previsione** (f)	[previ'zjone]
to forecast (vt)	**fare previsioni**	[fare previ'zjoni]
synthesis	**sintesi** (f)	['sintezi]
trend (tendency)	**tendenza** (f)	[ten'dentsa]
theorem	**teorema** (m)	[teo'rema]
teachings	**insegnamento** (m)	[inse'ɲamento]
fact	**fatto** (m)	['fatto]
expedition	**spedizione** (f)	[spedi'tsjone]
experiment	**esperimento** (m)	[esperi'mento]
academician	**accademico** (m)	[akka'demiko]
bachelor (e.g., ~ of Arts)	**laureato** (m)	[laure'ato]
doctor (PhD)	**dottore** (m)	[dot'tore]
Associate Professor	**professore** (m) **associato**	[profes'sore assoʧi'ato]
Master (e.g., ~ of Arts)	**Master** (m)	['master]
professor	**professore** (m)	[profes'sore]

Professions and occupations

123. Job search. Dismissal

job	**lavoro** (m)	[la'voro]
staff (work force)	**organico** (m)	[or'ganiko]
personnel	**personale** (m)	[perso'nale]
career	**carriera** (f)	[kar'rjera]
prospects (chances)	**prospettiva** (f)	[prospet'tiva]
skills (mastery)	**abilità** (f pl)	[abili'ta]
selection (screening)	**selezione** (f)	[sele'tsjone]
employment agency	**agenzia** (f) **di collocamento**	[adʒen'tsia di kolloka'mento]
résumé	**curriculum vitae** (f)	[kur'rikulum 'vite]
job interview	**colloquio** (m)	[kol'lokwio]
vacancy, opening	**posto** (m) **vacante**	['posto va'kante]
salary, pay	**salario** (m)	[sa'lario]
fixed salary	**stipendio** (m) **fisso**	[sti'pendio 'fisso]
pay, compensation	**compenso** (m)	[kom'penso]
position (job)	**carica** (f)	['karika]
duty (of employee)	**mansione** (f)	[man'sjone]
range of duties	**mansioni** (f pl) **di lavoro**	[man'sjoni di la'voro]
busy (I'm ~)	**occupato**	[okku'pato]
to fire (dismiss)	**licenziare** (vt)	[litʃen'tsjare]
dismissal	**licenziamento** (m)	[litʃentsja'mento]
unemployment	**disoccupazione** (f)	[disokkupa'tsjone]
unemployed (n)	**disoccupato** (m)	[disokku'pato]
retirement	**pensionamento** (m)	[pensjona'mento]
to retire (from job)	**andare in pensione**	[an'dare in pen'sjone]

124. Business people

director	**direttore** (m)	[diret'tore]
manager (director)	**dirigente** (m)	[diri'dʒente]
boss	**capo** (m)	['kapo]
superior	**capo** (m), **superiore** (m)	['kapo], [supe'rjore]
superiors	**capi** (m pl)	['kapi]

president	**presidente** (m)	[prezi'dente]
chairman	**presidente** (m)	[prezi'dente]
deputy (substitute)	**vice** (m)	['vitʃe]
assistant	**assistente** (m)	[assi'stente]
secretary	**segretario** (m)	[segre'tario]
personal assistant	**assistente** (m) **personale**	[assi'stente perso'nale]
businessman	**uomo** (m) **d'affari**	[u'omo daf'fari]
entrepreneur	**imprenditore** (m)	[imprendi'tore]
founder	**fondatore** (m)	[fonda'tore]
to found (vt)	**fondare** (vt)	[fon'dare]
incorporator	**socio** (m)	['sotʃo]
partner	**partner** (m)	['partner]
stockholder	**azionista** (m)	[atsio'nista]
millionaire	**milionario** (m)	[miljo'nario]
billionaire	**miliardario** (m)	[miljar'dario]
owner, proprietor	**proprietario** (m)	[proprie'tario]
landowner	**latifondista** (m)	[latifon'dista]
client	**cliente** (m)	[kli'ente]
regular client	**cliente** (m) **abituale**	[kli'ente abitu'ale]
buyer (customer)	**compratore** (m)	[kompra'tore]
visitor	**visitatore** (m)	[vizita'tore]
professional (n)	**professionista** (m)	[professjo'nista]
expert	**esperto** (m)	[e'sperto]
specialist	**specialista** (m)	[spetʃa'lista]
banker	**banchiere** (m)	[baŋ'kjere]
broker	**broker** (m)	['broker]
cashier, teller	**cassiere** (m)	[kas'sjere]
accountant	**contabile** (m)	[kon'tabile]
security guard	**guardia** (f) **giurata**	['gwardia dʒu'rata]
investor	**investitore** (m)	[investi'tore]
debtor	**debitore** (m)	[debi'tore]
creditor	**creditore** (m)	[kredi'tore]
borrower	**mutuatario** (m)	[mutua'tario]
importer	**importatore** (m)	[importa'tore]
exporter	**esportatore** (m)	[esporta'tore]
manufacturer	**produttore** (m)	[produt'tore]
distributor	**distributore** (m)	[distribu'tore]
middleman	**intermediario** (m)	[interme'djario]
consultant	**consulente** (m)	[konsu'lente]

sales representative	**rappresentante** (m)	[rapprezen'tante]
agent	**agente** (m)	[a'ʤente]
insurance agent	**assicuratore** (m)	[assikura'tore]

125. Service professions

cook	**cuoco** (m)	[ku'oko]
chef (kitchen chef)	**capocuoco** (m)	[kapo·ku'oko]
baker	**fornaio** (m)	[for'najo]
bartender	**barista** (m)	[ba'rista]
waiter	**cameriere** (m)	[kame'rjere]
waitress	**cameriera** (f)	[kame'rjera]
lawyer, attorney	**avvocato** (m)	[avvo'kato]
lawyer (legal expert)	**esperto** (m) **legale**	[e'sperto le'gale]
notary public	**notaio** (m)	[no'tajo]
electrician	**elettricista** (m)	[elettri'ʧista]
plumber	**idraulico** (m)	[i'drauliko]
carpenter	**falegname** (m)	[fale'ɲame]
masseur	**massaggiatore** (m)	[massaʤa'tore]
masseuse	**massaggiatrice** (f)	[massaʤa'triʧe]
doctor	**medico** (m)	['mediko]
taxi driver	**taxista** (m)	[ta'ksista]
driver	**autista** (m)	[au'tista]
delivery man	**fattorino** (m)	[fatto'rino]
chambermaid	**cameriera** (f)	[kame'rjera]
security guard	**guardia** (f) **giurata**	['gwardia ʤu'rata]
flight attendant (fem.)	**hostess** (f)	['ostess]
schoolteacher	**insegnante** (m, f)	[inse'ɲante]
librarian	**bibliotecario** (m)	[bibliote'kario]
translator	**traduttore** (m)	[tradut'tore]
interpreter	**interprete** (m)	[in'terprete]
guide	**guida** (f)	['gwida]
hairdresser	**parrucchiere** (m)	[parruk'kjere]
mailman	**postino** (m)	[po'stino]
salesman (store staff)	**commesso** (m)	[kom'messo]
gardener	**giardiniere** (m)	[ʤardi'njere]
domestic servant	**domestico** (m)	[do'mestiko]
maid (female servant)	**domestica** (f)	[do'mestika]
cleaner (cleaning lady)	**donna** (f) **delle pulizie**	['donna 'delle puli'tsie]

126. Military professions and ranks

private	**soldato** (m) **semplice**	[sol'dato 'sempliʧe]
sergeant	**sergente** (m)	[ser'ʤente]
lieutenant	**tenente** (m)	[te'nente]
captain	**capitano** (m)	[kapi'tano]
major	**maggiore** (m)	[ma'ʤore]
colonel	**colonnello** (m)	[kolon'nello]
general	**generale** (m)	[ʤene'rale]
marshal	**maresciallo** (m)	[mare'ʃallo]
admiral	**ammiraglio** (m)	[ammi'raʎʎo]
military (n)	**militare** (m)	[mili'tare]
soldier	**soldato** (m)	[sol'dato]
officer	**ufficiale** (m)	[uffi'ʧale]
commander	**comandante** (m)	[koman'dante]
border guard	**guardia** (f) **di frontiera**	['gwardia di fron'tjera]
radio operator	**marconista** (m)	[marko'nista]
scout (searcher)	**esploratore** (m)	[esplora'tore]
pioneer (sapper)	**geniere** (m)	[ʤe'njere]
marksman	**tiratore** (m)	[tira'tore]
navigator	**navigatore** (m)	[naviga'tore]

127. Officials. Priests

king	**re** (m)	[re]
queen	**regina** (f)	[re'ʤina]
prince	**principe** (m)	['prinʧipe]
princess	**principessa** (f)	[prinʧi'pessa]
czar	**zar** (m)	[tsar]
czarina	**zarina** (f)	[tsa'rina]
president	**presidente** (m)	[prezi'dente]
Secretary (minister)	**ministro** (m)	[mi'nistro]
prime minister	**primo ministro** (m)	['primo mi'nistro]
senator	**senatore** (m)	[sena'tore]
diplomat	**diplomatico** (m)	[diplo'matiko]
consul	**console** (m)	['konsole]
ambassador	**ambasciatore** (m)	[ambaʃa'tore]
counselor (diplomatic officer)	**consigliere** (m)	[konsiʎ'ʎere]
official, functionary (civil servant)	**funzionario** (m)	[funtsio'nario]

prefect	**prefetto** (m)	[pre'fetto]
mayor	**sindaco** (m)	['sindako]
judge	**giudice** (m)	['ʤuditʃe]
prosecutor (e.g., district attorney)	**procuratore** (m)	[prokura'tore]
missionary	**missionario** (m)	[missio'nario]
monk	**monaco** (m)	['monako]
abbot	**abate** (m)	[a'bate]
rabbi	**rabbino** (m)	[rab'bino]
vizier	**visir** (m)	[vi'zir]
shah	**scià** (m)	['ʃa]
sheikh	**sceicco** (m)	[ʃe'ikko]

128. Agricultural professions

beekeeper	**apicoltore** (m)	[apikol'tore]
herder, shepherd	**pastore** (m)	[pa'store]
agronomist	**agronomo** (m)	[a'gronomo]
cattle breeder	**allevatore** (m) **di bestiame**	[alleva'tore di bes'tjame]
veterinarian	**veterinario** (m)	[veteri'nario]
farmer	**fattore** (m)	[fat'tore]
winemaker	**vinificatore** (m)	[vinifika'tore]
zoologist	**zoologo** (m)	[ʣo'ologo]
cowboy	**cowboy** (m)	[kaw'boj]

129. Art professions

actor	**attore** (m)	[at'tore]
actress	**attrice** (f)	[at'tritʃe]
singer (masc.)	**cantante** (m)	[kan'tante]
singer (fem.)	**cantante** (f)	[kan'tante]
dancer (masc.)	**danzatore** (m)	[dantsa'tore]
dancer (fem.)	**ballerina** (f)	[balle'rina]
performer (masc.)	**artista** (m)	[ar'tista]
performer (fem.)	**artista** (f)	[ar'tista]
musician	**musicista** (m)	[muzi'ʧista]
pianist	**pianista** (m)	[pia'nista]
guitar player	**chitarrista** (m)	[kitar'rista]
conductor (orchestra ~)	**direttore** (m) **d'orchestra**	[diret'tore dor'kestra]

composer	**compositore** (m)	[kompozi'tore]
impresario	**impresario** (m)	[impre'zario]
film director	**regista** (m)	[re'dʒista]
producer	**produttore** (m)	[produt'tore]
scriptwriter	**sceneggiatore** (m)	[ʃenedʒa'tore]
critic	**critico** (m)	['kritiko]
writer	**scrittore** (m)	[skrit'tore]
poet	**poeta** (m)	[po'eta]
sculptor	**scultore** (m)	[skul'tore]
artist (painter)	**pittore** (m)	[pit'tore]
juggler	**giocoliere** (m)	[dʒoko'ljere]
clown	**pagliaccio** (m)	[paʎ'ʎatʃo]
acrobat	**acrobata** (m)	[a'krobata]
magician	**prestigiatore** (m)	[prestidʒa'tore]

130. Various professions

doctor	**medico** (m)	['mediko]
nurse	**infermiera** (f)	[infer'mjera]
psychiatrist	**psichiatra** (m)	[psiki'atra]
dentist	**dentista** (m)	[den'tista]
surgeon	**chirurgo** (m)	[ki'rurgo]
astronaut	**astronauta** (m)	[astro'nauta]
astronomer	**astronomo** (m)	[a'stronomo]
driver (of taxi, etc.)	**autista** (m)	[au'tista]
engineer (train driver)	**macchinista** (m)	[makki'nista]
mechanic	**meccanico** (m)	[mek'kaniko]
miner	**minatore** (m)	[mina'tore]
worker	**operaio** (m)	[ope'rajo]
locksmith	**operaio** (m) **metallurgico**	[ope'rajo metal'lurdʒiko]
joiner (carpenter)	**falegname** (m)	[fale'ɲame]
turner (lathe operator)	**tornitore** (m)	[torni'tore]
construction worker	**operaio** (m) **edile**	[ope'rajo e'dile]
welder	**saldatore** (m)	[salda'tore]
professor (title)	**professore** (m)	[profes'sore]
architect	**architetto** (m)	[arki'tetto]
historian	**storico** (m)	['storiko]
scientist	**scienziato** (m)	[ʃien'tsjato]
physicist	**fisico** (m)	['fiziko]
chemist (scientist)	**chimico** (m)	['kimiko]
archeologist	**archeologo** (m)	[arke'ologo]
geologist	**geologo** (m)	[dʒe'ologo]

researcher (scientist)	**ricercatore** (m)	[ritʃerka'tore]
babysitter	**baby-sitter** (f)	[bebi'siter]
teacher, educator	**insegnante** (m, f)	[inse'ɲante]
editor	**redattore** (m)	[redat'tore]
editor-in-chief	**redattore capo** (m)	[redat'tore 'kapo]
correspondent	**corrispondente** (m)	[korrispon'dente]
typist (fem.)	**dattilografa** (f)	[datti'lografa]
designer	**designer** (m)	[di'zajner]
computer expert	**esperto** (m) **informatico**	[e'sperto infor'matiko]
programmer	**programmatore** (m)	[programma'tore]
engineer (designer)	**ingegnere** (m)	[indʒe'ɲere]
sailor	**marittimo** (m)	[ma'rittimo]
seaman	**marinaio** (m)	[mari'najo]
rescuer	**soccorritore** (m)	[sokkorri'tore]
fireman	**pompiere** (m)	[pom'pjere]
police officer	**poliziotto** (m)	[poli'tsjotto]
watchman	**guardiano** (m)	[gwar'djano]
detective	**detective** (m)	[de'tektiv]
customs officer	**doganiere** (m)	[doga'njere]
bodyguard	**guardia** (f) **del corpo**	['gwardia del 'korpo]
prison guard	**guardia** (f) **carceraria**	['gwardia kartʃe'raria]
inspector	**ispettore** (m)	[ispet'tore]
sportsman	**sportivo** (m)	[spor'tivo]
trainer, coach	**allenatore** (m)	[allena'tore]
butcher	**macellaio** (m)	[matʃel'lajo]
cobbler (shoe repairer)	**calzolaio** (m)	[kaltso'lajo]
merchant	**uomo** (m) **d'affari**	[u'omo daf'fari]
loader (person)	**caricatore** (m)	[karika'tore]
fashion designer	**stilista** (m)	[sti'lista]
model (fem.)	**modella** (f)	[mo'della]

131. Occupations. Social status

schoolboy	**scolaro** (m)	[sko'laro]
student (college ~)	**studente** (m)	[stu'dente]
philosopher	**filosofo** (m)	[fi'lozofo]
economist	**economista** (m)	[ekono'mista]
inventor	**inventore** (m)	[inven'tore]
unemployed (n)	**disoccupato** (m)	[disokku'pato]
retiree	**pensionato** (m)	[pensjo'nato]
spy, secret agent	**spia** (f)	['spia]

prisoner	**detenuto** (m)	[dete'nuto]
striker	**scioperante** (m)	[ʃope'rante]
bureaucrat	**burocrate** (m)	[bu'rokrate]
traveler (globetrotter)	**viaggiatore** (m)	[vjadʒa'tore]
gay, homosexual (n)	**omosessuale** (m)	[omosessu'ale]
hacker	**hacker** (m)	['aker]
hippie	**hippy**	['ippi]
bandit	**bandito** (m)	[ban'dito]
hit man, killer	**sicario** (m)	[si'kario]
drug addict	**drogato** (m)	[dro'gato]
drug dealer	**trafficante** (m) **di droga**	[traffi'kante di 'droga]
prostitute (fem.)	**prostituta** (f)	[prosti'tuta]
pimp	**magnaccia** (m)	[ma'ɲatʃa]
sorcerer	**stregone** (m)	[stre'gone]
sorceress (evil ~)	**strega** (f)	['strega]
pirate	**pirata** (m)	[pi'rata]
slave	**schiavo** (m)	['skjavo]
samurai	**samurai** (m)	[samu'raj]
savage (primitive)	**selvaggio** (m)	[sel'vadʒo]

Sports

132. Kinds of sports. Sportspersons

sportsman	**sportivo** (m)	[spor'tivo]
kind of sports	**sport** (m)	[sport]
basketball	**pallacanestro** (m)	[pallaka'nestro]
basketball player	**cestista** (m)	[ʧes'tista]
baseball	**baseball** (m)	['bejzbol]
baseball player	**giocatore** (m) **di baseball**	[ʤoka'tore di 'bejzbol]
soccer	**calcio** (m)	['kalʧo]
soccer player	**calciatore** (m)	[kalʧa'tore]
goalkeeper	**portiere** (m)	[por'tjere]
hockey	**hockey** (m)	['okkej]
hockey player	**hockeista** (m)	[okke'ista]
volleyball	**pallavolo** (m)	[palla'volo]
volleyball player	**pallavolista** (m)	[pallavo'lista]
boxing	**pugilato** (m)	[puʤi'lato]
boxer	**pugile** (m)	['puʤile]
wrestling	**lotta** (f)	['lotta]
wrestler	**lottatore** (m)	[lotta'tore]
karate	**karate** (m)	[ka'rate]
karate fighter	**karateka** (m)	[kara'teka]
judo	**judo** (m)	['ʤudo]
judo athlete	**judoista** (m)	[ʤudo'ista]
tennis	**tennis** (m)	['tennis]
tennis player	**tennista** (m)	[ten'nista]
swimming	**nuoto** (m)	[nu'oto]
swimmer	**nuotatore** (m)	[nuota'tore]
fencing	**scherma** (f)	['skerma]
fencer	**schermitore** (m)	[skermi'tore]
chess	**scacchi** (m pl)	['skakki]
chess player	**scacchista** (m)	[skak'kista]

alpinism	**alpinismo** (m)	[alpi'nizmo]
alpinist	**alpinista** (m)	[alpi'nista]
running	**corsa** (f)	['korsa]
runner	**corridore** (m)	[korri'dore]
athletics	**atletica** (f) **leggera**	[a'tletika le'ʤera]
athlete	**atleta** (m)	[a'tleta]
horseback riding	**ippica** (f)	['ippika]
horse rider	**fantino** (m)	[fan'tino]
figure skating	**pattinaggio** (m) **artistico**	[patti'naʤo ar'tistiko]
figure skater (masc.)	**pattinatore** (m)	[pattina'tore]
figure skater (fem.)	**pattinatrice** (f)	[pattina'triʧe]
powerlifting	**pesistica** (f)	[pe'zistika]
powerlifter	**pesista** (m)	[pe'zista]
car racing	**automobilismo** (m)	[automobi'lizmo]
racer (driver)	**pilota** (m)	[pi'lota]
cycling	**ciclismo** (m)	[ʧik'lizmo]
cyclist	**ciclista** (m)	[ʧik'lista]
broad jump	**salto** (m) **in lungo**	['salto in 'lungo]
pole vault	**salto** (m) **con l'asta**	['salto kon 'lasta]
jumper	**saltatore** (m)	[salta'tore]

133. Kinds of sports. Miscellaneous

football	**football** (m) **americano**	['futboll ameri'kano]
badminton	**badminton** (m)	['badminton]
biathlon	**biathlon** (m)	['biatlon]
billiards	**biliardo** (m)	[bi'ljardo]
bobsled	**bob** (m)	[bob]
bodybuilding	**culturismo** (m)	[kultu'rizmo]
water polo	**pallanuoto** (m)	[pallanu'oto]
handball	**pallamano** (m)	[palla'mano]
golf	**golf** (m)	[golf]
rowing, crew	**canottaggio** (m)	[kanot'taʤo]
scuba diving	**immersione** (f) **subacquea**	[immer'sjone su'bakvea]
cross-country skiing	**sci** (m) **di fondo**	[ʃi di 'fondo]
table tennis (ping-pong)	**tennis** (m) **da tavolo**	['tennis da 'tavolo]
sailing	**vela** (f)	['vela]
rally racing	**rally** (m)	['relli]
rugby	**rugby** (m)	['ragbi]

snowboarding	**snowboard** (m)	['znobord]
archery	**tiro** (m) **con l'arco**	['tiro kon 'larko]

134. Gym

barbell	**bilanciere** (m)	[bilan'ʧere]
dumbbells	**manubri** (m pl)	[ma'nubri]
training machine	**attrezzo** (m) **sportivo**	[at'trettso spor'tivo]
exercise bicycle	**cyclette** (f)	[si'klett]
treadmill	**tapis roulant** (m)	[ta'pi ru'lan]
horizontal bar	**sbarra** (f)	['zbarra]
parallel bars	**parallele** (f pl)	[paral'lele]
vault (vaulting horse)	**cavallo** (m)	[ka'vallo]
mat (exercise ~)	**materassino** (m)	[materas'sino]
jump rope	**corda** (f) **per saltare**	['korda per sal'tare]
aerobics	**aerobica** (f)	[ae'robika]
yoga	**yoga** (m)	['joga]

135. Hockey

hockey	**hockey** (m)	['okkej]
hockey player	**hockeista** (m)	[okke'ista]
to play hockey	**giocare a hockey**	[ʤo'kare a 'okkej]
ice	**ghiaccio** (m)	['gjaʧo]
puck	**disco** (m)	['disko]
hockey stick	**bastone** (m) **da hockey**	[bas'tone da 'okkej]
ice skates	**pattini** (m pl)	['pattini]
board (ice hockey rink ~)	**bordo** (m)	['bordo]
shot	**tiro** (m)	['tiro]
goaltender	**portiere** (m)	[por'tjere]
goal (score)	**gol** (m)	[gol]
to score a goal	**segnare un gol**	[se'ɲare un gol]
period	**tempo** (m)	['tempo]
second period	**secondo tempo** (m)	[se'kondo 'temro]
substitutes bench	**panchina** (f)	[paŋ'kina]

136. Soccer

soccer	**calcio** (m)	['kalʧo]
soccer player	**calciatore** (m)	[kalʧa'tore]

to play soccer	**giocare a calcio**	[dʒo'kare a 'kaltʃo]
major league	**La Prima Divisione**	[la 'prima divi'zjone]
soccer club	**società** (f) **calcistica**	[sotʃe'ta kal'tʃistika]
coach	**allenatore** (m)	[allena'tore]
owner, proprietor	**proprietario** (m)	[proprie'tario]
team	**squadra** (f)	['skwadra]
team captain	**capitano** (m) **di squadra**	[kapi'tano di 'skwadra]
player	**giocatore** (m)	[dʒoka'tore]
substitute	**riserva** (f)	[ri'zerva]
forward	**attaccante** (m)	[attak'kante]
center forward	**centrocampista** (m)	[tʃentro·kam'pista]
scorer	**bomber** (m)	['bomber]
defender, back	**terzino** (m)	[ter'tsino]
midfielder, halfback	**mediano** (m)	[me'djano]
match	**partita** (f)	[par'tita]
to meet (vi, vt)	**incontrarsi** (vr)	[inkon'trarsi]
final	**finale** (m)	[fi'nale]
semi-final	**semifinale** (m)	[semifi'nale]
championship	**campionato** (m)	[kampjo'nato]
period, half	**tempo** (m)	['tempo]
first period	**primo tempo** (m)	['primo 'tempo]
half-time	**intervallo** (m)	[inter'vallo]
goal	**porta** (f)	['porta]
goalkeeper	**portiere** (m)	[por'tjere]
goalpost	**palo** (m)	['palo]
crossbar	**traversa** (f)	[tra'versa]
net	**rete** (f)	['rete]
to concede a goal	**subire un gol**	[su'bire un gol]
ball	**pallone** (m)	[pal'lone]
pass	**passaggio** (m)	[pas'sadʒo]
kick	**calcio** (m), **tiro** (m)	['kaltʃo], ['tiro]
to kick (~ the ball)	**tirare un calcio**	[ti'rare un 'kaltʃo]
free kick (direct ~)	**calcio** (m) **di punizione**	['kaltʃo di puni'tsjone]
corner kick	**calcio** (m) **d'angolo**	['kaltʃo 'dangolo]
attack	**attacco** (m)	[at'takko]
counterattack	**contrattacco** (m)	[kontrat'takko]
combination	**combinazione** (f)	[kombina'tsjone]
referee	**arbitro** (m)	['arbitro]
to blow the whistle	**fischiare** (vi)	[fis'kjare]
whistle (sound)	**fischio** (m)	['fiskio]
foul, misconduct	**fallo** (m)	['fallo]
to commit a foul	**fare un fallo**	['fare un 'fallo]
to send off	**espellere dal campo**	[e'spellere dal 'kampo]
yellow card	**cartellino** (m) **giallo**	[kartel'lino 'dʒallo]

red card	**cartellino** (m) **rosso**	[kartel'lino 'rosso]
disqualification	**squalifica** (f)	[skwa'lifika]
to disqualify (vt)	**squalificare** (vt)	[skwalifi'kare]
penalty kick	**rigore** (m)	[ri'gore]
wall	**barriera** (f)	[bar'rjera]
to score (vi, vt)	**segnare** (vt)	[se'ɲare]
goal (score)	**gol** (m)	[gol]
to score a goal	**segnare un gol**	[se'ɲare un gol]
substitution	**sostituzione** (f)	[sostitu'tsjone]
to replace (a player)	**sostituire** (vt)	[sostitu'ire]
rules	**regole** (f pl)	['regole]
tactics	**tattica** (f)	['tattika]
stadium	**stadio** (m)	['stadio]
stand (bleachers)	**tribuna** (f)	[tri'buna]
fan, supporter	**tifoso, fan** (m)	[ti'fozo], [fan]
to shout (vi)	**gridare** (vi)	[gri'dare]
scoreboard	**tabellone** (m) **segnapunti**	[tabel'lone seɲa'punti]
score	**punteggio** (m)	[pun'teʤo]
defeat	**sconfitta** (f)	[skon'fitta]
to lose (not win)	**perdere** (vi)	['perdere]
tie	**pareggio** (m)	[pa'reʤo]
to tie (vi)	**pareggiare** (vi)	[pare'ʤare]
victory	**vittoria** (f)	[vit'toria]
to win (vi, vt)	**vincere** (vi)	['vinʧere]
champion	**campione** (m)	[kam'pjone]
best (adj)	**migliore**	[miʎ'ʎore]
to congratulate (vt)	**congratularsi** (vr)	[kongratu'larsi]
commentator	**commentatore** (m)	[kommenta'tore]
to commentate (vt)	**commentare** (vt)	[kommen'tare]
broadcast	**trasmissione** (f)	[trazmis'sjone]

137. Alpine skiing

skis	**sci** (m pl)	[ʃi]
to ski (vi)	**sciare** (vi)	[ʃi'are]
mountain-ski resort	**stazione** (f) **sciistica**	[sta'tsjone ʃi'istika]
ski lift	**sciovia** (f)	[ʃio'via]
ski poles	**bastoni** (m pl) **da sci**	[bas'toni da ʃi]
slope	**pendio** (m)	[pen'dio]
slalom	**slalom** (m)	['zlalom]

138. Tennis. Golf

golf	**golf** (m)	[golf]
golf club	**golf club** (m)	[golf klab]
golfer	**golfista** (m)	[gol'fista]
hole	**buca** (f)	['buka]
club	**mazza** (f) **da golf**	['mattsa da golf]
golf trolley	**carrello** (m) **da golf**	[kar'rello da golf]
tennis	**tennis** (m)	['tennis]
tennis court	**campo** (m) **da tennis**	['kampo da 'tennis]
serve	**battuta** (f)	[bat'tuta]
to serve (vt)	**servire** (vt)	[ser'vire]
racket	**racchetta** (f)	[rak'ketta]
net	**rete** (f)	['rete]
ball	**palla** (f)	['palla]

139. Chess

chess	**scacchi** (m pl)	['skakki]
chessmen	**pezzi** (m pl) **degli scacchi**	['pettsi 'deʎʎi 'skakki]
chess player	**scacchista** (m)	[skak'kista]
chessboard	**scacchiera** (f)	[skak'kjera]
chessman	**pezzo** (m)	['pettso]
White (white pieces)	**Bianchi** (m pl)	['bjaŋki]
Black (black pieces)	**Neri** (m pl)	['neri]
pawn	**pedina** (f)	[pe'dina]
bishop	**alfiere** (m)	[al'fjere]
knight	**cavallo** (m)	[ka'vallo]
rook	**torre** (f)	['torre]
queen	**regina** (f)	[re'ʤina]
king	**re** (m)	[re]
move	**mossa** (m)	['mossa]
to move (vi, vt)	**muovere** (vt)	[mu'overe]
to sacrifice (vt)	**sacrificare** (vt)	[sakrifi'kare]
castling	**arrocco** (m)	[ar'rokko]
check	**scacco** (m)	['skakko]
checkmate	**scacco matto** (m)	['skakko 'matto]
chess tournament	**torneo** (m) **di scacchi**	[tor'neo di 'skakki]
Grand Master	**gran maestro** (m)	[gran ma'estro]
combination	**combinazione** (f)	[kombina'tsjone]
game (in chess)	**partita** (f)	[par'tita]
checkers	**dama** (f)	['dama]

140. Boxing

boxing	**pugilato** (m), **boxe** (f)	[puʤi'lato], [boks]
fight (bout)	**incontro** (m)	[in'kontro]
boxing match	**incontro** (m) **di boxe**	[in'kontro di boks]
round (in boxing)	**round** (m)	['raund]
ring	**ring** (m)	[ring]
gong	**gong** (m)	[gong]
punch	**pugno** (m)	['puɲo]
knockdown	**knock down** (m)	[nok 'daun]
knockout	**knock-out** (m)	[nok 'aut]
to knock out	**mettere knock-out**	['mettere nok 'aut]
boxing glove	**guantone** (m) **da pugile**	[gwan'tone da 'puʤile]
referee	**arbitro** (m)	['arbitro]
lightweight	**peso** (m) **leggero**	['pezo le'ʤero]
middleweight	**peso** (m) **medio**	['pezo 'medio]
heavyweight	**peso** (m) **massimo**	['pezo 'massimo]

141. Sports. Miscellaneous

Olympic Games	**Giochi** (m pl) **Olimpici**	['ʤoki o'limpiʧi]
winner	**vincitore** (m)	[vinʧi'tore]
to be winning	**ottenere la vittoria**	[otte'nere la vit'toria]
to win (vi)	**vincere** (vi)	['vinʧere]
leader	**leader** (m), **capo** (m)	['lider], ['kapo]
to lead (vi)	**essere alla guida**	['essere 'alla 'gwida]
first place	**primo posto** (m)	['primo 'posto]
second place	**secondo posto** (m)	[se'kondo 'posto]
third place	**terzo posto** (m)	['tertso 'posto]
medal	**medaglia** (f)	[me'daʎʎa]
trophy	**trofeo** (m)	[tro'feo]
prize cup (trophy)	**coppa** (f)	['koppa]
prize (in game)	**premio** (m)	['premio]
main prize	**primo premio** (m)	['primo 'premio]
record	**record** (m)	['rekord]
to set a record	**stabilire un record**	[stabi'lire un 'rekord]
final	**finale** (m)	[fi'nale]
final (adj)	**finale**	[fi'nale]
champion	**campione** (m)	[kam'pjone]
championship	**campionato** (m)	[kampjo'nato]

stadium	**stadio** (m)	['stadio]
stand (bleachers)	**tribuna** (f)	[tri'buna]
fan, supporter	**tifoso, fan** (m)	[ti'fozo], [fan]
opponent, rival	**avversario** (m)	[avver'sario]
start (start line)	**partenza** (f)	[par'tentsa]
finish line	**traguardo** (m)	[tra'gwardo]
defeat	**sconfitta** (f)	[skon'fitta]
to lose (not win)	**perdere** (vt)	['perdere]
referee	**arbitro** (m)	['arbitro]
jury (judges)	**giuria** (f)	[ʤu'ria]
score	**punteggio** (m)	[pun'teʤo]
tie	**pareggio** (m)	[pa'reʤo]
to tie (vi)	**pareggiare** (vi)	[pare'ʤare]
point	**punto** (m)	['punto]
result (final score)	**risultato** (m)	[rizul'tato]
period	**tempo** (m)	['tempo]
half-time	**intervallo** (m)	[inter'vallo]
doping	**doping** (m)	['doping]
to penalize (vt)	**penalizzare** (vt)	[penalid'ʣare]
to disqualify (vt)	**squalificare** (vt)	[skwalifi'kare]
apparatus	**attrezzatura** (f)	[attrettsa'tura]
javelin	**giavellotto** (m)	[ʤavel'lotto]
shot (metal ball)	**peso** (m)	['pezo]
ball (snooker, etc.)	**biglia** (f)	['biʎʎa]
aim (target)	**obiettivo** (m)	[objet'tivo]
target	**bersaglio** (m)	[ber'saʎʎo]
to shoot (vi)	**sparare** (vi)	[spa'rare]
accurate (~ shot)	**preciso**	[pre'ʧizo]
trainer, coach	**allenatore** (m)	[allena'tore]
to train (sb)	**allenare** (vt)	[alle'nare]
to train (vi)	**allenarsi** (vr)	[alle'narsi]
training	**allenamento** (m)	[allena'mento]
gym	**palestra** (f)	[pa'lestra]
exercise (physical)	**esercizio** (m)	[ezer'ʧitsio]
warm-up (athlete ~)	**riscaldamento** (m)	[riskalda'mento]

Education

142. School

school	**scuola** (f)	['skwola]
principal (headmaster)	**direttore** (m) **di scuola**	[diret'tore di 'skwola]
pupil (boy)	**allievo** (m)	[al'ljevo]
pupil (girl)	**allieva** (f)	[al'ljeva]
schoolboy	**scolaro** (m)	[sko'laro]
schoolgirl	**scolara** (f)	[sko'lara]
to teach (sb)	**insegnare**	[inse'ɲare]
to learn (language, etc.)	**imparare** (vt)	[impa'rare]
to learn by heart	**imparare a memoria**	[impa'rare a me'moria]
to learn (~ to count, etc.)	**studiare** (vi)	[stu'djare]
to be in school	**frequentare la scuola**	[frekwen'tare la 'skwola]
to go to school	**andare a scuola**	[an'dare a 'skwola]
alphabet	**alfabeto** (m)	[alfa'beto]
subject (at school)	**materia** (f)	[ma'teria]
classroom	**classe** (f)	['klasse]
lesson	**lezione** (f)	[le'tsjone]
recess	**ricreazione** (f)	[rikrea'tsjone]
school bell	**campanella** (f)	[kampa'nella]
school desk	**banco** (m)	['banko]
chalkboard	**lavagna** (f)	[la'vaɲa]
grade	**voto** (m)	['voto]
good grade	**voto** (m) **alto**	['voto 'alto]
bad grade	**voto** (m) **basso**	['voto 'basso]
to give a grade	**dare un voto**	['dare un 'voto]
mistake, error	**errore** (m)	[er'rore]
to make mistakes	**fare errori**	['fare er'rori]
to correct (an error)	**correggere** (vt)	[kor'redʒere]
cheat sheet	**bigliettino** (m)	[biʎʎet'tino]
homework	**compiti** (m pl)	['kompiti]
exercise (in education)	**esercizio** (m)	[ezer'ʧitsio]
to be present	**essere presente**	['essere pre'zente]
to be absent	**essere assente**	['essere as'sente]
to miss school	**mancare le lezioni**	[man'kare le le'tsjoni]

to punish (vt)	**punire** (vt)	[pu'nire]
punishment	**punizione** (f)	[puni'tsjone]
conduct (behavior)	**comportamento** (m)	[komporta'mento]
report card	**pagella** (f)	[pa'ʤella]
pencil	**matita** (f)	[ma'tita]
eraser	**gomma** (f) **per cancellare**	['gomma per kanʧel'lare]
chalk	**gesso** (m)	['ʤesso]
pencil case	**astuccio** (m) **portamatite**	[as'tuʧo portama'tite]
schoolbag	**cartella** (f)	[kar'tella]
pen	**penna** (f)	['penna]
school notebook	**quaderno** (m)	[kwa'derno]
textbook	**manuale** (m)	[manu'ale]
drafting compass	**compasso** (m)	[kom'passo]
to make technical drawings	**disegnare** (vt)	[dize'ɲare]
technical drawing	**disegno** (m) **tecnico**	[di'zeɲo 'tekniko]
poem	**poesia** (f)	[poe'zia]
by heart (adv)	**a memoria**	[a me'moria]
to learn by heart	**imparare a memoria**	[impa'rare a me'moria]
school vacation	**vacanze** (f pl) **scolastiche**	[va'kantse sko'lastike]
to be on vacation	**essere in vacanza**	['essere in va'kantsa]
to spend one's vacation	**passare le vacanze**	[pas'sare le va'kantse]
test (written math ~)	**prova** (f) **scritta**	['prova 'skritta]
essay (composition)	**composizione** (f)	[kompozi'tsjone]
dictation	**dettato** (m)	[det'tato]
exam (examination)	**esame** (m)	[e'zame]
to take an exam	**sostenere un esame**	[soste'neme un e'zame]
experiment (e.g., chemistry ~)	**esperimento** (m)	[esperi'mento]

143. College. University

academy	**accademia** (f)	[akka'demia]
university	**università** (f)	[universi'ta]
faculty (e.g., ~ of Medicine)	**facoltà** (f)	[fakol'ta]
student (masc.)	**studente** (m)	[stu'dente]
student (fem.)	**studentessa** (f)	[studen'tessa]
lecturer (teacher)	**docente** (m, f)	[do'ʧente]
lecture hall, room	**aula** (f)	['aula]
graduate	**diplomato** (m)	[diplo'mato]
diploma	**diploma** (m)	[di'ploma]

dissertation	**tesi** (f)	['tezi]
study (report)	**ricerca** (f)	[ri'tʃerka]
laboratory	**laboratorio** (m)	[labora'torio]
lecture	**lezione** (f)	[le'tsjone]
coursemate	**compagno** (m) **di corso**	[kom'paɲo di 'korso]
scholarship	**borsa** (f) **di studio**	['borsa di 'studio]
academic degree	**titolo** (m) **accademico**	['titolo akka'demiko]

144. Sciences. Disciplines

mathematics	**matematica** (f)	[mate'matika]
algebra	**algebra** (f)	['aldʒebra]
geometry	**geometria** (f)	[dʒeome'tria]
astronomy	**astronomia** (f)	[astrono'mia]
biology	**biologia** (f)	[biolo'dʒia]
geography	**geografia** (f)	[dʒeogra'fia]
geology	**geologia** (f)	[dʒeolo'dʒia]
history	**storia** (f)	['storia]
medicine	**medicina** (f)	[medi'tʃina]
pedagogy	**pedagogia** (f)	[pedago'dʒia]
law	**diritto** (m)	[di'ritto]
physics	**fisica** (f)	['fizika]
chemistry	**chimica** (f)	['kimika]
philosophy	**filosofia** (f)	[filozo'fia]
psychology	**psicologia** (f)	[psikolo'dʒia]

145. Writing system. Orthography

grammar	**grammatica** (f)	[gram'matika]
vocabulary	**lessico** (m)	['lessiko]
phonetics	**fonetica** (f)	[fo'netika]
noun	**sostantivo** (m)	[sostan'tivo]
adjective	**aggettivo** (m)	[adʒet'tivo]
verb	**verbo** (m)	['verbo]
adverb	**avverbio** (m)	[av'verbio]
pronoun	**pronome** (m)	[pro'nome]
interjection	**interiezione** (f)	[interje'tsjone]
preposition	**preposizione** (f)	[prepozi'tsjone]
root	**radice** (f)	[ra'ditʃe]
ending	**desinenza** (f)	[dezi'nentsa]
prefix	**prefisso** (m)	[pre'fisso]

syllable	**sillaba** (f)	['sillaba]
suffix	**suffisso** (m)	[suf'fisso]
stress mark	**accento** (m)	[a'tʃento]
apostrophe	**apostrofo** (m)	[a'postrofo]
period, dot	**punto** (m)	['punto]
comma	**virgola** (f)	['virgola]
semicolon	**punto** (m) **e virgola**	['punto e 'virgola]
colon	**due punti**	['due 'punti]
ellipsis	**puntini** (m pl) **di sospensione**	[pun'tini di sospen'sjone]
question mark	**punto** (m) **interrogativo**	['punto interroga'tivo]
exclamation point	**punto** (m) **esclamativo**	['punto esklama'tivo]
quotation marks	**virgolette** (f pl)	[virgo'lette]
in quotation marks	**tra virgolette**	[tra virgo'lette]
parenthesis	**parentesi** (f pl)	[pa'rentezi]
in parenthesis	**tra parentesi**	[tra pa'rentezi]
hyphen	**trattino** (m)	[trat'tino]
dash	**lineetta** (f)	[line'etta]
space (between words)	**spazio** (m)	['spatsio]
letter	**lettera** (f)	['lettera]
capital letter	**lettera** (f) **maiuscola**	['lettera ma'juskola]
vowel (n)	**vocale** (f)	[vo'kale]
consonant (n)	**consonante** (f)	[konso'nante]
sentence	**proposizione** (f)	[propozi'tsjone]
subject	**soggetto** (m)	[so'dʒetto]
predicate	**predicato** (m)	[predi'kato]
line	**riga** (f)	['riga]
on a new line	**a capo**	[a 'kapo]
paragraph	**capoverso** (m)	[kapo'verso]
word	**parola** (f)	[pa'rola]
group of words	**gruppo** (m) **di parole**	['gruppo di pa'role]
expression	**espressione** (f)	[espres'sjone]
synonym	**sinonimo** (m)	[si'nonimo]
antonym	**antonimo** (m)	[an'tonimo]
rule	**regola** (f)	['regola]
exception	**eccezione** (f)	[etʃe'tsjone]
correct (adj)	**corretto**	[kor'retto]
conjugation	**coniugazione** (f)	[konjuga'tsjone]
declension	**declinazione** (f)	[deklina'tsjone]
nominal case	**caso** (m) **nominativo**	['kazo nomina'tivo]

question	**domanda** (f)	[do'manda]
to underline (vt)	**sottolineare** (vt)	[sottoline'are]
dotted line	**linea** (f) **tratteggiata**	['linea tratte'dʒata]

146. Foreign languages

language	**lingua** (f)	['lingua]
foreign (adj)	**straniero**	[stra'njero]
foreign language	**lingua** (f) **straniera**	['lingua stra'njera]
to study (vt)	**studiare** (vt)	[stu'djare]
to learn (language, etc.)	**imparare** (vt)	[impa'rare]
to read (vi, vt)	**leggere** (vi, vt)	['ledʒere]
to speak (vi, vt)	**parlare** (vi, vt)	[par'lare]
to understand (vt)	**capire** (vt)	[ka'pire]
to write (vt)	**scrivere** (vi, vt)	['skrivere]
fast (adv)	**rapidamente**	[rapida'mente]
slowly (adv)	**lentamente**	[lenta'mente]
fluently (adv)	**correntemente**	[korrente'mente]
rules	**regole** (f pl)	['regole]
grammar	**grammatica** (f)	[gram'matika]
vocabulary	**lessico** (m)	['lessiko]
phonetics	**fonetica** (f)	[fo'netika]
textbook	**manuale** (m)	[manu'ale]
dictionary	**dizionario** (m)	[ditsjo'nario]
teach-yourself book	**manuale** (m) **autodidattico**	[manu'ale autodi'dattiko]
phrasebook	**frasario** (m)	[fra'zario]
cassette, tape	**cassetta** (f)	[kas'setta]
videotape	**videocassetta** (f)	[video·kas'setta]
CD, compact disc	**CD** (m)	[tʃi'di]
DVD	**DVD** (m)	[divu'di]
alphabet	**alfabeto** (m)	[alfa'beto]
to spell (vt)	**compitare** (vt)	[kompi'tare]
pronunciation	**pronuncia** (f)	[pro'nuntʃa]
accent	**accento** (m)	[a'tʃento]
with an accent	**con un accento**	[kon un a'tʃento]
without an accent	**senza accento**	['sentsa a'tʃento]
word	**vocabolo** (m)	[vo'kabolo]
meaning	**significato** (m)	[siɲifi'kato]
course (e.g., a French ~)	**corso** (m)	['korso]
to sign up	**iscriversi** (vr)	[is'kriversi]

teacher	**insegnante** (m, f)	[inse'ɲante]
translation (process)	**traduzione** (f)	[tradu'tsjone]
translation (text, etc.)	**traduzione** (f)	[tradu'tsjone]
translator	**traduttore** (m)	[tradut'tore]
interpreter	**interprete** (m)	[in'terprete]
polyglot	**poliglotta** (m)	[poli'glotta]
memory	**memoria** (f)	[me'moria]

147. Fairy tale characters

Santa Claus	**Babbo Natale** (m)	['babbo na'tale]
Cinderella	**Cenerentola** (f)	[ʧene'rentola]
mermaid	**sirena** (f)	[si'rena]
Neptune	**Nettuno** (m)	[net'tuno]
magician, wizard	**mago** (m)	['mago]
fairy	**fata** (f)	['fata]
magic (adj)	**magico**	['maʤiko]
magic wand	**bacchetta** (f) **magica**	[bak'ketta 'maʤika]
fairy tale	**fiaba** (f), **favola** (f)	['fjaba], ['favola]
miracle	**miracolo** (m)	[mi'rakolo]
dwarf	**nano** (m)	['nano]
to turn into ...	**trasformarsi in ...**	[trasfor'marsi in]
ghost	**spettro** (m)	['spettro]
phantom	**fantasma** (m)	[fan'tazma]
monster	**mostro** (m)	['mostro]
dragon	**drago** (m)	['drago]
giant	**gigante** (m)	[ʤi'gante]

148. Zodiac Signs

Aries	**Ariete** (m)	[a'rjete]
Taurus	**Toro** (m)	['toro]
Gemini	**Gemelli** (m pl)	[ʤe'melli]
Cancer	**Cancro** (m)	['kankro]
Leo	**Leone** (m)	[le'one]
Virgo	**Vergine** (f)	['verʤine]
Libra	**Bilancia** (f)	[bi'lanʧa]
Scorpio	**Scorpione** (m)	[skor'pjone]
Sagittarius	**Sagittario** (m)	[saʤit'tario]
Capricorn	**Capricorno** (m)	[kapri'korno]
Aquarius	**Acquario** (m)	[a'kwario]
Pisces	**Pesci** (m pl)	['peʃi]
character	**carattere** (m)	[ka'rattere]

character traits	**tratti** (m pl) **del carattere**	['tratti del ka'rattere]
behavior	**comportamento** (m)	[komporta'mento]
to tell fortunes	**predire il futuro**	[pre'dire il fu'turo]
fortune-teller	**cartomante** (f)	[karto'mante]
horoscope	**oroscopo** (m)	[o'roskopo]

Arts

149. Theater

theater	**teatro** (m)	[te'atro]
opera	**opera** (f)	['opera]
operetta	**operetta** (f)	[ope'retta]
ballet	**balletto** (m)	[bal'letto]
theater poster	**cartellone** (m)	[kartel'lone]
troupe (theatrical company)	**compagnia** (f) **teatrale**	[kompa'ɲia tea'trale]
tour	**tournée** (f)	[tur'ne]
to be on tour	**andare in tournée**	[an'dare in tur'ne]
to rehearse (vi, vt)	**fare le prove**	['fare le 'prove]
rehearsal	**prova** (f)	['prova]
repertoire	**repertorio** (m)	[reper'torio]
performance	**rappresentazione** (f)	[rapprezenta'tsjone]
theatrical show	**spettacolo** (m)	[spet'takolo]
play	**opera** (f) **teatrale**	['opera tea'trale]
ticket	**biglietto** (m)	[biʎ'ʎetto]
box office (ticket booth)	**botteghino** (m)	[botte'gino]
lobby, foyer	**hall** (f)	[oll]
coat check (cloakroom)	**guardaroba** (f)	[gwarda'roba]
coat check tag	**cartellino** (m) **del guardaroba**	[kartel'lino del gwarda'roba]
binoculars	**binocolo** (m)	[bi'nokolo]
usher	**maschera** (f)	['maskera]
orchestra seats	**platea** (f)	['platea]
balcony	**balconata** (f)	[balko'nata]
dress circle	**prima galleria** (f)	['prima galle'ria]
box	**palco** (m)	['palko]
row	**fila** (f)	['fila]
seat	**posto** (m)	['posto]
audience	**pubblico** (m)	['pubbliko]
spectator	**spettatore** (m)	[spetta'tore]
to clap (vi, vt)	**battere le mani**	['battere le 'mani]
applause	**applauso** (m)	[app'lauzo]
ovation	**ovazione** (f)	[ova'tsjone]
stage	**palcoscenico** (m)	[palko'ʃeniko]
curtain	**sipario** (m)	[si'pario]
scenery	**scenografia** (f)	[ʃenogra'fia]

backstage	**quinte** (f pl)	['kwinte]
scene (e.g., the last ~)	**scena** (f)	['ʃena]
act	**atto** (m)	['atto]
intermission	**intervallo** (m)	[inter'vallo]

150. Cinema

actor	**attore** (m)	[at'tore]
actress	**attrice** (f)	[at'tritʃe]
movies (industry)	**cinema** (m)	['tʃinema]
movie	**film** (m)	[film]
episode	**puntata** (f)	[pun'tata]
detective movie	**film** (m) **giallo**	[film 'dʒallo]
action movie	**film** (m) **d'azione**	[film da'tsjone]
adventure movie	**film** (m) **d'avventure**	[film davven'ture]
sci-fi movie	**film** (m) **di fantascienza**	['film de fanta'ʃentsa]
horror movie	**film** (m) **d'orrore**	[film dor'rore]
comedy movie	**film** (m) **comico**	[film 'komiko]
melodrama	**melodramma** (m)	[melo'dramma]
drama	**dramma** (m)	['dramma]
fictional movie	**film** (m) **a soggetto**	[film a so'dʒetto]
documentary	**documentario** (m)	[dokumen'tario]
cartoon	**cartoni** (m pl) **animati**	[kar'toni ani'mati]
silent movies	**cinema** (m) **muto**	['tʃinema 'muto]
role (part)	**parte** (f)	['parte]
leading role	**parte** (f) **principale**	['parte printʃi'pale]
to play (vi, vt)	**recitare** (vi, vt)	[retʃi'tare]
movie star	**star** (f), **stella** (f)	[star], ['stella]
well-known (adj)	**noto**	['noto]
famous (adj)	**famoso**	[fa'mozo]
popular (adj)	**popolare**	[popo'lare]
script (screenplay)	**sceneggiatura** (m)	[ʃenedʒa'tura]
scriptwriter	**sceneggiatore** (m)	[ʃenedʒa'tore]
movie director	**regista** (m)	[re'dʒista]
producer	**produttore** (m)	[produt'tore]
assistant	**assistente** (m)	[assi'stente]
cameraman	**cameraman** (m)	[kamera'men]
stuntman	**cascatore** (m)	[kaska'tore]
double (stand-in)	**controfigura** (f)	[kontrofi'gura]
to shoot a movie	**girare un film**	[dʒi'rare un film]
audition, screen test	**provino** (m)	[pro'vino]
shooting	**ripresa** (f)	[ri'preza]

movie crew	**troupe** (f) **cinematografica**	[trup ʧinemato'grafika]
movie set	**set** (m)	[set]
camera	**cinepresa** (f)	[ʧine'preza]
movie theater	**cinema** (m)	['ʧinema]
screen (e.g., big ~)	**schermo** (m)	['skermo]
to show a movie	**proiettare un film**	[projet'tare un film]
soundtrack	**colonna** (f) **sonora**	[ko'lonna so'nora]
special effects	**effetti** (m pl) **speciali**	[ef'fetti spe'ʧali]
subtitles	**sottotitoli** (m pl)	[sotto'titoli]
credits	**titoli** (m pl) **di coda**	['titoli di 'koda]
translation	**traduzione** (f)	[tradu'tsjone]

151. Painting

art	**arte** (f)	['arte]
fine arts	**belle arti** (f pl)	['belle 'arti]
art gallery	**galleria** (f) **d'arte**	[galle'ria 'darte]
art exhibition	**mostra** (f)	['mostra]
painting (art)	**pittura** (f)	[pit'tura]
graphic art	**grafica** (f)	['grafika]
abstract art	**astrattismo** (m)	[astrat'tizmo]
impressionism	**impressionismo** (m)	[impressio'nizmo]
picture (painting)	**quadro** (m)	['kwadro]
drawing	**disegno** (m)	[di'zeɲo]
poster	**cartellone** (m)	[kartel'lone]
illustration (picture)	**illustrazione** (f)	[illustra'tsjone]
miniature	**miniatura** (f)	[minia'tura]
copy (of painting, etc.)	**copia** (f)	['kopia]
reproduction	**riproduzione** (f)	[riprodu'tsjone]
mosaic	**mosaico** (m)	[mo'zaiko]
stained glass window	**vetrata** (f)	[ve'trata]
fresco	**affresco** (m)	[af'fresko]
engraving	**incisione** (f)	[inʧi'zjone]
bust (sculpture)	**busto** (m)	['busto]
sculpture	**scultura** (f)	[skul'tura]
statue	**statua** (f)	['statua]
plaster of Paris	**gesso** (m)	['ʤesso]
plaster (as adj)	**in gesso**	[in 'ʤesso]
portrait	**ritratto** (m)	[ri'tratto]
self-portrait	**autoritratto** (m)	[autori'tratto]
landscape painting	**paesaggio** (m)	[pae'zaʤʤo]

still life	**natura** (f) **morta**	[na'tura 'morta]
caricature	**caricatura** (f)	[karika'tura]
sketch	**abbozzo** (m)	[ab'bottso]
paint	**colore** (m)	[ko'lore]
watercolor paint	**acquerello** (m)	[akwe'rello]
oil (paint)	**olio** (m)	['oljo]
pencil	**matita** (f)	[ma'tita]
India ink	**inchiostro** (m) **di china**	[in'kjostro di 'kina]
charcoal	**carbone** (m)	[kar'bone]
to draw (vi, vt)	**disegnare** (vt)	[dize'ɲare]
to paint (vi, vt)	**dipingere** (vt)	[di'pindʒere]
to pose (vi)	**posare** (vi)	[po'zare]
artist's model (masc.)	**modello** (m)	[mo'dello]
artist's model (fem.)	**modella** (f)	[mo'della]
artist (painter)	**pittore** (m)	[pit'tore]
work of art	**opera** (f) **d'arte**	['opera 'darte]
masterpiece	**capolavoro** (m)	[kapo·la'voro]
studio (artist's workroom)	**laboratorio** (m)	[labora'torio]
canvas (cloth)	**tela** (f)	['tela]
easel	**cavalletto** (m)	[kaval'letto]
palette	**tavolozza** (f)	[tavo'lottsa]
frame (picture ~, etc.)	**cornice** (f)	[kor'nitʃe]
restoration	**restauro** (m)	[re'stauro]
to restore (vt)	**restaurare** (vt)	[restau'rare]

152. Literature & Poetry

literature	**letteratura** (f)	[lettera'tura]
author (writer)	**autore** (m)	[au'tore]
pseudonym	**pseudonimo** (m)	[pseu'donimo]
book	**libro** (m)	['libro]
volume	**volume** (m)	[vo'lume]
table of contents	**sommario** (m), **indice** (m)	[som'mario], ['inditʃe]
page	**pagina** (f)	['padʒina]
main character	**protagonista** (m)	[protago'nista]
autograph	**autografo** (m)	[au'tografo]
short story	**racconto** (m)	[rak'konto]
story (novella)	**romanzo** (m) **breve**	[ro'mandzo 'breve]
novel	**romanzo** (m)	[ro'mandzo]
work (writing)	**opera** (f)	['opera]
fable	**favola** (f)	['favola]
detective novel	**giallo** (m)	['dʒallo]

poem (verse)	**verso** (m)	['verso]
poetry	**poesia** (f)	[poe'zia]
poem (epic, ballad)	**poema** (m)	[po'ema]
poet	**poeta** (m)	[po'eta]
fiction	**narrativa** (f)	[narra'tiva]
science fiction	**fantascienza** (f)	[fanta'ʃentsa]
adventures	**avventure** (f pl)	[avven'ture]
educational literature	**letteratura** (f) **formativa**	[lettera'tura forma'tiva]
children's literature	**libri** (m pl) **per l'infanzia**	['libri per lin'fansia]

153. Circus

circus	**circo** (m)	['ʧirko]
traveling circus	**tendone** (m) **del circo**	[ten'done del 'ʧirko]
program	**programma** (m)	[pro'gramma]
performance	**spettacolo** (m)	[spet'takolo]
act (circus ~)	**numero** (m)	['numero]
circus ring	**arena** (f)	[a'rena]
pantomime (act)	**pantomima** (m)	[panto'mima]
clown	**pagliaccio** (m)	[paʎ'ʎaʧo]
acrobat	**acrobata** (m)	[a'krobata]
acrobatics	**acrobatica** (f)	[akro'batika]
gymnast	**ginnasta** (m)	[ʤin'nasta]
acrobatic gymnastics	**ginnastica** (m)	[ʤin'nastika]
somersault	**salto** (m) **mortale**	['salto mor'tale]
athlete (strongman)	**forzuto** (m)	[for'tsuto]
tamer (e.g., lion ~)	**domatore** (m)	[doma'tore]
rider (circus horse ~)	**cavallerizzo** (m)	[kavalle'riddzo]
assistant	**assistente** (m)	[assi'stente]
stunt	**acrobazia** (f)	[akroba'tsia]
magic trick	**gioco** (m) **di prestigio**	['ʤoko di pre'stiʤo]
conjurer, magician	**prestigiatore** (m)	[prestiʤa'tore]
juggler	**giocoliere** (m)	[ʤoko'ljere]
to juggle (vi, vt)	**giocolare** (vi)	[ʤoko'lare]
animal trainer	**ammaestratore** (m)	[ammaestra'tore]
animal training	**ammaestramento** (m)	[ammaestra'mento]
to train (animals)	**ammaestrare** (vt)	[ammae'strare]

154. Music. Pop music

music	**musica** (f)	['muzika]
musician	**musicista** (m)	[muzi'ʧista]

musical instrument	**strumento** (m) **musicale**	[stru'mento muzi'kale]
to play ...	**suonare ...**	[suo'nare]
guitar	**chitarra** (f)	[ki'tarra]
violin	**violino** (m)	[vio'lino]
cello	**violoncello** (m)	[violon'tʃello]
double bass	**contrabbasso** (m)	[kontrab'basso]
harp	**arpa** (f)	['arpa]
piano	**pianoforte** (m)	[pjano'forte]
grand piano	**pianoforte** (m) **a coda**	[pjano'forte a 'koda]
organ	**organo** (m)	['organo]
wind instruments	**strumenti** (m pl) **a fiato**	[stru'menti a 'fjato]
oboe	**oboe** (m)	['oboe]
saxophone	**sassofono** (m)	[sas'sofono]
clarinet	**clarinetto** (m)	[klari'netto]
flute	**flauto** (m)	['flauto]
trumpet	**tromba** (f)	['tromba]
accordion	**fisarmonica** (f)	[fizar'monika]
drum	**tamburo** (m)	[tam'buro]
duo	**duetto** (m)	[du'etto]
trio	**trio** (m)	['trio]
quartet	**quartetto** (m)	[kwar'tetto]
choir	**coro** (m)	['koro]
orchestra	**orchestra** (f)	[or'kestra]
pop music	**musica** (f) **pop**	['muzika pop]
rock music	**musica** (f) **rock**	['muzika rok]
rock group	**gruppo** (m) **rock**	['gruppo rok]
jazz	**jazz** (m)	[dʒaz]
idol	**idolo** (m)	['idolo]
admirer, fan	**ammiratore** (m)	[ammira'tore]
concert	**concerto** (m)	[kon'tʃerto]
symphony	**sinfonia** (f)	[sinfo'nia]
composition	**composizione** (f)	[kompozi'tsjone]
to compose (write)	**comporre** (vt)	[kom'porre]
singing (n)	**canto** (m)	['kanto]
song	**canzone** (f)	[kan'tsone]
tune (melody)	**melodia** (f)	[melo'dia]
rhythm	**ritmo** (m)	['ritmo]
blues	**blues** (m)	[bluz]
sheet music	**note** (f pl)	['note]
baton	**bacchetta** (f)	[bak'ketta]
bow	**arco** (m)	['arko]
string	**corda** (f)	['korda]
case (e.g., guitar ~)	**custodia** (f)	[ku'stodia]

Rest. Entertainment. Travel

155. Trip. Travel

tourism, travel	**turismo** (m)	[tu'rizmo]
tourist	**turista** (m)	[tu'rista]
trip, voyage	**viaggio** (m)	['vjadʒo]
adventure	**avventura** (f)	[avven'tura]
trip, journey	**viaggio** (m)	['vjadʒo]
vacation	**vacanza** (f)	[va'kantsa]
to be on vacation	**essere in vacanza**	['essere in va'kantsa]
rest	**riposo** (m)	[ri'pozo]
train	**treno** (m)	['treno]
by train	**in treno**	[in 'treno]
airplane	**aereo** (m)	[a'ereo]
by airplane	**in aereo**	[in a'ereo]
by car	**in macchina**	[in 'makkina]
by ship	**in nave**	[in 'nave]
luggage	**bagaglio** (m)	[ba'gaʎʎo]
suitcase	**valigia** (f)	[va'lidʒa]
luggage cart	**carrello** (m)	[kar'rello]
passport	**passaporto** (m)	[passa'porto]
visa	**visto** (m)	['visto]
ticket	**biglietto** (m)	[biʎ'ʎetto]
air ticket	**biglietto** (m) **aereo**	[biʎ'ʎetto a'ereo]
guidebook	**guida** (f)	['gwida]
map (tourist ~)	**carta** (f) **geografica**	['karta dʒeo'grafika]
area (rural ~)	**località** (f)	[lokali'ta]
place, site	**luogo** (m)	[lu'ogo]
exotica (n)	**ogetti** (m pl) **esotici**	[o'dʒetti e'zotitʃi]
exotic (adj)	**esotico**	[e'zotiko]
amazing (adj)	**sorprendente**	[sorpren'dente]
group	**gruppo** (m)	['gruppo]
excursion, sightseeing tour	**escursione** (f)	[eskur'sjone]
guide (person)	**guida** (f)	['gwida]

156. Hotel

hotel	**albergo, hotel** (m)	[al'bergo], [o'tel]
motel	**motel** (m)	[mo'tel]
three-star (~ hotel)	**tre stelle**	[tre 'stelle]
five-star	**cinque stelle**	['ʧinkwe 'stelle]
to stay (in a hotel, etc.)	**alloggiare** (vi)	[allo'ʤare]
room	**camera** (f)	['kamera]
single room	**camera** (f) **singola**	['kamera 'singola]
double room	**camera** (f) **doppia**	['kamera 'doppia]
to book a room	**prenotare una camera**	[preno'tare 'una 'kamera]
half board	**mezza pensione** (f)	['meddza pen'sjone]
full board	**pensione** (f) **completa**	[pen'sjone kom'pleta]
with bath	**con bagno**	[kon 'baɲo]
with shower	**con doccia**	[kon 'doʧa]
satellite television	**televisione** (f) **satellitare**	[televi'zjone satelli'tare]
air-conditioner	**condizionatore** (m)	[konditsiona'tore]
towel	**asciugamano** (m)	[aʃuga'mano]
key	**chiave** (f)	['kjave]
administrator	**amministratore** (m)	[amministra'tore]
chambermaid	**cameriera** (f)	[kame'rjera]
porter, bellboy	**portabagagli** (m)	[porta·ba'gaʎʎi]
doorman	**portiere** (m)	[por'tjere]
restaurant	**ristorante** (m)	[risto'rante]
pub, bar	**bar** (m)	[bar]
breakfast	**colazione** (f)	[kola'tsjone]
dinner	**cena** (f)	['ʧena]
buffet	**buffet** (m)	[buf'fe]
lobby	**hall** (f)	[oll]
elevator	**ascensore** (m)	[aʃen'sore]
DO NOT DISTURB	**NON DISTURBARE**	[non distur'bare]
NO SMOKING	**VIETATO FUMARE!**	[vje'tato fu'mare]

157. Books. Reading

book	**libro** (m)	['libro]
author	**autore** (m)	[au'tore]
writer	**scrittore** (m)	[skrit'tore]
to write (~ a book)	**scrivere** (vi, vt)	['skrivere]
reader	**lettore** (m)	[let'tore]
to read (vi, vt)	**leggere** (vi, vt)	['leʤere]

reading (activity)	**lettura** (f)	[let'tura]
silently (to oneself)	**in silenzio**	[in si'lentsio]
aloud (adv)	**ad alta voce**	[ad 'alta 'votʃe]
to publish (vt)	**pubblicare** (vt)	[pubbli'kare]
publishing (process)	**pubblicazione** (f)	[publika'tsjone]
publisher	**editore** (m)	[edi'tore]
publishing house	**casa** (f) **editrice**	['kaza edi'tritʃe]
to come out (be released)	**uscire** (vi)	[u'ʃire]
release (of a book)	**uscita** (f)	[u'ʃita]
print run	**tiratura** (f)	[tira'tura]
bookstore	**libreria** (f)	[libre'ria]
library	**biblioteca** (f)	[biblio'teka]
story (novella)	**romanzo** (m) **breve**	[ro'mandzo 'breve]
short story	**racconto** (m)	[rak'konto]
novel	**romanzo** (m)	[ro'mandzo]
detective novel	**giallo** (m)	['dʒallo]
memoirs	**memorie** (f pl)	[me'morie]
legend	**leggenda** (f)	[le'dʒenda]
myth	**mito** (m)	['mito]
poetry, poems	**poesia** (f), **versi** (m pl)	[poe'zia], ['versi]
autobiography	**autobiografia** (f)	[auto·biogra'fia]
selected works	**opere** (f pl) **scelte**	['opere 'ʃelte]
science fiction	**fantascienza** (f)	[fanta'ʃentsa]
title	**titolo** (m)	['titolo]
introduction	**introduzione** (f)	[introdu'tsjone]
title page	**frontespizio** (m)	[fronte'spitsio]
chapter	**capitolo** (m)	[ka'pitolo]
extract	**frammento** (m)	[fram'mento]
episode	**episodio** (m)	[epi'zodio]
plot (storyline)	**soggetto** (m)	[so'dʒetto]
contents	**contenuto** (m)	[konte'nuto]
table of contents	**sommario** (m)	[som'mario]
main character	**protagonista** (m)	[protago'nista]
volume	**volume** (m)	[vo'lume]
cover	**copertina** (f)	[koper'tina]
binding	**rilegatura** (f)	[rilega'tura]
bookmark	**segnalibro** (m)	[seɲa'libro]
page	**pagina** (f)	['padʒina]
to page through	**sfogliare** (vt)	[sfoʎ'ʎare]
margins	**margini** (m pl)	['mardʒini]
annotation (marginal note, etc.)	**annotazione** (f)	[annota'tsjone]

footnote	**nota** (f)	['nota]
text	**testo** (m)	['testo]
type, font	**carattere** (m)	[ka'rattere]
misprint, typo	**refuso** (m)	[re'fuzo]
translation	**traduzione** (f)	[tradu'tsjone]
to translate (vt)	**tradurre** (vt)	[tra'durre]
original (n)	**originale** (m)	[oridʒi'nale]
famous (adj)	**famoso**	[fa'mozo]
unknown (not famous)	**sconosciuto**	[skono'ʃuto]
interesting (adj)	**interessante**	[interes'sante]
bestseller	**best seller** (m)	[best 'seller]
dictionary	**dizionario** (m)	[ditsjo'nario]
textbook	**manuale** (m)	[manu'ale]
encyclopedia	**enciclopedia** (f)	[entʃiklope'dia]

158. Hunting. Fishing

hunting	**caccia** (f)	['katʃa]
to hunt (vi, vt)	**cacciare** (vt)	[ka'tʃare]
hunter	**cacciatore** (m)	[katʃa'tore]
to shoot (vi)	**sparare** (vi)	[spa'rare]
rifle	**fucile** (m)	[fu'tʃile]
bullet (shell)	**cartuccia** (f)	[kar'tutʃa]
shot (lead balls)	**pallini** (m pl)	[pal'lini]
steel trap	**tagliola** (f)	[taʎ'ʎoʎa]
snare (for birds, etc.)	**trappola** (f)	['trappola]
to fall into the steel trap	**cadere in trappola**	[ka'dere in 'trappola]
to lay a steel trap	**tendere una trappola**	['tendere 'una 'trappola]
poacher	**bracconiere** (m)	[brakko'njere]
game (in hunting)	**cacciagione** (m)	[katʃa'dʒone]
hound dog	**cane** (m) **da caccia**	['kane da 'katʃa]
safari	**safari** (m)	[sa'fari]
mounted animal	**animale** (m) **impagliato**	[ani'male impaʎ'ʎato]
fisherman, angler	**pescatore** (m)	[peska'tore]
fishing (angling)	**pesca** (f)	['peska]
to fish (vi)	**pescare** (vi)	[pe'skare]
fishing rod	**canna** (f) **da pesca**	['kanna da 'peska]
fishing line	**lenza** (f)	['lentsa]
hook	**amo** (m)	['amo]
float, bobber	**galleggiante** (m)	[galle'dʒante]
bait	**esca** (f)	['eska]
to cast a line	**lanciare la canna**	[lan'tʃare la 'kanna]

to bite (ab. fish)	**abboccare** (vi)	[abbok'kare]
catch (of fish)	**pescato** (m)	[pe'skato]
ice-hole	**buco** (m) **nel ghiaccio**	['buko nel 'gjatʃo]
fishing net	**rete** (f)	['rete]
boat	**barca** (f)	['barka]
to net (to fish with a net)	**prendere con la rete**	['prendere kon la 'rete]
to cast[throw] the net	**gettare la rete**	[dʒet'tare la 'rete]
to haul the net in	**tirare le reti**	[ti'rare le 'reti]
to fall into the net	**cadere nella rete**	[ka'dere 'nella 'rete]
whaler (person)	**baleniere** (m)	[bale'njere]
whaleboat	**baleniera** (f)	[bale'njera]
harpoon	**rampone** (m)	[ram'pone]

159. Games. Billiards

billiards	**biliardo** (m)	[bi'ljardo]
billiard room, hall	**sala** (f) **da biliardo**	['sala da bi'ljardo]
ball (snooker, etc.)	**bilia** (f)	['bilia]
to pocket a ball	**imbucare** (vt)	[imbu'kare]
cue	**stecca** (f) **da biliardo**	['stekka da bi'ljardo]
pocket	**buca** (f)	['buka]

160. Games. Playing cards

diamonds	**quadri** (m pl)	['kwadri]
spades	**picche** (f pl)	['pikke]
hearts	**cuori** (m pl)	[ku'ori]
clubs	**fiori** (m pl)	['fjori]
ace	**asso** (m)	['asso]
king	**re** (m)	[re]
queen	**donna** (f)	['donna]
jack, knave	**fante** (m)	['fante]
playing card	**carta** (f) **da gioco**	['karta da 'dʒoko]
cards	**carte** (f pl)	['karte]
trump	**briscola** (f)	['briskola]
deck of cards	**mazzo** (m) **di carte**	['mattso di 'karte]
point	**punto** (m)	['punto]
to deal (vi, vt)	**dare le carte**	['dare le 'karte]
to shuffle (cards)	**mescolare** (vt)	[mesko'lare]
lead, turn (n)	**turno** (m)	['turno]
cardsharp	**baro** (m)	['baro]

161. Casino. Roulette

casino	**casinò** (m)	[kazi'no]
roulette (game)	**roulette** (f)	[ru'lett]
bet	**puntata** (f)	[pun'tata]
to place bets	**puntare su ...**	[pun'tare su]
red	**rosso**	['rosso]
black	**nero** (m)	['nero]
to bet on red	**puntare sul rosso**	[pun'tare sul 'rosso]
to bet on black	**puntare sul nero**	[pun'tare sul 'nero]
croupier (dealer)	**croupier** (m)	[kru'pje]
to spin the wheel	**far girare la ruota**	[far ʤi'rare la ru'ota]
rules (of game)	**regole** (f pl) **del gioco**	['regole del 'ʤoko]
chip	**fiche** (f)	[fiʃ]
to win (vi, vt)	**vincere** (vi, vt)	['vinʧere]
win (winnings)	**vincita** (f)	['vinʧita]
to lose (~ 100 dollars)	**perdere** (vt)	['perdere]
loss (losses)	**perdita** (f)	['perdita]
player	**giocatore** (m)	[ʤoka'tore]
blackjack (card game)	**black jack** (m)	[blek 'ʤek]
craps (dice game)	**gioco** (m) **dei dadi**	['ʤoko dei 'dadi]
dice (a pair of ~)	**dadi** (m pl)	['dadi]
slot machine	**slot machine** (f)	[zlot ma'ʃin]

162. Rest. Games. Miscellaneous

to stroll (vi, vt)	**passeggiare** (vi)	[passe'ʤare]
stroll (leisurely walk)	**passeggiata** (f)	[passe'ʤata]
car ride	**gita** (f)	['ʤita]
adventure	**avventura** (f)	[avven'tura]
picnic	**picnic** (m)	['piknik]
game (chess, etc.)	**gioco** (m)	['ʤoko]
player	**giocatore** (m)	[ʤoka'tore]
game (one ~ of chess)	**partita** (f)	[par'tita]
collector (e.g., philatelist)	**collezionista** (m)	[kolletsjo'nista]
to collect (stamps, etc.)	**collezionare** (vt)	[kolletsio'nare]
collection	**collezione** (f)	[kolle'tsjone]
crossword puzzle	**cruciverba** (m)	[kruʧi'verba]
racetrack (horse racing venue)	**ippodromo** (m)	[ip'podromo]
disco (discotheque)	**discoteca** (f)	[disko'teka]

sauna	**sauna** (f)	['sauna]
lottery	**lotteria** (f)	[lotte'ria]
camping trip	**campeggio** (m)	[kam'pedʒo]
camp	**campo** (m)	['kampo]
tent (for camping)	**tenda** (f) **da campeggio**	['tenda da kam'pedʒo]
compass	**bussola** (f)	['bussola]
camper	**campeggiatore** (m)	[kampedʒa'tore]
to watch (movie, etc.)	**guardare** (vt)	[gwar'dare]
viewer	**telespettatore** (m)	[telespetta'tore]
TV show (TV program)	**trasmissione** (f)	[trazmis'sjone]

163. Photography

camera (photo)	**macchina** (f) **fotografica**	['makkina foto'grafika]
photo, picture	**fotografia** (f)	[fotogra'fia]
photographer	**fotografo** (m)	[fo'tografo]
photo studio	**studio** (m) **fotografico**	['studio foto'grafiko]
photo album	**album** (m) **di fotografie**	['album di fotogra'fie]
camera lens	**obiettivo** (m)	[objet'tivo]
telephoto lens	**teleobiettivo** (m)	[teleobjet'tivo]
filter	**filtro** (m)	['filtro]
lens	**lente** (f)	['lente]
optics (high-quality ~)	**ottica** (f)	['ottika]
diaphragm (aperture)	**diaframma** (m)	[dia'framma]
exposure time (shutter speed)	**tempo** (m) **di esposizione**	['tempo di espozi'tsjone]
viewfinder	**mirino** (m)	[mi'rino]
digital camera	**fotocamera** (f) **digitale**	[foto'kamera didʒi'tale]
tripod	**cavalletto** (m)	[kaval'letto]
flash	**flash** (m)	[fleʃ]
to photograph (vt)	**fotografare** (vt)	[fotogra'fare]
to take pictures	**fare foto**	['fare 'foto]
to have one's picture taken	**fotografarsi**	[fotogra'farsi]
focus	**fuoco** (m)	[fu'oko]
to focus	**mettere a fuoco**	['mettere a fu'oko]
sharp, in focus (adj)	**nitido**	['nitido]
sharpness	**nitidezza** (f)	[niti'dettsa]
contrast	**contrasto** (m)	[kon'trasto]
contrast (as adj)	**contrastato**	[kontra'stato]
picture (photo)	**foto** (f)	['foto]
negative (n)	**negativa** (f)	[nega'tiva]

film (a roll of ~)	**pellicola** (f) **fotografica**	[pel'likola foto'grafika]
frame (still)	**fotogramma** (m)	[foto'gramma]
to print (photos)	**stampare** (vt)	[stam'pare]

164. Beach. Swimming

beach	**spiaggia** (f)	['spjadʒa]
sand	**sabbia** (f)	['sabbia]
deserted (beach)	**deserto**	[de'zerto]
suntan	**abbronzatura** (f)	[abbrondza'tura]
to get a tan	**abbronzarsi** (vr)	[abbron'dzarsi]
tan (adj)	**abbronzato**	[abbron'dzato]
sunscreen	**crema** (f) **solare**	['krema so'lare]
bikini	**bikini** (m)	[bi'kini]
bathing suit	**costume** (m) **da bagno**	[ko'stume da 'baɲo]
swim trunks	**slip** (m) **da bagno**	[zlip da 'baɲo]
swimming pool	**piscina** (f)	[pi'ʃina]
to swim (vi)	**nuotare** (vi)	[nuo'tare]
shower	**doccia** (f)	['dotʃa]
to change (one's clothes)	**cambiarsi** (vr)	[kam'bjarsi]
towel	**asciugamano** (m)	[aʃuga'mano]
boat	**barca** (f)	['barka]
motorboat	**motoscafo** (m)	[moto'skafo]
water ski	**sci** (m) **nautico**	[ʃi 'nautiko]
paddle boat	**pedalò** (m)	[peda'lo]
surfing	**surf** (m)	[serf]
surfer	**surfista** (m)	[sur'fista]
scuba set	**autorespiratore** (m)	[autorespira'tore]
flippers (swim fins)	**pinne** (f pl)	['pinne]
mask (diving ~)	**maschera** (f)	['maskera]
diver	**subacqueo** (m)	[su'bakveo]
to dive (vi)	**tuffarsi** (vr)	[tuf'farsi]
underwater (adv)	**sott'acqua**	[so'takva]
beach umbrella	**ombrellone** (m)	[ombrel'lone]
sunbed (lounger)	**sdraio** (f)	['zdrajo]
sunglasses	**occhiali** (m pl) **da sole**	[ok'kjali da 'sole]
air mattress	**materasso** (m) **ad aria**	[mate'rasso ad 'aria]
to play (amuse oneself)	**giocare** (vi)	[dʒo'kare]
to go for a swim	**fare il bagno**	['fare il 'baɲo]
beach ball	**pallone** (m)	[pal'lone]
to inflate (vt)	**gonfiare** (vt)	[gon'fjare]

inflatable, air (adj)	**gonfiabile**	[gon'fjabile]
wave	**onda** (f)	['onda]
buoy (line of ~s)	**boa** (f)	['boa]
to drown (ab. person)	**annegare** (vi)	[anne'gare]
to save, to rescue	**salvare** (vt)	[sal'vare]
life vest	**giubbotto** (m) **di salvataggio**	[dʒub'botto di salva'tadʒo]
to observe, to watch	**osservare** (vt)	[osser'vare]
lifeguard	**bagnino** (m)	[ba'ɲɪno]

TECHNICAL EQUIPMENT. TRANSPORTATION

Technical equipment

165. Computer

computer	**computer** (m)	[kom'pjuter]
notebook, laptop	**computer** (m) **portatile**	[kom'pjuter por'tatile]
to turn on	**accendere** (vt)	[a'tʃendere]
to turn off	**spegnere** (vt)	['speɲere]
keyboard	**tastiera** (f)	[tas'tjera]
key	**tasto** (m)	['tasto]
mouse	**mouse** (m)	['maus]
mouse pad	**tappetino** (m) **del mouse**	[tappe'tino del 'maus]
button	**tasto** (m)	['tasto]
cursor	**cursore** (m)	[kur'sore]
monitor	**monitor** (m)	['monitor]
screen	**schermo** (m)	['skermo]
hard disk	**disco** (m) **rigido**	['disko 'ridʒido]
hard disk capacity	**spazio** (m) **sul disco rigido**	['spatsio sul 'disko 'ridʒido]
memory	**memoria** (f)	[me'moria]
random access memory	**memoria** (f) **operativa**	[me'moria opera'tiva]
file	**file** (m)	[fajl]
folder	**cartella** (f)	[kar'tella]
to open (vt)	**aprire** (vt)	[a'prire]
to close (vt)	**chiudere** (vt)	['kjudere]
to save (vt)	**salvare** (vt)	[sal'vare]
to delete (vt)	**eliminare** (vt)	[elimi'nare]
to copy (vt)	**copiare** (vt)	[ko'pjare]
to sort (vt)	**ordinare** (vt)	[ordi'nare]
to transfer (copy)	**trasferire** (vt)	[trasfe'rire]
program	**programma** (m)	[pro'gramma]
software	**software** (m)	['softwea]
programmer	**programmatore** (m)	[programma'tore]
to program (vt)	**programmare** (vt)	[program'mare]
hacker	**hacker** (m)	['aker]

password	**password** (f)	['password]
virus	**virus** (m)	['virus]
to find, to detect	**trovare** (vt)	[tro'vare]
byte	**byte** (m)	[bajt]
megabyte	**megabyte** (m)	['megabajt]
data	**dati** (m pl)	['dati]
database	**database** (m)	['databejz]
cable (USB, etc.)	**cavo** (m)	['kavo]
to disconnect (vt)	**sconnettere** (vt)	[skon'nettere]
to connect (sth to sth)	**collegare** (vt)	[kolle'gare]

166. Internet. E-mail

Internet	**internet** (f)	['internet]
browser	**navigatore** (m)	[naviga'tore]
search engine	**motore** (m) **di ricerca**	[mo'tore di ri'tʃerka]
provider	**provider** (m)	[pro'vajder]
webmaster	**webmaster** (m)	web'master]
website	**sito web** (m)	['sito web]
webpage	**pagina web** (f)	['padʒina web]
address (e-mail ~)	**indirizzo** (m)	[indi'rittso]
address book	**rubrica** (f) **indirizzi**	[ru'brika indi'rittsi]
mailbox	**casella** (f) **di posta**	[ka'zella di 'posta]
mail	**posta** (f)	['posta]
full (adj)	**battaglia** (f)	[bat'taʎʎa]
message	**messaggio** (m)	[mes'sadʒo]
incoming messages	**messaggi** (m pl) **in arrivo**	[mes'sadʒi in ar'rivo]
outgoing messages	**messaggi** (m pl) **in uscita**	[mes'sadʒo in u'ʃita]
sender	**mittente** (m)	[mit'tente]
to send (vt)	**inviare** (vt)	[in'vjare]
sending (of mail)	**invio** (m)	[in'vio]
receiver	**destinatario** (m)	[destina'tario]
to receive (vt)	**ricevere** (vt)	[ri'tʃevere]
correspondence	**corrispondenza** (f)	[korrispon'dentsa]
to correspond (vi)	**essere in corrispondenza**	['essere in korrispon'dentsa]
file	**file** (m)	[fajl]
to download (vt)	**scaricare** (vt)	[skari'kare]
to create (vt)	**creare** (vt)	[kre'are]
to delete (vt)	**eliminare** (vt)	[elimi'nare]

deleted (adj)	**eliminato**	[elimi'nato]
connection (ADSL, etc.)	**connessione** (f)	[konne'sjone]
speed	**velocità** (f)	[velotʃi'ta]
modem	**modem** (m)	['modem]
access	**accesso** (m)	[a'tʃesso]
port (e.g., input ~)	**porta** (f)	['porta]
connection (make a ~)	**collegamento** (m)	[kollega'mento]
to connect to ... (vi)	**collegarsi a ...**	[kolle'garsi a]
to select (vt)	**scegliere** (vt)	['ʃeʎʎere]
to search (for ...)	**cercare** (vt)	[tʃer'kare]

167. Electricity

electricity	**elettricità** (f)	[elettritʃi'ta]
electric, electrical (adj)	**elettrico**	[e'lettriko]
electric power plant	**centrale** (f) **elettrica**	[tʃen'trale e'lettrika]
energy	**energia** (f)	[ener'dʒia]
electric power	**energia** (f) **elettrica**	[ener'dʒia e'lettrika]
light bulb	**lampadina** (f)	[lampa'dina]
flashlight	**torcia** (f) **elettrica**	['tortʃa e'lettrika]
street light	**lampione** (m)	[lam'pjone]
light	**luce** (f)	['lutʃe]
to turn on	**accendere** (vt)	[a'tʃendere]
to turn off	**spegnere** (vt)	['speɲere]
to turn off the light	**spegnere la luce**	['speɲere la 'lutʃe]
to burn out (vi)	**fulminarsi** (vr)	[fulmi'narsi]
short circuit	**corto circuito** (m)	['korto tʃir'kwito]
broken wire	**rottura** (f)	[rot'tura]
contact (electrical ~)	**contatto** (m)	[kon'tatto]
light switch	**interruttore** (m)	[interrut'tore]
wall socket	**presa** (f) **elettrica**	['preza e'lettrika]
plug	**spina** (f)	['spina]
extension cord	**prolunga** (f)	[pro'lunga]
fuse	**fusibile** (m)	[fu'zibile]
cable, wire	**filo** (m)	['filo]
wiring	**impianto** (m) **elettrico**	[im'pjanto e'lettriko]
ampere	**ampere** (m)	[am'pere]
amperage	**intensità di corrente**	[intensi'ta di kor'rente]
volt	**volt** (m)	[volt]
voltage	**tensione** (f)	[ten'sjone]
electrical device	**apparecchio** (m) **elettrico**	[appa'rekkjo e'lettriko]
indicator	**indicatore** (m)	[indika'tore]

electrician	**elettricista** (m)	[elettri'tʃista]
to solder (vt)	**saldare** (vt)	[sal'dare]
soldering iron	**saldatoio** (m)	[salda'tojo]
electric current	**corrente** (f)	[kor'rente]

168. Tools

tool, instrument	**utensile** (m)	[uten'sile]
tools	**utensili** (m pl)	[uten'sili]
equipment (factory ~)	**impianto** (m)	[im'pjanto]
hammer	**martello** (m)	[mar'tello]
screwdriver	**giravite** (m)	[dʒira'vite]
ax	**ascia** (f)	['aʃa]
saw	**sega** (f)	['sega]
to saw (vt)	**segare** (vt)	[se'gare]
plane (tool)	**pialla** (f)	['pjalla]
to plane (vt)	**piallare** (vt)	[pjal'lare]
soldering iron	**saldatoio** (m)	[salda'tojo]
to solder (vt)	**saldare** (vt)	[sal'dare]
file (tool)	**lima** (f)	['lima]
carpenter pincers	**tenaglie** (f pl)	[te'naʎʎe]
lineman's pliers	**pinza** (f) **a punte piatte**	['pintsa a 'punte 'pjatte]
chisel	**scalpello** (m)	[skal'pello]
drill bit	**punta** (f) **da trapano**	['punta da 'trapano]
electric drill	**trapano** (m) **elettrico**	['trapano e'lettriko]
to drill (vi, vt)	**trapanare** (vt)	[trapa'nare]
knife	**coltello** (m)	[kol'tello]
pocket knife	**coltello** (m) **da tasca**	[kol'tello da 'taska]
blade	**lama** (f)	['lama]
sharp (blade, etc.)	**affilato**	[affi'lato]
dull, blunt (adj)	**smussato**	[zmu'sato]
to get blunt (dull)	**smussarsi** (vr)	[zmus'sarsi]
to sharpen (vt)	**affilare** (vt)	[affi'lare]
bolt	**bullone** (m)	[bul'lone]
nut	**dado** (m)	['dado]
thread (of a screw)	**filettatura** (f)	[filetta'tura]
wood screw	**vite** (f)	['vite]
nail	**chiodo** (m)	[ki'odo]
nailhead	**testa** (f) **di chiodo**	['testa di ki'odo]
ruler (for measuring)	**regolo** (m)	['regolo]
tape measure	**nastro** (m) **metrico**	['nastro 'metriko]

spirit level	**livella** (f)	[li'vella]
magnifying glass	**lente** (f) **d'ingradimento**	['lente dingrandi'mento]
measuring instrument	**strumento** (m) **di misurazione**	[stru'mento di mizura'tsjone]
to measure (vt)	**misurare** (vt)	[mizu'rare]
scale (of thermometer, etc.)	**scala** (f) **graduata**	['skala gradu'ata]
readings	**lettura, indicazione** (f)	[let'tura], [indika'tsjone]
compressor	**compressore** (m)	[kompres'sore]
microscope	**microscopio** (m)	[mikro'skopio]
pump (e.g., water ~)	**pompa** (f)	['pompa]
robot	**robot** (m)	[ro'bo]
laser	**laser** (m)	['lazer]
wrench	**chiave** (f)	['kjave]
adhesive tape	**nastro** (m) **adesivo**	['nastro ade'zivo]
glue	**colla** (f)	['kolla]
sandpaper	**carta** (f) **smerigliata**	['karta zmeriʎ'ʎata]
spring	**molla** (f)	['molla]
magnet	**magnete** (m)	[ma'ɲete]
gloves	**guanti** (m pl)	['gwanti]
rope	**corda** (f)	['korda]
cord	**cordone** (m)	[kor'done]
wire (e.g., telephone ~)	**filo** (m)	['filo]
cable	**cavo** (m)	['kavo]
sledgehammer	**mazza** (f)	['mattsa]
prybar	**palanchino** (m)	[palaŋ'kino]
ladder	**scala** (f) **a pioli**	['skala a pi'oli]
stepladder	**scala** (m) **a libretto**	['skala a li'bretto]
to screw (tighten)	**avvitare** (vt)	[avvi'tare]
to unscrew (lid, filter, etc.)	**svitare** (vt)	[zvi'tare]
to tighten (e.g., with a clamp)	**stringere** (vt)	['strindʒere]
to glue, to stick	**incollare** (vt)	[inkol'lare]
to cut (vt)	**tagliare** (vt)	[taʎ'ʎare]
malfunction (fault)	**guasto** (m)	['gwasto]
repair (mending)	**riparazione** (f)	[ripara'tsjone]
to repair, to fix (vt)	**riparare** (vt)	[ripa'rare]
to adjust (machine, etc.)	**regolare** (vt)	[rego'lare]
to check (to examine)	**verificare** (vt)	[verifi'kare]
checking	**controllo** (m)	[kon'trollo]
readings	**lettura, indicazione** (f)	[let'tura], [indika'tsjone]
reliable, solid (machine)	**sicuro**	[si'kuro]

complex (adj)	**complesso**	[kom'plesso]
to rust (get rusted)	**arrugginire** (vi)	[arrudʒi'nire]
rusty, rusted (adj)	**arrugginito**	[arrudʒi'nito]
rust	**ruggine** (f)	['rudʒine]

Transportation

169. Airplane

airplane	**aereo** (m)	[a'ereo]
air ticket	**biglietto** (m) **aereo**	[biʎ'ʎetto a'ereo]
airline	**compagnia** (f) **aerea**	[kompa'ɲia a'erea]
airport	**aeroporto** (m)	[aero'porto]
supersonic (adj)	**supersonico**	[super'soniko]
captain	**comandante** (m)	[koman'dante]
crew	**equipaggio** (m)	[ekwi'padʒo]
pilot	**pilota** (m)	[pi'lota]
flight attendant (fem.)	**hostess** (f)	['ostess]
navigator	**navigatore** (m)	[naviga'tore]
wings	**ali** (f pl)	['ali]
tail	**coda** (f)	['koda]
cockpit	**cabina** (f)	[ka'bina]
engine	**motore** (m)	[mo'tore]
undercarriage (landing gear)	**carrello** (m) **d'atterraggio**	[kar'rello datter'radʒo]
turbine	**turbina** (f)	[tur'bina]
propeller	**elica** (f)	['elika]
black box	**scatola** (f) **nera**	['skatola 'nera]
yoke (control column)	**barra** (f) **di comando**	['barra di ko'mando]
fuel	**combustibile** (m)	[kombu'stibile]
safety card	**safety card** (f)	['sejfti kard]
oxygen mask	**maschera** (f) **ad ossigeno**	['maskera ad os'sidʒeno]
uniform	**uniforme** (f)	[uni'forme]
life vest	**giubbotto** (m) **di salvataggio**	[dʒub'botto di salva'tadʒo]
parachute	**paracadute** (m)	[paraka'dute]
takeoff	**decollo** (m)	[de'kollo]
to take off (vi)	**decollare** (vi)	[dekol'lare]
runway	**pista** (f) **di decollo**	['pista di de'kollo]
visibility	**visibilità** (f)	[vizibili'ta]
flight (act of flying)	**volo** (m)	['volo]
altitude	**altitudine** (f)	[alti'tudine]
air pocket	**vuoto** (m) **d'aria**	[vu'oto 'daria]
seat	**posto** (m)	['posto]
headphones	**cuffia** (f)	['kuffia]

folding tray (tray table)	**tavolinetto** (m) **pieghevole**	[tavoli'netto pje'gevole]
airplane window	**oblò** (m), **finestrino** (m)	[ob'lo], [fine'strino]
aisle	**corridoio** (m)	[korri'dojo]

170. Train

train	**treno** (m)	['treno]
commuter train	**elettrotreno** (m)	[elettro'treno]
express train	**treno** (m) **rapido**	['treno 'rapido]
diesel locomotive	**locomotiva** (f) **diesel**	[lokomo'tiva 'dizel]
steam locomotive	**locomotiva** (f) **a vapore**	[lokomo'tiva a va'pore]
passenger car	**carrozza** (f)	[kar'rottsa]
dining car	**vagone** (m) **ristorante**	[va'gone risto'rante]
rails	**rotaie** (f pl)	[ro'taje]
railroad	**ferrovia** (f)	[ferro'via]
railway tie	**traversa** (f)	[tra'versa]
platform (railway ~)	**banchina** (f)	[baŋ'kina]
track (~ 1, 2, etc.)	**binario** (m)	[bi'nario]
semaphore	**semaforo** (m)	[se'maforo]
station	**stazione** (f)	[sta'tsjone]
engineer (train driver)	**macchinista** (m)	[makki'nista]
porter (of luggage)	**portabagagli** (m)	[porta·ba'gaʎʎi]
car attendant	**cuccettista** (m, f)	[kuʧet'tista]
passenger	**passeggero** (m)	[passe'ʤero]
conductor (ticket inspector)	**controllore** (m)	[kontrol'lore]
corridor (in train)	**corridoio** (m)	[korri'dojo]
emergency brake	**freno** (m) **di emergenza**	['freno di emer'ʤentsa]
compartment	**scompartimento** (m)	[skomparti'mento]
berth	**cuccetta** (f)	[ku'ʧetta]
upper berth	**cuccetta** (f) **superiore**	[ku'ʧetta supe'rjore]
lower berth	**cuccetta** (f) **inferiore**	[ku'ʧetta infe'rjore]
bed linen, bedding	**biancheria** (f) **da letto**	[bjanke'ria da 'letto]
ticket	**biglietto** (m)	[biʎ'ʎetto]
schedule	**orario** (m)	[o'rario]
information display	**tabellone** (m) **orari**	[tabel'lone o'rari]
to leave, to depart	**partire** (vi)	[par'tire]
departure (of train)	**partenza** (f)	[par'tentsa]
to arrive (ab. train)	**arrivare** (vi)	[arri'vare]
arrival	**arrivo** (m)	[ar'rivo]
to arrive by train	**arrivare con il treno**	[arri'vare kon il 'treno]
to get on the train	**salire sul treno**	[sa'lire sul 'treno]

to get off the train	**scendere dal treno**	['ʃendere dal 'treno]
train wreck	**deragliamento** (m)	[deraʎʎa'mento]
to derail (vi)	**deragliare** (vi)	[deraʎ'ʎare]
steam locomotive	**locomotiva** (f) **a vapore**	[lokomo'tiva a va'pore]
stoker, fireman	**fuochista** (m)	[fo'kista]
firebox	**forno** (m)	['forno]
coal	**carbone** (m)	[kar'bone]

171. Ship

ship	**nave** (f)	['nave]
vessel	**imbarcazione** (f)	[imbarka'tsjone]
steamship	**piroscafo** (m)	[pi'roskafo]
riverboat	**barca** (f) **fluviale**	['barka flu'vjale]
cruise ship	**transatlantico** (m)	[transat'lantiko]
cruiser	**incrociatore** (m)	[inkrotʃa'tore]
yacht	**yacht** (m)	[jot]
tugboat	**rimorchiatore** (m)	[rimorkja'tore]
barge	**chiatta** (f)	['kjatta]
ferry	**traghetto** (m)	[tra'getto]
sailing ship	**veliero** (m)	[ve'ljero]
brigantine	**brigantino** (m)	[brigan'tino]
ice breaker	**rompighiaccio** (m)	[rompi'gjatʃo]
submarine	**sottomarino** (m)	[sottoma'rino]
boat (flat-bottomed ~)	**barca** (f)	['barka]
dinghy	**scialuppa** (f)	[ʃa'luppa]
lifeboat	**scialuppa** (f) **di salvataggio**	[ʃa'luppa di salva'tadʒo]
motorboat	**motoscafo** (m)	[moto'skafo]
captain	**capitano** (m)	[kapi'tano]
seaman	**marittimo** (m)	[ma'rittimo]
sailor	**marinaio** (m)	[mari'najo]
crew	**equipaggio** (m)	[ekwi'padʒo]
boatswain	**nostromo** (m)	[no'stromo]
ship's boy	**mozzo** (m) **di nave**	['mottso di 'nave]
cook	**cuoco** (m)	[ku'oko]
ship's doctor	**medico** (m) **di bordo**	['mediko di 'bordo]
deck	**ponte** (m)	['ponte]
mast	**albero** (m)	['albero]
sail	**vela** (f)	['vela]
hold	**stiva** (f)	['stiva]

bow (prow)	**prua** (f)	['prua]
stern	**poppa** (f)	['poppa]
oar	**remo** (m)	['remo]
screw propeller	**elica** (f)	['elika]
cabin	**cabina** (f)	[ka'bina]
wardroom	**quadrato** (m) **degli ufficiali**	[kwa'drato 'deʎʎi uffi'tʃali]
engine room	**sala** (f) **macchine**	['sala 'makkine]
bridge	**ponte** (m) **di comando**	['ponte di ko'mando]
radio room	**cabina** (f) **radiotelegrafica**	[ka'bina radiotele'grafika]
wave (radio)	**onda** (f)	['onda]
logbook	**giornale** (m) **di bordo**	[dʒor'nale di 'bordo]
spyglass	**cannocchiale** (m)	[kannok'kjale]
bell	**campana** (f)	[kam'pana]
flag	**bandiera** (f)	[ban'djera]
hawser (mooring ~)	**cavo** (m) **d'ormeggio**	['kavo dor'medʒo]
knot (bowline, etc.)	**nodo** (m)	['nodo]
deckrails	**ringhiera** (f)	[rin'gjera]
gangway	**passerella** (f)	[passe'rella]
anchor	**ancora** (f)	['ankora]
to weigh anchor	**levare l'ancora**	[le'vare 'lankora]
to drop anchor	**gettare l'ancora**	[dʒet'tare 'lankora]
anchor chain	**catena** (f) **dell'ancora**	[ka'tena dell 'ankora]
port (harbor)	**porto** (m)	['porto]
quay, wharf	**banchina** (f)	[baŋ'kina]
to berth (moor)	**ormeggiarsi** (vr)	[orme'dʒarsi]
to cast off	**salpare** (vi)	[sal'pare]
trip, voyage	**viaggio** (m)	['vjadʒo]
cruise (sea trip)	**crociera** (f)	[kro'tʃera]
course (route)	**rotta** (f)	['rotta]
route (itinerary)	**itinerario** (m)	[itine'rario]
fairway (safe water channel)	**tratto** (m) **navigabile**	['tratto navi'gabile]
shallows	**secca** (f)	['sekka]
to run aground	**arenarsi** (vr)	[are'narsi]
storm	**tempesta** (f)	[tem'pesta]
signal	**segnale** (m)	[se'ɲale]
to sink (vi)	**affondare** (vi)	[affon'dare]
Man overboard!	**Uomo in mare!**	[u'omo in 'mare]
SOS (distress signal)	**SOS**	['esse o 'esse]
ring buoy	**salvagente** (m) **anulare**	[salva'dʒente anu'lare]

172. Airport

airport	**aeroporto** (m)	[aero'porto]
airplane	**aereo** (m)	[a'ereo]
airline	**compagnia** (f) **aerea**	[kompa'ɲia a'erea]
air traffic controller	**controllore** (m) **di volo**	[kontrol'lore di 'volo]
departure	**partenza** (f)	[par'tentsa]
arrival	**arrivo** (m)	[ar'rivo]
to arrive (by plane)	**arrivare** (vi)	[arri'vare]
departure time	**ora** (f) **di partenza**	['ora di par'tentsa]
arrival time	**ora** (f) **di arrivo**	['ora di ar'rivo]
to be delayed	**essere ritardato**	['essere ritar'dato]
flight delay	**volo** (m) **ritardato**	['volo ritar'dato]
information board	**tabellone** (m) **orari**	[tabel'lone o'rari]
information	**informazione** (f)	[informa'tsjone]
to announce (vt)	**annunciare** (vt)	[annun'ʧare]
flight (e.g., next ~)	**volo** (m)	['volo]
customs	**dogana** (f)	[do'gana]
customs officer	**doganiere** (m)	[doga'njere]
customs declaration	**dichiarazione** (f)	[dikjara'tsjone]
to fill out (vt)	**riempire** (vt)	[riem'pire]
to fill out the declaration	**riempire una dichiarazione**	[riem'pire 'una dikjara'tsjone]
passport control	**controllo** (m) **passaporti**	[kon'trollo passa'porti]
luggage	**bagaglio** (m)	[ba'gaʎʎo]
hand luggage	**bagaglio** (m) **a mano**	[ba'gaʎʎo a 'mano]
luggage cart	**carrello** (m)	[kar'rello]
landing	**atterraggio** (m)	[atter'raʤo]
landing strip	**pista** (f) **di atterraggio**	['pista di atter'raʤo]
to land (vi)	**atterrare** (vi)	[atter'rare]
airstair (passenger stair)	**scaletta** (f) **dell'aereo**	[ska'letta dell a'ereo]
check-in	**check-in** (m)	[ʧek-in]
check-in counter	**banco** (m) **del check-in**	['banko del ʧek-in]
to check-in (vi)	**fare il check-in**	['fare il ʧek-in]
boarding pass	**carta** (f) **d'imbarco**	['karta dim'barko]
departure gate	**porta** (f) **d'imbarco**	['porta dim'barko]
transit	**transito** (m)	['tranzito]
to wait (vt)	**aspettare** (vt)	[aspet'tare]
departure lounge	**sala** (f) **d'attesa**	['sala dat'teza]
to see off	**accompagnare** (vt)	[akkompa'ɲare]
to say goodbye	**congedarsi** (vr)	[konʤe'darsi]

173. Bicycle. Motorcycle

bicycle	**bicicletta** (f)	[bitʃi'kletta]
scooter	**motorino** (m)	[moto'rino]
motorcycle, bike	**motocicletta** (f)	[mototʃi'kletta]
to go by bicycle	**andare in bicicletta**	[an'dare in bitʃi'kletta]
handlebars	**manubrio** (m)	[ma'nubrio]
pedal	**pedale** (m)	[pe'dale]
brakes	**freni** (m pl)	['freni]
bicycle seat (saddle)	**sellino** (m)	[sel'lino]
pump	**pompa** (f)	['pompa]
luggage rack	**portabagagli** (m)	[porta·ba'gaʎʎi]
front lamp	**fanale** (m) **anteriore**	[fa'nale ante'rjore]
helmet	**casco** (m)	['kasko]
wheel	**ruota** (f)	[ru'ota]
fender	**parafango** (m)	[para'fango]
rim	**cerchione** (m)	[tʃer'kjone]
spoke	**raggio** (m)	['radʒo]

Cars

174. Types of cars

automobile, car	**automobile** (f)	[auto'mobile]
sports car	**auto** (f) **sportiva**	['auto spor'tiva]
limousine	**limousine** (f)	[limu'zin]
off-road vehicle	**fuoristrada** (m)	[fuori'strada]
convertible (n)	**cabriolet** (m)	[kabrio'le]
minibus	**pulmino** (m)	[pul'mino]
ambulance	**ambulanza** (f)	[ambu'lantsa]
snowplow	**spazzaneve** (m)	[spattsa'neve]
truck	**camion** (m)	['kamjon]
tanker truck	**autocisterna** (f)	[auto·ʧi'sterna]
van (small truck)	**furgone** (m)	[fur'gone]
road tractor (trailer truck)	**motrice** (f)	[mo'triʧe]
trailer	**rimorchio** (m)	[ri'morkio]
comfortable (adj)	**confortevole**	[konfor'tevole]
used (adj)	**di seconda mano**	[di se'konda 'mano]

175. Cars. Bodywork

hood	**cofano** (m)	['kofano]
fender	**parafango** (m)	[para'fango]
roof	**tetto** (m)	['tetto]
windshield	**parabrezza** (m)	[para'breddza]
rear-view mirror	**retrovisore** (m)	[retrovi'zore]
windshield washer	**lavacristallo** (m)	[lava kris'tallo]
windshield wipers	**tergicristallo** (m)	[terdʒikris'tallo]
side window	**finestrino** (m) **laterale**	[fine'strino late'rale]
window lift (power window)	**alzacristalli** (m)	[altsa·kri'stalli]
antenna	**antenna** (f)	[an'tenna]
sunroof	**tettuccio** (m) **apribile**	[tet'tuʧo a'pribile]
bumper	**paraurti** (m)	[para'urti]
trunk	**bagagliaio** (m)	[bagaʎ'ʎajo]
roof luggage rack	**portapacchi** (m)	[porta'pakki]
door	**portiera** (f)	[por'tjera]

door handle	**maniglia** (f)	[ma'niʎʎa]
door lock	**serratura** (f)	[serra'tura]
license plate	**targa** (f)	['targa]
muffler	**marmitta** (f)	[mar'mitta]
gas tank	**serbatoio** (m) **della benzina**	[serba'tojo della ben'dzina]
tailpipe	**tubo** (m) **di scarico**	['tubo di 'skariko]
gas, accelerator	**acceleratore** (m)	[atʃelera'tore]
pedal	**pedale** (m)	[pe'dale]
gas pedal	**pedale** (m) **dell'acceleratore**	[pe'dale dell atʃelera'tore]
brake	**freno** (m)	['freno]
brake pedal	**pedale** (m) **del freno**	[pe'dale del 'freno]
to brake (use the brake)	**frenare** (vi)	[fre'nare]
parking brake	**freno** (m) **a mano**	['freno a 'mano]
clutch	**frizione** (f)	[fri'tsjone]
clutch pedal	**pedale** (m) **della frizione**	[pe'dale 'della fri'tsjone]
clutch disc	**disco** (m) **della frizione**	['disko 'della fri'tsjone]
shock absorber	**ammortizzatore** (m)	[ammortiddza'tore]
wheel	**ruota** (f)	[ru'ota]
spare tire	**ruota** (f) **di scorta**	[ru'ota di 'skorta]
tire	**pneumatico** (m)	[pneu'matiko]
hubcap	**copriruota** (m)	[kopri·ru'ota]
driving wheels	**ruote** (f pl) **motrici**	[ru'ote mo'tritʃi]
front-wheel drive (as adj)	**a trazione anteriore**	[a tra'tsjone ante'rjore]
rear-wheel drive (as adj)	**a trazione posteriore**	[a tra'tsjone poste'rjore]
all-wheel drive (as adj)	**a trazione integrale**	[a tra'tsjone inte'grale]
gearbox	**scatola** (f) **del cambio**	['skatola del 'kambio]
automatic (adj)	**automatico**	[auto'matiko]
mechanical (adj)	**meccanico**	[mek'kaniko]
gear shift	**leva** (f) **del cambio**	['leva del 'kambio]
headlight	**faro** (m)	['faro]
headlights	**luci** (f pl), **fari** (m pl)	['lutʃi], ['fari]
low beam	**luci** (f pl) **anabbaglianti**	['lutʃi anabbaʎ'ʎanti]
high beam	**luci** (f pl) **abbaglianti**	['lutʃi abbaʎ'ʎanti]
brake light	**luci** (f pl) **di arresto**	['lutʃi di ar'resto]
parking lights	**luci** (f pl) **di posizione**	['lutʃi di pozi'tsjone]
hazard lights	**luci** (f pl) **di emergenza**	['lutʃi di emer'dʒentsa]
fog lights	**fari** (m pl) **antinebbia**	['fari anti'nebbia]
turn signal	**freccia** (f)	['fretʃa]
back-up light	**luci** (f pl) **di retromarcia**	['lutʃi di retro'martʃa]

176. Cars. Passenger compartment

car inside (interior)	**abitacolo** (m)	[abi'takolo]
leather (as adj)	**di pelle**	[di 'pelle]
velour (as adj)	**in velluto**	[in vel'luto]
upholstery	**rivestimento** (m)	[rivesti'mento]
instrument (gage)	**strumento** (m) **di bordo**	[stru'mento di 'bordo]
dashboard	**cruscotto** (m)	[kru'skotto]
speedometer	**tachimetro** (m)	[ta'kimetro]
needle (pointer)	**lancetta** (f)	[lan'tʃetta]
odometer	**contachilometri** (m)	[kontaki'lometri]
indicator (sensor)	**indicatore** (m)	[indika'tore]
level	**livello** (m)	[li'vello]
warning light	**spia** (f) **luminosa**	['spia lumi'noza]
steering wheel	**volante** (m)	[vo'lante]
horn	**clacson** (m)	['klakson]
button	**pulsante** (m)	[pul'sante]
switch	**interruttore** (m)	[interrut'tore]
seat	**sedile** (m)	[se'dile]
backrest	**spalliera** (f)	[spal'ljera]
headrest	**appoggiatesta** (m)	[appodʒa'testa]
seat belt	**cintura** (f) **di sicurezza**	[tʃin'tura di siku'rettsa]
to fasten the belt	**allacciare la cintura**	[ala'tʃare la tʃin'tura]
adjustment (of seats)	**regolazione** (f)	[regola'tsjone]
airbag	**airbag** (m)	['erbeg]
air-conditioner	**condizionatore** (m)	[konditsiona'tore]
radio	**radio** (f)	['radio]
CD player	**lettore** (m) **CD**	[let'tore tʃi'di]
to turn on	**accendere** (vt)	[a'tʃendere]
antenna	**antenna** (f)	[an'tenna]
glove box	**vano** (m) **portaoggetti**	['vano porta·o'dʒetti]
ashtray	**portacenere** (m)	[porta·'tʃenere]

177. Cars. Engine

engine, motor	**motore** (m)	[mo'tore]
diesel (as adj)	**a diesel**	[a 'dizel]
gasoline (as adj)	**a benzina**	[a ben'dzina]
engine volume	**cilindrata** (f)	[tʃilin'drata]
power	**potenza** (f)	[po'tentsa]
horsepower	**cavallo vapore** (m)	[ka'vallo va'pore]
piston	**pistone** (m)	[pi'stone]

cylinder	**cilindro** (m)	[tʃi'lindro]
valve	**valvola** (f)	['valvola]
injector	**iniettore** (m)	[injet'tore]
generator (alternator)	**generatore** (m)	[dʒenera'tore]
carburetor	**carburatore** (m)	[karbura'tore]
motor oil	**olio** (m) **motore**	['olio mo'tore]
radiator	**radiatore** (m)	[radia'tore]
coolant	**liquido** (m) **di raffreddamento**	['likwido di raffredda'mento]
cooling fan	**ventilatore** (m)	[ventila'tore]
battery (accumulator)	**batteria** (m)	[batte'ria]
starter	**motorino** (m) **d'avviamento**	[moto'rino davvja'mento]
ignition	**accensione** (f)	[atʃen'sjone]
spark plug	**candela** (f) **d'accensione**	[kan'dela datʃen'sjone]
terminal (of battery)	**morsetto** (m)	[mor'setto]
positive terminal	**più** (m)	['pju]
negative terminal	**meno** (m)	['meno]
fuse	**fusibile** (m)	[fu'zibile]
air filter	**filtro** (m) **dell'aria**	['filtro dell 'aria]
oil filter	**filtro** (m) **dell'olio**	['filtro dell 'olio]
fuel filter	**filtro** (m) **del carburante**	['filtro del karbu'rante]

178. Cars. Crash. Repair

car crash	**incidente** (m)	[intʃi'dente]
traffic accident	**incidente** (m) **stradale**	[intʃi'dente stra'dale]
to crash (into the wall, etc.)	**sbattere contro ...**	['zbattere 'kontro]
to get smashed up	**avere un incidente**	[a'vere un intʃi'dente]
damage	**danno** (m)	['danno]
intact (unscathed)	**illeso**	[il'lezo]
breakdown	**guasto** (m), **avaria** (f)	['gwasto], [ava'ria]
to break down (vi)	**essere rotto**	['essere 'rotto]
towrope	**cavo** (m) **di rimorchio**	['kavo di ri'morkio]
puncture	**foratura** (f)	[fora'tura]
to be flat	**essere a terra**	['essere a 'terra]
to pump up	**gonfiare** (vt)	[gon'fjare]
pressure	**pressione** (f)	[pres'sjone]
to check (to examine)	**verificare** (vt)	[verifi'kare]
repair	**riparazione** (f)	[ripara'tsjone]
auto repair shop	**officina** (f) **meccanica**	[offi'tʃina me'kanika]

spare part	**pezzo** (m) **di ricambio**	['pettso di ri'kambio]
part	**pezzo** (m)	['pettso]
bolt (with nut)	**bullone** (m)	[bul'lone]
screw (fastener)	**bullone** (m) **a vite**	[bul'lone a 'vite]
nut	**dado** (m)	['dado]
washer	**rondella** (f)	[ron'della]
bearing (e.g., ball ~)	**cuscinetto** (m)	[kuʃi'netto]
tube	**tubo** (m)	['tubo]
gasket (head ~)	**guarnizione** (f)	[gwarni'tsjone]
cable, wire	**filo** (m), **cavo** (m)	['filo], ['kavo]
jack	**cric** (m)	[krik]
wrench	**chiave** (f)	['kjave]
hammer	**martello** (m)	[mar'tello]
pump	**pompa** (f)	['pompa]
screwdriver	**giravite** (m)	[dʒira'vite]
fire extinguisher	**estintore** (m)	[estin'tore]
warning triangle	**triangolo** (m) **di emergenza**	[tri'angolo di emer'dʒentsa]
to stall (vi)	**spegnersi** (vr)	['speɲersi]
stall (n)	**spegnimento** (m) **motore**	[speɲi'mento mo'tore]
to be broken	**essere rotto**	['essere 'rotto]
to overheat (vi)	**surriscaldarsi** (vr)	[surriskal'darsi]
to be clogged up	**intasarsi** (vr)	[inta'zarsi]
to freeze up (pipes, etc.)	**ghiacciarsi** (vr)	[gja'tʃarsi]
to burst (vi, ab. tube)	**spaccarsi** (vr)	[spak'karsi]
pressure	**pressione** (f)	[pres'sjone]
level	**livello** (m)	[li'vello]
slack (~ belt)	**lento**	['lento]
dent	**ammaccatura** (f)	[ammakka'tura]
knocking noise (engine)	**battito** (m)	['battito]
crack	**fessura** (f)	[fes'sura]
scratch	**graffiatura** (f)	[graffja'tura]

179. Cars. Road

road	**strada** (f)	['strada]
highway	**superstrada** (f)	[super'strada]
freeway	**autostrada** (f)	[auto'strada]
direction (way)	**direzione** (f)	[dire'tsjone]
distance	**distanza** (f)	[di'stantsa]
bridge	**ponte** (m)	['ponte]
parking lot	**parcheggio** (m)	[par'kedʒo]

square	**piazza** (f)	['pjattsa]
interchange	**svincolo** (m)	['zvinkolo]
tunnel	**galleria** (f), **tunnel** (m)	[galle'ria], ['tunnel]
gas station	**distributore** (m) **di benzina**	[distribu'tore di ben'dzina]
parking lot	**parcheggio** (m)	[par'kedʒo]
gas pump (fuel dispenser)	**pompa** (f) **di benzina**	['pompa di ben'dzina]
auto repair shop	**officina** (f) **meccanica**	[offi'tʃina me'kanika]
to get gas (to fill up)	**fare benzina**	['fare ben'dzina]
fuel	**carburante** (m)	[karbu'rante]
jerrycan	**tanica** (f)	['tanika]
asphalt	**asfalto** (m)	[as'falto]
road markings	**segnaletica** (f) **stradale**	[seɲa'letika stra'dale]
curb	**cordolo** (m)	['kordolo]
guardrail	**barriera** (f) **di sicurezza**	[bar'rjera di siku'rettsa]
ditch	**fosso** (m)	['fosso]
roadside (shoulder)	**ciglio** (m) **della strada**	['tʃiʎʎo della 'strada]
lamppost	**lampione** (m)	[lam'pjone]
to drive (a car)	**guidare, condurre**	[gwi'dare], [kon'durre]
to turn (e.g., ~ left)	**girare** (vi)	[dʒi'rare]
to make a U-turn	**fare un'inversione a U**	['fare un inver'sjone a u:]
reverse (~ gear)	**retromarcia** (m)	[retro'martʃa]
to honk (vi)	**suonare il clacson**	[suo'nare il 'klakson]
honk (sound)	**colpo** (m) **di clacson**	['kolpo di 'klakson]
to get stuck (in the mud, etc.)	**incastrarsi** (vr)	[inka'strarsi]
to spin the wheels	**impantanarsi** (vr)	[impanta'narsi]
to cut, to turn off (vt)	**spegnere** (vt)	['speɲere]
speed	**velocità** (f)	[velotʃi'ta]
to exceed the speed limit	**superare i limiti di velocità**	[supe'rare i 'limiti di velotʃi'ta]
to give a ticket	**multare** (vt)	[mul'tare]
traffic lights	**semaforo** (m)	[se'maforo]
driver's license	**patente** (f) **di guida**	[pa'tente di 'gwida]
grade crossing	**passaggio** (m) **a livello**	[pas'sadʒo a li'vello]
intersection	**incrocio** (m)	[in'krotʃo]
crosswalk	**passaggio** (m) **pedonale**	[pas'sadʒo pedo'nale]
bend, curve	**curva** (f)	['kurva]
pedestrian zone	**zona** (f) **pedonale**	['dzona pedo'nale]

180. Traffic signs

rules of the road	**codice** (m) **stradale**	['koditʃe stra'dale]
road sign (traffic sign)	**segnale** (m) **stradale**	[se'ɲale stra'dale]

passing (overtaking)	**sorpasso** (m)	[sor'passo]
curve	**curva** (f)	['kurva]
U-turn	**inversione a U**	[inver'sjone a 'u:]
traffic circle	**rotatoria** (f)	[rota'toria]
No entry	**divieto d'accesso**	[di'vjeto da'ʧesso]
No vehicles allowed	**divieto di transito**	[di'vjeto di 'tranzito]
No passing	**divieto di sorpasso**	[di'vjeto di sor'passo]
No parking	**divieto di sosta**	[di'vjeto di 'sosta]
No stopping	**divieto di fermata**	[di'vjeto di fer'mata]
dangerous bend	**curva** (f) **pericolosa**	['kurva periko'loza]
steep descent	**discesa** (f) **ripida**	[di'ʃeza 'ripida]
one-way traffic	**senso** (m) **unico**	['senso 'uniko]
crosswalk	**passaggio** (m) **pedonale**	[pas'saʤo pedo'nale]
slippery road	**strada** (f) **scivolosa**	['strada ʃivo'loza]
YIELD	**dare la precedenza**	['dare la preʧe'dentsa]

PEOPLE. LIFE EVENTS

Life events

181. Holidays. Event

celebration, holiday	**festa** (f)	['festa]
national day	**festa** (f) **nazionale**	['festa natsjo'nale]
public holiday	**festività** (f) **civile**	[festivi'ta ʧi'vile]
to commemorate (vt)	**festeggiare** (vt)	[feste'ʤare]
event (happening)	**avvenimento** (m)	[avveni'mento]
event (organized activity)	**evento** (m)	[e'vento]
banquet (party)	**banchetto** (m)	[baŋ'ketto]
reception (formal party)	**ricevimento** (m)	[riʧevi'mento]
feast	**festino** (m)	[fes'tino]
anniversary	**anniversario** (m)	[anniver'sario]
jubilee	**giubileo** (m)	[ʤubi'leo]
to celebrate (vt)	**festeggiare** (vt)	[feste'ʤare]
New Year	**Capodanno** (m)	[kapo'danno]
Happy New Year!	**Buon Anno!**	[buo'nanno]
Christmas	**Natale** (m)	[na'tale]
Merry Christmas!	**Buon Natale!**	[bu'on na'tale]
Christmas tree	**Albero** (m) **di Natale**	['albero di na'tale]
fireworks (fireworks show)	**fuochi** (m pl) **artificiali**	[fu'oki artifi'ʧali]
wedding	**nozze** (f pl)	['nottse]
groom	**sposo** (m)	['spozo]
bride	**sposa** (f)	['spoza]
to invite (vt)	**invitare** (vt)	[invi'tare]
invitation card	**invito** (m)	[in'vito]
guest	**ospite** (m)	['ospite]
to visit (~ your parents, etc.)	**andare a trovare**	[an'dare a tro'vare]
to meet the guests	**accogliere gli invitati**	[ak'koʎʎere ʎi invi'tati]
gift, present	**regalo** (m)	[re'galo]
to give (sth as present)	**offrire** (vt)	[of'frire]
to receive gifts	**ricevere i regali**	[ri'ʧevere i re'gali]
bouquet (of flowers)	**mazzo** (m) **di fiori**	['mattso di 'fjori]

congratulations	**auguri** (m pl)	[au'guri]
to congratulate (vt)	**augurare** (vt)	[augu'rare]
greeting card	**cartolina** (f)	[karto'lina]
to send a postcard	**mandare una cartolina**	[man'dare 'una karto'lina]
to get a postcard	**ricevere una cartolina**	[ri'ʧevere 'una karto'lina]
toast	**brindisi** (m)	['brindizi]
to offer (a drink, etc.)	**offrire** (vt)	[of'frire]
champagne	**champagne** (m)	[ʃam'paɲ]
to enjoy oneself	**divertirsi** (vr)	[diver'tirsi]
merriment (gaiety)	**allegria** (f)	[alle'gria]
joy (emotion)	**gioia** (f)	['ʤoja]
dance	**danza** (f), **ballo** (m)	['dantsa], ['ballo]
to dance (vi, vt)	**ballare** (vi, vt)	[bal'lare]
waltz	**valzer** (m)	['valtser]
tango	**tango** (m)	['tango]

182. Funerals. Burial

cemetery	**cimitero** (m)	[ʧimi'tero]
grave, tomb	**tomba** (f)	['tomba]
cross	**croce** (f)	['kroʧe]
gravestone	**pietra** (f) **tombale**	['pjetra tom'bale]
fence	**recinto** (m)	[re'ʧinto]
chapel	**cappella** (f)	[kap'pella]
death	**morte** (f)	['morte]
to die (vi)	**morire** (vi)	[mo'rire]
the deceased	**defunto** (m)	[de'funto]
mourning	**lutto** (m)	['lutto]
to bury (vt)	**seppellire** (vt)	[seppel'lire]
funeral home	**sede** (f) **di pompe funebri**	['sede di 'pompe 'funebri]
funeral	**funerale** (m)	[fune'rale]
wreath	**corona** (f) **di fiori**	[ko'rona di 'fjori]
casket, coffin	**bara** (f)	['bara]
hearse	**carro** (m) **funebre**	['karro 'funebre]
shroud	**lenzuolo** (m) **funebre**	[lentsu'olo 'funebre]
funeral procession	**corteo** (m) **funebre**	[kor'teo 'funebre]
funerary urn	**urna** (f) **funeraria**	['urna fune'raria]
crematory	**crematorio** (m)	[krema'torio]
obituary	**necrologio** (m)	[nekro'loʤo]
to cry (weep)	**piangere** (vi)	['pjanʤere]
to sob (vi)	**singhiozzare** (vi)	[singjot'tsare]

183. War. Soldiers

platoon	**plotone** (m)	[plo'tone]
company	**compagnia** (f)	[kompa'ɲia]
regiment	**reggimento** (m)	[redʒi'mento]
army	**esercito** (m)	[e'zertʃito]
division	**divisione** (f)	[divi'zjone]
section, squad	**distaccamento** (m)	[distakka'mento]
host (army)	**armata** (f)	[ar'mata]
soldier	**soldato** (m)	[sol'dato]
officer	**ufficiale** (m)	[uffi'tʃale]
private	**soldato** (m) **semplice**	[sol'dato 'semplitʃe]
sergeant	**sergente** (m)	[ser'dʒente]
lieutenant	**tenente** (m)	[te'nente]
captain	**capitano** (m)	[kapi'tano]
major	**maggiore** (m)	[ma'dʒore]
colonel	**colonnello** (m)	[kolon'nello]
general	**generale** (m)	[dʒene'rale]
sailor	**marinaio** (m)	[mari'najo]
captain	**capitano** (m)	[kapi'tano]
boatswain	**nostromo** (m)	[no'stromo]
artilleryman	**artigliere** (m)	[artiʎ'ʎere]
paratrooper	**paracadutista** (m)	[parakadu'tista]
pilot	**pilota** (m)	[pi'lota]
navigator	**navigatore** (m)	[naviga'tore]
mechanic	**meccanico** (m)	[mek'kaniko]
pioneer (sapper)	**geniere** (m)	[dʒe'njere]
parachutist	**paracadutista** (m)	[parakadu'tista]
reconnaissance scout	**esploratore** (m)	[esplora'tore]
sniper	**cecchino** (m)	[tʃek'kino]
patrol (group)	**pattuglia** (f)	[pat'tuʎʎa]
to patrol (vt)	**pattugliare** (vt)	[pattuʎ'ʎare]
sentry, guard	**sentinella** (f)	[senti'nella]
warrior	**guerriero** (m)	[gwer'rjero]
patriot	**patriota** (m)	[patri'ota]
hero	**eroe** (m)	[e'roe]
heroine	**eroina** (f)	[ero'ina]
traitor	**traditore** (m)	[tradi'tore]
deserter	**disertore** (m)	[dizer'tore]
to desert (vi)	**disertare** (vi)	[dizer'tare]
mercenary	**mercenario** (m)	[mertʃe'nario]
recruit	**recluta** (f)	['rekluta]

volunteer	**volontario** (m)	[volon'tario]
dead (n)	**ucciso** (m)	[u'tʃizo]
wounded (n)	**ferito** (m)	[fe'rito]
prisoner of war	**prigioniero** (m) **di guerra**	[pridʒo'njero di 'gwerra]

184. War. Military actions. Part 1

war	**guerra** (f)	['gwerra]
to be at war	**essere in guerra**	['essere in 'gwerra]
civil war	**guerra** (f) **civile**	['gwerra tʃi'vile]
treacherously (adv)	**perfidamente**	[perfida'mente]
declaration of war	**dichiarazione** (f) **di guerra**	[dikjara'tsjone di 'gwerra]
to declare (~ war)	**dichiarare** (vt)	[dikja'rare]
aggression	**aggressione** (f)	[aggres'sjone]
to attack (invade)	**attaccare** (vt)	[attak'kare]
to invade (vt)	**invadere** (vt)	[in'vadere]
invader	**invasore** (m)	[inva'zore]
conqueror	**conquistatore** (m)	[konkwista'tore]
defense	**difesa** (f)	[di'feza]
to defend (a country, etc.)	**difendere** (vt)	[di'fendere]
to defend (against ...)	**difendersi** (vr)	[di'fendersi]
enemy	**nemico** (m)	[ne'miko]
foe, adversary	**avversario** (m)	[avver'sario]
enemy (as adj)	**ostile**	[o'stile]
strategy	**strategia** (f)	[strate'dʒia]
tactics	**tattica** (f)	['tattika]
order	**ordine** (m)	['ordine]
command (order)	**comando** (m)	[ko'mando]
to order (vt)	**ordinare** (vt)	[ordi'nare]
mission	**missione** (f)	[mis'sjone]
secret (adj)	**segreto**	[se'greto]
battle	**battaglia** (f)	[bat'taʎʎa]
combat	**combattimento** (m)	[kombatti'mento]
attack	**attacco** (m)	[at'takko]
charge (assault)	**assalto** (m)	[as'salto]
to storm (vt)	**assalire** (vt)	[assa'lire]
siege (to be under ~)	**assedio** (m)	[as'sedio]
offensive (n)	**offensiva** (f)	[offen'siva]
to go on the offensive	**passare all'offensiva**	[pas'sare all ofen'siva]
retreat	**ritirata** (f)	[riti'rata]
to retreat (vi)	**ritirarsi** (vr)	[riti'rarsi]

encirclement	**accerchiamento** (m)	[atʃerkja'mento]
to encircle (vt)	**accerchiare** (vt)	[atʃer'kjare]
bombing (by aircraft)	**bombardamento** (m)	[bombarda'mento]
to drop a bomb	**lanciare una bomba**	[lan'tʃare 'una 'bomba]
to bomb (vt)	**bombardare** (vt)	[bomar'dare]
explosion	**esplosione** (f)	[esplo'zjone]
shot	**sparo** (m)	['sparo]
to fire (~ a shot)	**sparare un colpo**	[spa'rare un 'kolpo]
firing (burst of ~)	**sparatoria** (f)	[spara'toria]
to aim (to point a weapon)	**puntare su ...**	[pun'tare su]
to point (a gun)	**puntare** (vt)	[pun'tare]
to hit (the target)	**colpire** (vt)	[kol'pire]
to sink (~ a ship)	**affondare** (vt)	[affon'dare]
hole (in a ship)	**falla** (f)	['falla]
to founder, to sink (vi)	**affondare** (vi)	[affon'dare]
front (war ~)	**fronte** (m)	['fronte]
evacuation	**evacuazione** (f)	[evakua'tsjone]
to evacuate (vt)	**evacuare** (vt)	[evaku'are]
trench	**trincea** (f)	[trin'tʃea]
barbwire	**filo** (m) **spinato**	['filo spi'nato]
barrier (anti tank ~)	**sbarramento** (m)	[zbarra'mento]
watchtower	**torretta** (f) **di osservazione**	[tor'retta di oserva'tsjone]
military hospital	**ospedale** (m) **militare**	[ospe'dale mili'tare]
to wound (vt)	**ferire** (vt)	[fe'rire]
wound	**ferita** (f)	[fe'rita]
wounded (n)	**ferito** (m)	[fe'rito]
to be wounded	**rimanere ferito**	[rima'nere fe'rito]
serious (wound)	**grave**	['grave]

185. War. Military actions. Part 2

captivity	**prigionia** (f)	[pridʒo'nia]
to take captive	**fare prigioniero**	['fare pridʒo'njero]
to be held captive	**essere prigioniero**	['essere pridʒo'njero]
to be taken captive	**essere fatto prigioniero**	['essere 'fatto pridʒo'njero]
concentration camp	**campo** (m) **di concentramento**	['kampo di kontʃentra'mento]
prisoner of war	**prigioniero** (m) **di guerra**	[pridʒo'njero di 'gwerra]
to escape (vi)	**fuggire** (vi)	[fu'dʒire]
to betray (vt)	**tradire** (vt)	[tra'dire]
betrayer	**traditore** (m)	[tradi'tore]

betrayal	**tradimento** (m)	[tradi'mento]
to execute (by firing squad)	**fucilare** (vt)	[futʃi'lare]
execution (by firing squad)	**fucilazione** (f)	[futʃila'tsjone]
equipment (military gear)	**divisa** (f) **militare**	[di'viza mili'tare]
shoulder board	**spallina** (f)	[spal'lina]
gas mask	**maschera** (f) **antigas**	['maskera anti'gas]
field radio	**radiotrasmettitore** (m)	['radio transmetti'tore]
cipher, code	**codice** (m)	['koditʃe]
secrecy	**complotto** (m)	[kom'plotto]
password	**parola** (f) **d'ordine**	[pa'rola 'dordine]
land mine	**mina** (f)	['mina]
to mine (road, etc.)	**minare** (vt)	[mi'nare]
minefield	**campo** (m) **minato**	['kampo mi'nato]
air-raid warning	**allarme** (m) **aereo**	[al'larme a'ereo]
alarm (alert signal)	**allarme** (m)	[al'larme]
signal	**segnale** (m)	[se'ɲale]
signal flare	**razzo** (m) **di segnalazione**	['raddzo di seɲala'tsjone]
headquarters	**quartier** (m) **generale**	[kwar'tje dʒene'rale]
reconnaissance	**esplorazione** (m)	[esplora'tore]
situation	**situazione** (f)	[situa'tsjone]
report	**rapporto** (m)	[rap'porto]
ambush	**agguato** (m)	[ag'gwato]
reinforcement (of army)	**rinforzo** (m)	[rin'fortso]
target	**bersaglio** (m)	[ber'saʎʎo]
proving ground	**terreno** (m) **di caccia**	[ter'reno di 'katʃa]
military exercise	**manovre** (f pl)	[ma'novre]
panic	**panico** (m)	['paniko]
devastation	**devastazione** (f)	[devasta'tsjone]
destruction, ruins	**distruzione** (m)	[distru'tsjone]
to destroy (vt)	**distruggere** (vt)	[di'strudʒere]
to survive (vi, vt)	**sopravvivere** (vi, vt)	[soprav'vivere]
to disarm (vt)	**disarmare** (vt)	[dizar'mare]
to handle (~ a gun)	**maneggiare** (vt)	[mane'dʒare]
Attention!	**Attenti!**	[at'tenti]
At ease!	**Riposo!**	[ri'pozo]
feat, act of courage	**atto** (m) **eroico**	['atto e'roiko]
oath (vow)	**giuramento** (m)	[dʒura'mento]
to swear (an oath)	**giurare** (vi)	[dʒu'rare]
decoration (medal, etc.)	**decorazione** (f)	[dekora'tsjone]
to award (give medal to)	**decorare qn**	[deko'rare]

medal	**medaglia** (f)	[me'daʎʎa]
order (e.g., ~ of Merit)	**ordine** (m)	['ordine]
victory	**vittoria** (f)	[vit'toria]
defeat	**sconfitta** (m)	[skon'fitta]
armistice	**armistizio** (m)	[armi'stitsio]
standard (battle flag)	**bandiera** (f)	[ban'djera]
glory (honor, fame)	**gloria** (f)	['gloria]
parade	**parata** (f)	[pa'rata]
to march (on parade)	**marciare** (vi)	[mar'ʧare]

186. Weapons

weapons	**armi** (f pl)	['armi]
firearms	**arma** (f) **da fuoco**	['arma da fu'oko]
cold weapons (knives, etc.)	**arma** (f) **bianca**	['arma 'bjanka]
chemical weapons	**armi** (f pl) **chimiche**	['armi 'kimike]
nuclear (adj)	**nucleare**	[nukle'are]
nuclear weapons	**armi** (f pl) **nucleari**	['armi nukle'ari]
bomb	**bomba** (f)	['bomba]
atomic bomb	**bomba** (f) **atomica**	['bomba a'tomika]
pistol (gun)	**pistola** (f)	[pi'stola]
rifle	**fucile** (m)	[fu'ʧile]
submachine gun	**mitra** (m)	['mitra]
machine gun	**mitragliatrice** (f)	[mitraʎʎa'triʧe]
muzzle	**bocca** (f)	['bokka]
barrel	**canna** (f)	['kanna]
caliber	**calibro** (m)	['kalibro]
trigger	**grilletto** (m)	[gril'letto]
sight (aiming device)	**mirino** (m)	[mi'rino]
magazine	**caricatore** (m)	[karika'tore]
butt (shoulder stock)	**calcio** (m)	['kalʧo]
hand grenade	**bomba** (f) **a mano**	['bomba a 'mano]
explosive	**esplosivo** (m)	[esplo'zivo]
bullet	**pallottola** (f)	[pal'lottola]
cartridge	**cartuccia** (f)	[kar'tuʧa]
charge	**carica** (f)	['karika]
ammunition	**munizioni** (f pl)	[muni'tsjoni]
bomber (aircraft)	**bombardiere** (m)	[bombar'djere]
fighter	**aereo** (m) **da caccia**	[a'ereo da 'kaʧa]

helicopter	**elicottero** (m)	[eli'kottero]
anti-aircraft gun	**cannone** (m) **antiaereo**	[kan'none anti·a'ereo]
tank	**carro** (m) **armato**	['karro ar'mato]
tank gun	**cannone** (m)	[kan'none]
artillery	**artiglieria** (f)	[artiʎʎe'ria]
gun (cannon, howitzer)	**cannone** (m)	[kan'none]
to lay (a gun)	**mirare a ...**	[mi'rare a]
shell (projectile)	**proiettile** (m)	[pro'jettile]
mortar bomb	**granata** (f) **da mortaio**	[gra'nata da mor'tajo]
mortar	**mortaio** (m)	[mor'tajo]
splinter (shell fragment)	**scheggia** (f)	['skedʒa]
submarine	**sottomarino** (m)	[sottoma'rino]
torpedo	**siluro** (m)	[si'luro]
missile	**missile** (m)	['missile]
to load (gun)	**caricare** (vt)	[kari'kare]
to shoot (vi)	**sparare** (vi)	[spa'rare]
to point at (the cannon)	**puntare su ...**	[pun'tare su]
bayonet	**baionetta** (f)	[bajo'netta]
rapier	**spada** (f)	['spada]
saber (e.g., cavalry ~)	**sciabola** (f)	['ʃabola]
spear (weapon)	**lancia** (f)	['lantʃa]
bow	**arco** (m)	['arko]
arrow	**freccia** (f)	['fretʃa]
musket	**moschetto** (m)	[mos'ketto]
crossbow	**balestra** (f)	[ba'lestra]

187. Ancient people

primitive (prehistoric)	**primitivo**	[primi'tivo]
prehistoric (adj)	**preistorico**	[preis'toriko]
ancient (~ civilization)	**antico**	[an'tiko]
Stone Age	**Età** (f) **della pietra**	[e'ta 'della 'pjetra]
Bronze Age	**Età** (f) **del bronzo**	[e'ta del 'brondzo]
Ice Age	**epoca** (f) **glaciale**	['epoka gla'tʃale]
tribe	**tribù** (f)	[tri'bu]
cannibal	**cannibale** (m)	[kan'nibale]
hunter	**cacciatore** (m)	[katʃa'tore]
to hunt (vi, vt)	**cacciare** (vt)	[ka'tʃare]
mammoth	**mammut** (m)	[mam'mut]
cave	**caverna** (f), **grotta** (f)	[ka'verna], ['grotta]
fire	**fuoco** (m)	[fu'oko]
campfire	**falò** (m)	[fa'lo]

cave painting	**pittura** (f) **rupestre**	[pit'tura ru'pestre]
tool (e.g., stone ax)	**strumento** (m) **di lavoro**	[stru'mento di la'voro]
spear	**lancia** (f)	['lantʃa]
stone ax	**ascia** (f) **di pietra**	['aʃa di 'pjetra]
to be at war	**essere in guerra**	['essere in 'gwerra]
to domesticate (vt)	**addomesticare** (vt)	[addomesti'kare]
idol	**idolo** (m)	['idolo]
to worship (vt)	**idolatrare** (vt)	[idola'trare]
superstition	**superstizione** (f)	[supersti'tsjone]
rite	**rito** (m)	['rito]
evolution	**evoluzione** (f)	[evolu'tsjone]
development	**sviluppo** (m)	[zvi'luppo]
disappearance (extinction)	**estinzione** (f)	[estin'tsjone]
to adapt oneself	**adattarsi** (vr)	[adat'tarsi]
archeology	**archeologia** (f)	[arkeolo'dʒia]
archeologist	**archeologo** (m)	[arke'ologo]
archeological (adj)	**archeologico**	[arkeo'lodʒiko]
excavation site	**sito** (m) **archeologico**	['sito arkeo'lodʒiko]
excavations	**scavi** (m pl)	['skavi]
find (object)	**reperto** (m)	[re'perto]
fragment	**frammento** (m)	[fram'mento]

188. Middle Ages

people (ethnic group)	**popolo** (m)	['popolo]
peoples	**popoli** (m pl)	['popoli]
tribe	**tribù** (f)	[tri'bu]
tribes	**tribù** (f pl)	[tri'bu]
barbarians	**barbari** (m pl)	['barbari]
Gauls	**galli** (m pl)	['galli]
Goths	**goti** (m pl)	['goti]
Slavs	**slavi** (m pl)	['zlavi]
Vikings	**vichinghi** (m pl)	[vi'kingi]
Romans	**romani** (m pl)	[ro'mani]
Roman (adj)	**romano**	[ro'mano]
Byzantines	**bizantini** (m pl)	[bidzan'tini]
Byzantium	**Bisanzio** (m)	[bi'zansio]
Byzantine (adj)	**bizantino**	[bidzan'tino]
emperor	**imperatore** (m)	[impera'tore]
leader, chief (tribal ~)	**capo** (m)	['kapo]
powerful (~ king)	**potente**	[po'tente]
king	**re** (m)	[re]

ruler (sovereign)	**governante** (m)	[gover'nante]
knight	**cavaliere** (m)	[kava'ljere]
feudal lord	**feudatario** (m)	[feuda'tario]
feudal (adj)	**feudale**	[feu'dale]
vassal	**vassallo** (m)	[vas'sallo]
duke	**duca** (m)	['duka]
earl	**conte** (m)	['konte]
baron	**barone** (m)	[ba'rone]
bishop	**vescovo** (m)	['veskovo]
armor	**armatura** (f)	[arma'tura]
shield	**scudo** (m)	['skudo]
sword	**spada** (f)	['spada]
visor	**visiera** (f)	[vi'zjera]
chainmail	**cotta** (f) **di maglia**	['kotta di 'maʎʎa]
Crusade	**crociata** (f)	[kro'ʧata]
crusader	**crociato** (m)	[kro'ʧato]
territory	**territorio** (m)	[terri'torio]
to attack (invade)	**attaccare** (vt)	[attak'kare]
to conquer (vt)	**conquistare** (vt)	[konkwi'stare]
to occupy (invade)	**occupare** (vt)	[okku'pare]
siege (to be under ~)	**assedio** (m)	[as'sedio]
besieged (adj)	**assediato**	[asse'djato]
to besiege (vt)	**assediare** (vt)	[asse'djare]
inquisition	**inquisizione** (f)	[inkwizi'tsjone]
inquisitor	**inquisitore** (m)	[inkwizi'tore]
torture	**tortura** (f)	[tor'tura]
cruel (adj)	**crudele**	[kru'dele]
heretic	**eretico** (m)	[e'retiko]
heresy	**eresia** (f)	[ere'zia]
seafaring	**navigazione** (f)	[naviga'tsjone]
pirate	**pirata** (m)	[pi'rata]
piracy	**pirateria** (f)	[pirate'ria]
boarding (attack)	**arrembaggio** (m)	[arrem'badʒo]
loot, booty	**bottino** (m)	[bot'tino]
treasures	**tesori** (m)	[te'zori]
discovery	**scoperta** (f)	[sko'perta]
to discover (new land, etc.)	**scoprire** (vt)	[sko'prire]
expedition	**spedizione** (f)	[spedi'tsjone]
musketeer	**moschettiere** (m)	[mosket'tjere]
cardinal	**cardinale** (m)	[kardi'nale]
heraldry	**araldica** (f)	[a'raldika]
heraldic (adj)	**araldico**	[a'raldiko]

189. Leader. Chief. Authorities

king	**re** (m)	[re]
queen	**regina** (f)	[re'dʒina]
royal (adj)	**reale**	[re'ale]
kingdom	**regno** (m)	['reɲo]
prince	**principe** (m)	['printʃipe]
princess	**principessa** (f)	[printʃi'pessa]
president	**presidente** (m)	[prezi'dente]
vice-president	**vicepresidente** (m)	[vitʃe·prezi'dente]
senator	**senatore** (m)	[sena'tore]
monarch	**monarca** (m)	[mo'narka]
ruler (sovereign)	**governante** (m)	[gover'nante]
dictator	**dittatore** (m)	[ditta'tore]
tyrant	**tiranno** (m)	[ti'ranno]
magnate	**magnate** (m)	[ma'ɲate]
director	**direttore** (m)	[diret'tore]
chief	**capo** (m)	['kapo]
manager (director)	**dirigente** (m)	[diri'dʒente]
boss	**capo** (m)	['kapo]
owner	**proprietario** (m)	[proprie'tario]
head (~ of delegation)	**capo** (m)	['kapo]
authorities	**autorità** (f pl)	[autori'ta]
superiors	**superiori** (m pl)	[supe'rjori]
governor	**governatore** (m)	[governa'tore]
consul	**console** (m)	['konsole]
diplomat	**diplomatico** (m)	[diplo'matiko]
mayor	**sindaco** (m)	['sindako]
sheriff	**sceriffo** (m)	[ʃe'riffo]
emperor	**imperatore** (m)	[impera'tore]
tsar, czar	**zar** (m)	[tsar]
pharaoh	**faraone** (m)	[fara'one]
khan	**khan** (m)	['kan]

190. Road. Way. Directions

road	**strada** (f)	['strada]
way (direction)	**cammino** (m)	[kam'mino]
freeway	**superstrada** (f)	[super'strada]
highway	**autostrada** (f)	[auto'strada]
interstate	**strada** (f) **statale**	['strada sta'tale]

main road	**strada** (f) **principale**	['strada printʃi'pale]
dirt road	**strada** (f) **sterrata**	['strada ster'rata]
pathway	**viottolo** (m)	[vi'ottolo]
footpath (troddenpath)	**sentiero** (m)	[sen'tjero]
Where?	**Dove?**	['dove]
Where (to)?	**Dove?**	['dove]
From where?	**Di dove?, Da dove?**	[di 'dove], [da 'dove]
direction (way)	**direzione** (f)	[dire'tsjone]
to point (~ the way)	**indicare** (vt)	[indi'kare]
to the left	**a sinistra**	[a si'nistra]
to the right	**a destra**	[a 'destra]
straight ahead (adv)	**dritto**	['dritto]
back (e.g., to turn ~)	**indietro**	[in'djetro]
bend, curve	**curva** (f)	['kurva]
to turn (e.g., ~ left)	**girare** (vi)	[dʒi'rare]
to make a U-turn	**fare un'inversione a U**	['fare un inver'sjone a u:]
to be visible (mountains, castle, etc.)	**essere visibile**	['essere vi'zibile]
to appear (come into view)	**apparire** (vi)	[appa'rire]
stop, halt (e.g., during a trip)	**sosta** (f)	['sosta]
to rest, to pause (vi)	**riposarsi** (vr)	[ripo'zarsi]
rest (pause)	**riposo** (m)	[ri'pozo]
to lose one's way	**perdersi** (vr)	['perdersi]
to lead to ... (ab. road)	**portare verso ...**	[por'tare 'verso]
to come out (e.g., on the highway)	**raggiungere** (vt)	[ra'dʒundʒere]
stretch (of road)	**tratto** (m) **di strada**	['tratto di 'strada]
asphalt	**asfalto** (m)	[as'falto]
curb	**cordolo** (m)	['kordolo]
ditch	**fosso** (m)	['fosso]
manhole	**tombino** (m)	[tom'bino]
roadside (shoulder)	**ciglio** (m) **della strada**	['tʃiʎʎo della 'strada]
pit, pothole	**buca** (f)	['buka]
to go (on foot)	**andare** (vi)	[an'dare]
to pass (overtake)	**sorpassare** (vt)	[sorpas'sare]
step (footstep)	**passo** (m)	['passo]
on foot (adv)	**a piedi**	[a 'pjedi]
to block (road)	**sbarrare** (vt)	[zbar'rare]
boom gate	**sbarra** (f)	['zbarra]
dead end	**vicolo** (m) **cieco**	['vikolo 'tʃjeko]

191. Breaking the law. Criminals. Part 1

bandit	**bandito** (m)	[ban'dito]
crime	**delitto** (m)	[de'litto]
criminal (person)	**criminale** (m)	[krimi'nale]
thief	**ladro** (m)	['ladro]
to steal (vi, vt)	**rubare** (vi, vt)	[ru'bare]
stealing (larceny)	**ruberia** (f)	[rube'ria]
theft	**furto** (m)	['furto]
to kidnap (vt)	**rapire** (vt)	[ra'pire]
kidnapping	**rapimento** (m)	[rapi'mento]
kidnapper	**rapitore** (m)	[rapi'tore]
ransom	**riscatto** (m)	[ris'katto]
to demand ransom	**chiedere il riscatto**	['kjedere il ris'katto]
to rob (vt)	**rapinare** (vt)	[rapi'nare]
robber	**rapinatore** (m)	[rapina'tore]
to extort (vt)	**estorcere** (vt)	[es'tortʃere]
extortionist	**estorsore** (m)	[estor'sore]
extortion	**estorsione** (f)	[estor'sjone]
to murder, to kill	**uccidere** (vt)	[u'tʃidere]
murder	**assassinio** (m)	[assas'sinio]
murderer	**assassino** (m)	[assas'sino]
gunshot	**sparo** (m)	['sparo]
to fire (~ a shot)	**tirare un colpo**	[ti'rare un 'kolpo]
to shoot to death	**abbattere** (vt)	[ab'battere]
to shoot (vi)	**sparare** (vi)	[spa'rare]
shooting	**sparatoria** (f)	[spara'toria]
incident (fight, etc.)	**incidente** (m)	[intʃi'dente]
fight, brawl	**rissa** (f)	['rissa]
Help!	**Aiuto!**	[a'juto]
victim	**vittima** (f)	['vittima]
to damage (vt)	**danneggiare** (vt)	[danne'dʒare]
damage	**danno** (m)	['danno]
dead body, corpse	**cadavere** (m)	[ka'davere]
grave (~ crime)	**grave**	['grave]
to attack (vt)	**aggredire** (vt)	[aggre'dire]
to beat (to hit)	**picchiare** (vt)	[pik'kjare]
to beat up	**picchiare** (vt)	[pik'kjare]
to take (rob of sth)	**sottrarre** (vt)	[sot'trarre]
to stab to death	**accoltellare a morte**	[akkolte'lare a 'morte]
to maim (vt)	**mutilare** (vt)	[muti'lare]

to wound (vt)	**ferire** (vt)	[fe'rire]
blackmail	**ricatto** (m)	[ri'katto]
to blackmail (vt)	**ricattare** (vt)	[rikat'tare]
blackmailer	**ricattatore** (m)	[rikatta'tore]
protection racket	**estorsione** (f)	[estor'sjone]
racketeer	**estorsore** (m)	[estor'sore]
gangster	**gangster** (m)	['gangster]
mafia, Mob	**mafia** (f)	['mafia]
pickpocket	**borseggiatore** (m)	[borsedʒa'tore]
burglar	**scassinatore** (m)	[skassina'tore]
smuggling	**contrabbando** (m)	[kontrab'bando]
smuggler	**contrabbandiere** (m)	[kontrabban'djere]
forgery	**falsificazione** (f)	[falsifika'tsjone]
to forge (counterfeit)	**falsificare** (vt)	[falsifi'kare]
fake (forged)	**falso, falsificato**	['falso], [falsifi'kato]

192. Breaking the law. Criminals. Part 2

rape	**stupro** (m)	['stupro]
to rape (vt)	**stuprare** (vt)	[stu'prare]
rapist	**stupratore** (m)	[stupra'tore]
maniac	**maniaco** (m)	[ma'njako]
prostitute (fem.)	**prostituta** (f)	[prosti'tuta]
prostitution	**prostituzione** (f)	[prostitu'tsjone]
pimp	**magnaccia** (m)	[ma'ɲatʃa]
drug addict	**drogato** (m)	[dro'gato]
drug dealer	**trafficante** (m) **di droga**	[traffi'kante di 'droga]
to blow up (bomb)	**far esplodere**	[far e'splodere]
explosion	**esplosione** (f)	[esplo'zjone]
to set fire	**incendiare** (vt)	[intʃen'djare]
arsonist	**incendiario** (m)	[intʃen'djario]
terrorism	**terrorismo** (m)	[terro'rizmo]
terrorist	**terrorista** (m)	[terro'rista]
hostage	**ostaggio** (m)	[os'tadʒo]
to swindle (deceive)	**imbrogliare** (vt)	[imbroʎ'ʎare]
swindle, deception	**imbroglio** (m)	[im'broʎʎo]
swindler	**imbroglione** (m)	[imbroʎ'ʎone]
to bribe (vt)	**corrompere** (vt)	[kor'rompere]
bribery	**corruzione** (f)	[korru'tsjone]
bribe	**bustarella** (f)	[busta'rella]
poison	**veleno** (m)	[ve'leno]

to poison (vt)	**avvelenare** (vt)	[avvele'nare]
to poison oneself	**avvelenarsi** (vr)	[avvele'narsi]
suicide (act)	**suicidio** (m)	[sui'ʧidio]
suicide (person)	**suicida** (m)	[sui'ʧida]
to threaten (vt)	**minacciare** (vt)	[mina'ʧare]
threat	**minaccia** (f)	[mi'naʧa]
to make an attempt	**attentare** (vi)	[atten'tare]
attempt (attack)	**attentato** (m)	[atten'tato]
to steal (a car)	**rubare** (vt)	[ru'bare]
to hijack (a plane)	**dirottare** (vt)	[dirot'tare]
revenge	**vendetta** (f)	[ven'detta]
to avenge (get revenge)	**vendicare** (vt)	[vendi'kare]
to torture (vt)	**torturare** (vt)	[tortu'rare]
torture	**tortura** (f)	[tor'tura]
to torment (vt)	**maltrattare** (vt)	[maltrat'tare]
pirate	**pirata** (m)	[pi'rata]
hooligan	**teppista** (m)	[tep'pista]
armed (adj)	**armato**	[ar'mato]
violence	**violenza** (f)	[vio'lentsa]
illegal (unlawful)	**illegale**	[ille'gale]
spying (espionage)	**spionaggio** (m)	[spio'naʤo]
to spy (vi)	**spiare** (vi)	[spi'are]

193. Police. Law. Part 1

justice	**giustizia** (f)	[ʤu'stitsia]
court (see you in ~)	**tribunale** (m)	[tribu'nale]
judge	**giudice** (m)	['ʤuditʃe]
jurors	**giurati** (m)	[ʤu'rati]
jury trial	**processo** (m) **con giuria**	[pro'ʧesso kon ʤu'ria]
to judge, to try (vt)	**giudicare** (vt)	[ʤudi'kare]
lawyer, attorney	**avvocato** (m)	[avvo'kato]
defendant	**imputato** (m)	[impu'tato]
dock	**banco** (m) **degli imputati**	['banko 'deʎʎi impu'tati]
charge	**accusa** (f)	[ak'kuza]
accused	**accusato** (m)	[akku'zato]
sentence	**condanna** (f)	[kon'danna]
to sentence (vt)	**condannare** (vt)	[kondan'nare]
guilty (culprit)	**colpevole** (m)	[kol'pevole]

to punish (vt)	**punire** (vt)	[pu'nire]
punishment	**punizione** (f)	[puni'tsjone]
fine (penalty)	**multa** (f), **ammenda** (f)	['multa], [am'menda]
life imprisonment	**ergastolo** (m)	[er'gastolo]
death penalty	**pena** (f) **di morte**	['pena di 'morte]
electric chair	**sedia** (f) **elettrica**	['sedia e'lettrika]
gallows	**impiccagione** (f)	[impikka'ʤone]
to execute (vt)	**giustiziare** (vt)	[ʤusti'tsjare]
execution	**esecuzione** (f)	[ezeku'tsjone]
prison, jail	**prigione** (f)	[pri'ʤone]
cell	**cella** (f)	['ʧella]
escort (convoy)	**scorta** (f)	['skorta]
prison guard	**guardia** (f) **carceraria**	['gwardia karʧe'raria]
prisoner	**prigioniero** (m)	[priʤo'njero]
handcuffs	**manette** (f pl)	[ma'nette]
to handcuff (vt)	**mettere le manette**	['mettere le ma'nette]
prison break	**fuga** (f)	['fuga]
to break out (vi)	**fuggire** (vi)	[fu'ʤire]
to disappear (vi)	**scomparire** (vi)	[skompa'rire]
to release (from prison)	**liberare** (vt)	[libe'rare]
amnesty	**amnistia** (f)	[amni'stia]
police	**polizia** (f)	[poli'tsia]
police officer	**poliziotto** (m)	[poli'tsjotto]
police station	**commissariato** (m)	[kommissa'rjato]
billy club	**manganello** (m)	[manga'nello]
bullhorn	**altoparlante** (m)	[altopar'lante]
patrol car	**macchina** (f) **di pattuglia**	['makkina di pat'tuʎʎa]
siren	**sirena** (f)	[si'rena]
to turn on the siren	**mettere la sirena**	['mettere la si'rena]
siren call	**suono** (m) **della sirena**	[su'ono 'della si'rena]
crime scene	**luogo** (m) **del crimine**	[lu'ogo del 'krimine]
witness	**testimone** (m)	[testi'mone]
freedom	**libertà** (f)	[liber'ta]
accomplice	**complice** (m)	['kompliʧe]
to flee (vi)	**fuggire** (vi)	[fu'ʤire]
trace (to leave a ~)	**traccia** (f)	['traʧa]

194. Police. Law. Part 2

search (investigation)	**ricerca** (f)	[ri'ʧerka]
to look for ...	**cercare** (vt)	[ʧer'kare]

suspicion	**sospetto** (m)	[so'spetto]
suspicious (e.g., ~ vehicle)	**sospetto**	[so'spetto]
to stop (cause to halt)	**fermare** (vt)	[fer'mare]
to detain (keep in custody)	**arrestare**	[arre'stare]
case (lawsuit)	**causa** (f)	['kauza]
investigation	**inchiesta** (f)	[in'kjesta]
detective	**detective** (m)	[de'tektiv]
investigator	**investigatore** (m)	[investiga'tore]
hypothesis	**versione** (f)	[ver'sjone]
motive	**movente** (m)	[mo'vente]
interrogation	**interrogatorio** (m)	[interroga'torio]
to interrogate (vt)	**interrogare** (vt)	[interro'gare]
to question (~ neighbors, etc.)	**interrogare** (vt)	[interro'gare]
check (identity ~)	**controllo** (m)	[kon'trollo]
round-up (raid)	**retata** (f)	[re'tata]
search (~ warrant)	**perquisizione** (f)	[perkwizi'tsjone]
chase (pursuit)	**inseguimento** (m)	[insegwi'mento]
to pursue, to chase	**inseguire** (vt)	[inse'gwire]
to track (a criminal)	**essere sulle tracce**	['essere sulle 'tratʃe]
arrest	**arresto** (m)	[ar'resto]
to arrest (sb)	**arrestare**	[arre'stare]
to catch (thief, etc.)	**catturare** (vt)	[kattu'rare]
capture	**cattura** (f)	[kat'tura]
document	**documento** (m)	[doku'mento]
proof (evidence)	**prova** (f)	['prova]
to prove (vt)	**provare** (vt)	[pro'vare]
footprint	**impronta** (f) **del piede**	[im'pronta del 'pjede]
fingerprints	**impronte** (f pl) **digitali**	[im'pronte didʒi'tali]
piece of evidence	**elemento** (m) **di prova**	[ele'mento di 'prova]
alibi	**alibi** (m)	['alibi]
innocent (not guilty)	**innocente**	[inno'tʃente]
injustice	**ingiustizia** (f)	[indʒu'stitsia]
unjust, unfair (adj)	**ingiusto**	[in'dʒusto]
criminal (adj)	**criminale**	[krimi'nale]
to confiscate (vt)	**confiscare** (vt)	[konfis'kare]
drug (illegal substance)	**droga** (f)	['droga]
weapon, gun	**armi** (f pl)	['armi]
to disarm (vt)	**disarmare** (vt)	[dizar'mare]
to order (command)	**ordinare** (vt)	[ordi'nare]
to disappear (vi)	**sparire** (vi)	[spa'rire]
law	**legge** (f)	['ledʒe]
legal, lawful (adj)	**legale**	[le'gale]
illegal, illicit (adj)	**illegale**	[ille'gale]

responsibility (blame)	**responsabilità** (f)	[responsabili'ta]
responsible (adj)	**responsabile**	[respon'sabile]

NATURE

The Earth. Part 1

195. Outer space

space	**cosmo** (m)	['kozmo]
space (as adj)	**cosmico, spaziale**	['kozmiko], [spa'tsjale]
outer space	**spazio** (m) **cosmico**	['spatsio 'kozmiko]
world	**mondo** (m)	['mondo]
universe	**universo** (m)	[uni'verso]
galaxy	**galassia** (f)	[ga'lassia]
star	**stella** (f)	['stella]
constellation	**costellazione** (f)	[kostella'tsjone]
planet	**pianeta** (m)	[pja'neta]
satellite	**satellite** (m)	[sa'tellite]
meteorite	**meteorite** (m)	[meteo'rite]
comet	**cometa** (f)	[ko'meta]
asteroid	**asteroide** (m)	[aste'roide]
orbit	**orbita** (f)	['orbita]
to revolve (~ around the Earth)	**ruotare** (vi)	[ruo'tare]
atmosphere	**atmosfera** (f)	[atmo'sfera]
the Sun	**il Sole**	[il 'sole]
solar system	**sistema** (m) **solare**	[si'stema so'lare]
solar eclipse	**eclisse** (f) **solare**	[e'klisse so'lare]
the Earth	**la Terra**	[la 'terra]
the Moon	**la Luna**	[la 'luna]
Mars	**Marte** (m)	['marte]
Venus	**Venere** (f)	['venere]
Jupiter	**Giove** (m)	['dʒove]
Saturn	**Saturno** (m)	[sa'turno]
Mercury	**Mercurio** (m)	[mer'kurio]
Uranus	**Urano** (m)	[u'rano]
Neptune	**Nettuno** (m)	[net'tuno]
Pluto	**Plutone** (m)	[plu'tone]
Milky Way	**Via** (f) **Lattea**	['via 'lattea]

Great Bear (Ursa Major)	**Orsa** (f) **Maggiore**	['orsa ma'dʒore]
North Star	**Stella** (f) **Polare**	['stella po'lare]
Martian	**marziano** (m)	[mar'tsjano]
extraterrestrial (n)	**extraterrestre** (m)	[ekstrater'restre]
alien	**alieno** (m)	[a'ljeno]
flying saucer	**disco** (m) **volante**	['disko vo'lante]
spaceship	**nave** (f) **spaziale**	['nave spa'tsjale]
space station	**stazione** (f) **spaziale**	[sta'tsjone spa'tsjale]
blast-off	**lancio** (m)	['lantʃo]
engine	**motore** (m)	[mo'tore]
nozzle	**ugello** (m)	[u'dʒello]
fuel	**combustibile** (m)	[kombu'stibile]
cockpit, flight deck	**cabina** (f) **di pilotaggio**	[ka'bina di pilo'tadʒio]
antenna	**antenna** (f)	[an'tenna]
porthole	**oblò** (m)	[ob'lo]
solar panel	**batteria** (f) **solare**	[batte'ria so'lare]
spacesuit	**scafandro** (m)	[ska'fandro]
weightlessness	**imponderabilità** (f)	[imponderabili'ta]
oxygen	**ossigeno** (m)	[os'sidʒeno]
docking (in space)	**aggancio** (m)	[ag'gantʃo]
to dock (vi, vt)	**agganciarsi** (vr)	[aggan'tʃarsi]
observatory	**osservatorio** (m)	[osserva'torio]
telescope	**telescopio** (m)	[tele'skopio]
to observe (vt)	**osservare** (vt)	[osser'vare]
to explore (vt)	**esplorare** (vt)	[esplo'rare]

196. The Earth

the Earth	**la Terra**	[la 'terra]
the globe (the Earth)	**globo** (m) **terrestre**	['globo ter'restre]
planet	**pianeta** (m)	[pja'neta]
atmosphere	**atmosfera** (f)	[atmo'sfera]
geography	**geografia** (f)	[dʒeogra'fia]
nature	**natura** (f)	[na'tura]
globe (table ~)	**mappamondo** (m)	[mappa'mondo]
map	**carta** (f) **geografica**	['karta dʒeo'grafika]
atlas	**atlante** (m)	[a'tlante]
Europe	**Europa** (f)	[eu'ropa]
Asia	**Asia** (f)	['azia]
Africa	**Africa** (f)	['afrika]

Australia	**Australia** (f)	[au'stralia]
America	**America** (f)	[a'merika]
North America	**America** (f) **del Nord**	[a'merika del nord]
South America	**America** (f) **del Sud**	[a'merika del sud]
Antarctica	**Antartide** (f)	[an'tartide]
the Arctic	**Artico** (m)	['artiko]

197. Cardinal directions

north	**nord** (m)	[nord]
to the north	**a nord**	[a nord]
in the north	**al nord**	[al nord]
northern (adj)	**del nord**	[del nord]
south	**sud** (m)	[sud]
to the south	**a sud**	[a sud]
in the south	**al sud**	[al sud]
southern (adj)	**del sud**	[del sud]
west	**ovest** (m)	['ovest]
to the west	**a ovest**	[a 'ovest]
in the west	**all'ovest**	[all 'ovest]
western (adj)	**dell'ovest, occidentale**	[dell 'ovest], [otʃiden'tale]
east	**est** (m)	[est]
to the east	**a est**	[a est]
in the east	**all'est**	[all 'est]
eastern (adj)	**dell'est, orientale**	[dell 'est], [orien'tale]

198. Sea. Ocean

sea	**mare** (m)	['mare]
ocean	**oceano** (m)	[o'tʃeano]
gulf (bay)	**golfo** (m)	['golfo]
straits	**stretto** (m)	['stretto]
land (solid ground)	**terra** (f)	['terra]
continent (mainland)	**continente** (m)	[konti'nente]
island	**isola** (f)	['izola]
peninsula	**penisola** (f)	[pe'nizola]
archipelago	**arcipelago** (m)	[artʃi'pelago]
bay, cove	**baia** (f)	['baja]
harbor	**porto** (m)	['porto]
lagoon	**laguna** (f)	[la'guna]
cape	**capo** (m)	['kapo]
atoll	**atollo** (m)	[a'tollo]

reef	**scogliera** (f)	[skoʎ'ʎera]
coral	**corallo** (m)	[ko'rallo]
coral reef	**barriera** (f) **corallina**	[bar'rjera koral'lina]
deep (adj)	**profondo**	[pro'fondo]
depth (deep water)	**profondità** (f)	[profondi'ta]
abyss	**abisso** (m)	[a'bisso]
trench (e.g., Mariana ~)	**fossa** (f)	['fossa]
current (Ocean ~)	**corrente** (f)	[kor'rente]
to surround (bathe)	**circondare** (vt)	[ʧirkon'dare]
shore	**litorale** (m)	[lito'rale]
coast	**costa** (f)	['kosta]
flow (flood tide)	**alta marea** (f)	['alta ma'rea]
ebb (ebb tide)	**bassa marea** (f)	['bassa ma'rea]
shoal	**banco** (m) **di sabbia**	['banko di 'sabbia]
bottom (~ of the sea)	**fondo** (m)	['fondo]
wave	**onda** (f)	['onda]
crest (~ of a wave)	**cresta** (f) **dell'onda**	['kresta dell 'onda]
spume (sea foam)	**schiuma** (f)	['skjuma]
storm (sea storm)	**tempesta** (f)	[tem'pesta]
hurricane	**uragano** (m)	[ura'gano]
tsunami	**tsunami** (m)	[tsu'nami]
calm (dead ~)	**bonaccia** (f)	[bo'naʧa]
quiet, calm (adj)	**tranquillo**	[tran'kwillo]
pole	**polo** (m)	['polo]
polar (adj)	**polare**	[po'lare]
latitude	**latitudine** (f)	[lati'tudine]
longitude	**longitudine** (f)	[lonʤi'tudine]
parallel	**parallelo** (m)	[paral'lelo]
equator	**equatore** (m)	[ekwa'tore]
sky	**cielo** (m)	['ʧelo]
horizon	**orizzonte** (m)	[orid'ʣonte]
air	**aria** (f)	['aria]
lighthouse	**faro** (m)	['faro]
to dive (vi)	**tuffarsi** (vr)	[tuf'farsi]
to sink (ab. boat)	**affondare** (vi)	[affon'dare]
treasures	**tesori** (m)	[te'zori]

199. Seas' and Oceans' names

Atlantic Ocean	**Oceano** (m) **Atlantico**	[o'ʧeano at'lantiko]
Indian Ocean	**Oceano** (m) **Indiano**	[o'ʧeano indi'ano]

Pacific Ocean	**Oceano** (m) **Pacifico**	[o'ʧeano pa'ʧifiko]
Arctic Ocean	**mar** (m) **Glaciale Artico**	[mar gla'ʧale 'artiko]
Black Sea	**mar** (m) **Nero**	[mar 'nero]
Red Sea	**mar** (m) **Rosso**	[mar 'rosso]
Yellow Sea	**mar** (m) **Giallo**	[mar 'ʤallo]
White Sea	**mar** (m) **Bianco**	[mar 'bjanko]
Caspian Sea	**mar** (m) **Caspio**	[mar 'kaspio]
Dead Sea	**mar** (m) **Morto**	[mar 'morto]
Mediterranean Sea	**mar** (m) **Mediterraneo**	[mar mediter'raneo]
Aegean Sea	**mar** (m) **Egeo**	[mar e'ʤeo]
Adriatic Sea	**mar** (m) **Adriatico**	[mar adri'atiko]
Arabian Sea	**mar** (m) **Arabico**	[mar a'rabiko]
Sea of Japan	**mar** (m) **del Giappone**	[mar del ʤap'pone]
Bering Sea	**mare** (m) **di Bering**	['mare di 'bering]
South China Sea	**mar** (m) **Cinese meridionale**	[mar ʧi'neze meridio'nale]
Coral Sea	**mar** (m) **dei Coralli**	[mar 'dei ko'ralli]
Tasman Sea	**mar** (m) **di Tasmania**	[mar di taz'mania]
Caribbean Sea	**mar** (m) **dei Caraibi**	[mar dei kara'ibi]
Barents Sea	**mare** (m) **di Barents**	['mare di 'barents]
Kara Sea	**mare** (m) **di Kara**	['mare di 'kara]
North Sea	**mare** (m) **del Nord**	['mare del nord]
Baltic Sea	**mar** (m) **Baltico**	[mar 'baltiko]
Norwegian Sea	**mare** (m) **di Norvegia**	['mare di nor'veʤa]

200. Mountains

mountain	**monte** (m), **montagna** (f)	['monte], [mon'taɲa]
mountain range	**catena** (f) **montuosa**	[ka'tena montu'oza]
mountain ridge	**crinale** (m)	[kri'nale]
summit, top	**cima** (f)	['ʧima]
peak	**picco** (m)	['pikko]
foot (~ of the mountain)	**piedi** (m pl)	['pjede]
slope (mountainside)	**pendio** (m)	[pen'dio]
volcano	**vulcano** (m)	[vul'kano]
active volcano	**vulcano** (m) **attivo**	[vul'kano at'tivo]
dormant volcano	**vulcano** (m) **inattivo**	[vul'kano inat'tivo]
eruption	**eruzione** (f)	[eru'tsjone]
crater	**cratere** (m)	[kra'tere]
magma	**magma** (m)	['magma]

lava	**lava** (f)	['lava]
molten (~ lava)	**fuso**	['fuzo]
canyon	**canyon** (m)	['kenjon]
gorge	**gola** (f)	['gola]
crevice	**crepaccio** (m)	[kre'patʃo]
abyss (chasm)	**precipizio** (m)	[pretʃi'pitsio]
pass, col	**passo** (m), **valico** (m)	['passo], ['valiko]
plateau	**altopiano** (m)	[alto'pjano]
cliff	**falesia** (f)	[fa'lezia]
hill	**collina** (f)	[kol'lina]
glacier	**ghiacciaio** (m)	[gja'tʃajo]
waterfall	**cascata** (f)	[kas'kata]
geyser	**geyser** (m)	['gejzer]
lake	**lago** (m)	['lago]
plain	**pianura** (f)	[pja'nura]
landscape	**paesaggio** (m)	[pae'zadʒo]
echo	**eco** (f)	['eko]
alpinist	**alpinista** (m)	[alpi'nista]
rock climber	**scalatore** (m)	[skala'tore]
to conquer (in climbing)	**conquistare** (vt)	[konkwi'stare]
climb (an easy ~)	**scalata** (f)	[ska'lata]

201. Mountains names

The Alps	**Alpi** (f pl)	['alpi]
Mont Blanc	**Monte** (m) **Bianco**	['monte 'bjanko]
The Pyrenees	**Pirenei** (m pl)	[pire'nei]
The Carpathians	**Carpazi** (m pl)	[kar'patsi]
The Ural Mountains	**gli Urali** (m pl)	[ʎi u'rali]
The Caucasus Mountains	**Caucaso** (m)	['kaukazo]
Mount Elbrus	**Monte** (m) **Elbrus**	['monte 'elbrus]
The Altai Mountains	**Monti** (m pl) **Altai**	['monti al'taj]
The Tian Shan	**Tien Shan** (m)	[tjen 'ʃan]
The Pamir Mountains	**Pamir** (m)	[pa'mir]
The Himalayas	**Himalaia** (m)	[ima'laja]
Mount Everest	**Everest** (m)	['everest]
The Andes	**Ande** (f pl)	['ande]
Mount Kilimanjaro	**Kilimangiaro** (m)	[kiliman'dʒaro]

202. Rivers

river	**fiume** (m)	['fjume]
spring (natural source)	**fonte** (f)	['fonte]
riverbed (river channel)	**letto** (m)	['letto]
basin (river valley)	**bacino** (m)	[ba'ʧino]
to flow into ...	**sfociare nel ...**	[sfo'ʧare nel]
tributary	**affluente** (m)	[afflu'ente]
bank (of river)	**riva** (f)	['riva]
current (stream)	**corrente** (f)	[kor'rente]
downstream (adv)	**a valle**	[a 'valle]
upstream (adv)	**a monte**	[a 'monte]
inundation	**inondazione** (f)	[inonda'tsjone]
flooding	**piena** (f)	['pjena]
to overflow (vi)	**straripare** (vi)	[strari'pare]
to flood (vt)	**inondare** (vt)	[inon'dare]
shallow (shoal)	**secca** (f)	['sekka]
rapids	**rapida** (f)	['rapida]
dam	**diga** (f)	['diga]
canal	**canale** (m)	[ka'nale]
reservoir (artificial lake)	**bacino** (m) **di riserva**	[ba'ʧino di ri'zerva]
sluice, lock	**chiusa** (f)	['kjuza]
water body (pond, etc.)	**bacino** (m) **idrico**	[ba'ʧino 'idriko]
swamp (marshland)	**palude** (f)	[pa'lude]
bog, marsh	**pantano** (m)	[pan'tano]
whirlpool	**vortice** (m)	['vortiʧe]
stream (brook)	**ruscello** (m)	[ru'ʃello]
drinking (ab. water)	**potabile**	[po'tabile]
fresh (~ water)	**dolce**	['dolʧe]
ice	**ghiaccio** (m)	['gjaʧo]
to freeze over (ab. river, etc.)	**ghiacciarsi** (vr)	[gja'ʧarsi]

203. Rivers' names

Seine	**Senna** (f)	['senna]
Loire	**Loira** (f)	['loira]
Thames	**Tamigi** (m)	[ta'midʒi]
Rhine	**Reno** (m)	['reno]
Danube	**Danubio** (m)	[da'nubio]

Volga	**Volga** (m)	['volga]
Don	**Don** (m)	[don]
Lena	**Lena** (f)	['lena]
Yellow River	**Fiume** (m) **Giallo**	['fjume 'dʒallo]
Yangtze	**Fiume** (m) **Azzurro**	['fjume ad'dzurro]
Mekong	**Mekong** (m)	[me'kong]
Ganges	**Gange** (m)	['gandʒe]
Nile River	**Nilo** (m)	['nilo]
Congo River	**Congo** (m)	['kongo]
Okavango River	**Okavango**	[oka'vango]
Zambezi River	**Zambesi** (m)	[dzam'bezi]
Limpopo River	**Limpopo** (m)	['limpopo]
Mississippi River	**Mississippi** (m)	[missis'sippi]

204. Forest

forest, wood	**foresta** (f)	[fo'resta]
forest (as adj)	**forestale**	[fores'tale]
thick forest	**foresta** (f) **fitta**	[fo'resta 'fitta]
grove	**boschetto** (m)	[bos'ketto]
forest clearing	**radura** (f)	[ra'dura]
thicket	**roveto** (m)	[ro'veto]
scrubland	**boscaglia** (f)	[bos'kaʎʎa]
footpath (troddenpath)	**sentiero** (m)	[sen'tjero]
gully	**calanco** (m)	[ka'lanko]
tree	**albero** (m)	['albero]
leaf	**foglia** (f)	['foʎʎa]
leaves (foliage)	**fogliame** (m)	[foʎ'ʎame]
fall of leaves	**caduta** (f) **delle foglie**	[ka'duta 'delle 'foʎʎe]
to fall (ab. leaves)	**cadere** (vi)	[ka'dere]
top (of the tree)	**cima** (f)	['tʃima]
branch	**ramo** (m), **ramoscello** (m)	['ramo], [ramo'ʃello]
bough	**ramo** (m)	['ramo]
bud (on shrub, tree)	**gemma** (f)	['dʒemma]
needle (of pine tree)	**ago** (m)	['ago]
pine cone	**pigna** (f)	['piɲa]
tree hollow	**cavità** (f)	[kavi'ta]
nest	**nido** (m)	['nido]
burrow (animal hole)	**tana** (f)	['tana]
trunk	**tronco** (m)	['tronko]
root	**radice** (f)	[ra'ditʃe]

bark	**corteccia** (f)	[kor'tetʃa]
moss	**musco** (m)	['musko]
to uproot (remove trees or tree stumps)	**sradicare** (vt)	[zradi'kare]
to chop down	**abbattere** (vt)	[ab'battere]
to deforest (vt)	**disboscare** (vt)	[dizbo'skare]
tree stump	**ceppo** (m)	['tʃeppo]
campfire	**falò** (m)	[fa'lo]
forest fire	**incendio** (m) **boschivo**	[in'tʃendio bos'kivo]
to extinguish (vt)	**spegnere** (vt)	['speɲere]
forest ranger	**guardia** (f) **forestale**	['gwardia fores'tale]
protection	**protezione** (f)	[prote'tsjone]
to protect (~ nature)	**proteggere** (vt)	[pro'tedʒere]
poacher	**bracconiere** (m)	[brakko'njere]
steel trap	**tagliola** (f)	[taʎ'ʎoʎa]
to gather, to pick (vt)	**raccogliere** (vt)	[rak'koʎʎere]
to lose one's way	**perdersi** (vr)	['perdersi]

205. Natural resources

natural resources	**risorse** (f pl) **naturali**	[ri'sorse natu'rali]
minerals	**minerali** (m pl)	[mine'rali]
deposits	**deposito** (m)	[de'pozito]
field (e.g., oilfield)	**giacimento** (m)	[dʒatʃi'mento]
to mine (extract)	**estrarre** (vt)	[e'strarre]
mining (extraction)	**estrazione** (f)	[estra'tsjone]
ore	**minerale** (m) **grezzo**	[mine'rale 'greddzo]
mine (e.g., for coal)	**miniera** (f)	[mi'njera]
shaft (mine ~)	**pozzo** (m) **di miniera**	['pottso di mi'njera]
miner	**minatore** (m)	[mina'tore]
gas (natural ~)	**gas** (m)	[gas]
gas pipeline	**gasdotto** (m)	[gas'dotto]
oil (petroleum)	**petrolio** (m)	[pe'trolio]
oil pipeline	**oleodotto** (m)	[oleo'dotto]
oil well	**torre** (f) **di estrazione**	['torre di estra'tsjone]
derrick (tower)	**torre** (f) **di trivellazione**	['torre di trivella'tsjone]
tanker	**petroliera** (f)	[petro'ljera]
sand	**sabbia** (f)	['sabbia]
limestone	**calcare** (m)	[kal'kare]
gravel	**ghiaia** (f)	['gjaja]
peat	**torba** (f)	['torba]
clay	**argilla** (f)	[ar'dʒilla]

coal	**carbone** (m)	[kar'bone]
iron (ore)	**ferro** (m)	['ferro]
gold	**oro** (m)	['oro]
silver	**argento** (m)	[ar'dʒento]
nickel	**nichel** (m)	['nikel]
copper	**rame** (m)	['rame]
zinc	**zinco** (m)	['dzinko]
manganese	**manganese** (m)	[manga'neze]
mercury	**mercurio** (m)	[mer'kurio]
lead	**piombo** (m)	['pjombo]
mineral	**minerale** (m)	[mine'rale]
crystal	**cristallo** (m)	[kris'tallo]
marble	**marmo** (m)	['marmo]
uranium	**uranio** (m)	[u'ranio]

The Earth. Part 2

206. Weather

weather	**tempo** (m)	['tempo]
weather forecast	**previsione** (f) **del tempo**	[previ'zjone del 'tempo]
temperature	**temperatura** (f)	[tempera'tura]
thermometer	**termometro** (m)	[ter'mometro]
barometer	**barometro** (m)	[ba'rometro]
humid (adj)	**umido**	['umido]
humidity	**umidità** (f)	[umidi'ta]
heat (extreme ~)	**caldo** (m), **afa** (f)	['kaldo], ['afa]
hot (torrid)	**molto caldo**	['molto 'kaldo]
it's hot	**fa molto caldo**	[fa 'molto 'kaldo]
it's warm	**fa caldo**	[fa 'kaldo]
warm (moderately hot)	**caldo**	['kaldo]
it's cold	**fa freddo**	[fa 'freddo]
cold (adj)	**freddo**	['freddo]
sun	**sole** (m)	['sole]
to shine (vi)	**splendere** (vi)	['splendere]
sunny (day)	**di sole**	[di 'sole]
to come up (vi)	**levarsi** (vr)	[le'varsi]
to set (vi)	**tramontare** (vi)	[tramon'tare]
cloud	**nuvola** (f)	['nuvola]
cloudy (adj)	**nuvoloso**	[nuvo'lozo]
rain cloud	**nube** (f) **di pioggia**	['nube di 'pjodʒa]
somber (gloomy)	**nuvoloso**	[nuvo'lozo]
rain	**pioggia** (f)	['pjodʒa]
it's raining	**piove**	['pjove]
rainy (~ day, weather)	**piovoso**	[pjo'vozo]
to drizzle (vi)	**piovigginare** (vi)	[pjovidʒi'nare]
pouring rain	**pioggia** (f) **torrenziale**	['pjodʒa torren'tsjale]
downpour	**acquazzone** (m)	[akwat'tsone]
heavy (e.g., ~ rain)	**forte**	['forte]
puddle	**pozzanghera** (f)	[pot'tsangera]
to get wet (in rain)	**bagnarsi** (vr)	[ba'ɲarsi]
fog (mist)	**foschia** (f), **nebbia** (f)	[fos'kia], ['nebbia]
foggy	**nebbioso**	[neb'bjozo]

snow	**neve** (f)	['neve]
it's snowing	**nevica**	['nevika]

207. Severe weather. Natural disasters

thunderstorm	**temporale** (m)	[tempo'rale]
lightning (~ strike)	**fulmine** (f)	['fulmine]
to flash (vi)	**lampeggiare** (vi)	[lampe'ʤare]
thunder	**tuono** (m)	[tu'ono]
to thunder (vi)	**tuonare** (vi)	[tuo'nare]
it's thundering	**tuona**	[tu'ona]
hail	**grandine** (f)	['grandine]
it's hailing	**grandina**	['grandina]
to flood (vt)	**inondare** (vt)	[inon'dare]
flood, inundation	**inondazione** (f)	[inonda'tsjone]
earthquake	**terremoto** (m)	[terre'moto]
tremor, shoke	**scossa** (f)	['skossa]
epicenter	**epicentro** (m)	[epi'ʧentro]
eruption	**eruzione** (f)	[eru'tsjone]
lava	**lava** (f)	['lava]
twister	**tromba** (f) **d'aria**	['tromba 'daria]
tornado	**tornado** (m)	[tor'nado]
typhoon	**tifone** (m)	[ti'fone]
hurricane	**uragano** (m)	[ura'gano]
storm	**tempesta** (f)	[tem'pesta]
tsunami	**tsunami** (m)	[tsu'nami]
cyclone	**ciclone** (m)	[ʧi'klone]
bad weather	**maltempo** (m)	[mal'tempo]
fire (accident)	**incendio** (m)	[in'ʧendio]
disaster	**disastro** (m)	[di'zastro]
meteorite	**meteorite** (m)	[meteo'rite]
avalanche	**valanga** (f)	[va'langa]
snowslide	**slavina** (f)	[zla'vina]
blizzard	**tempesta** (f) **di neve**	[tem'pesta di 'neve]
snowstorm	**bufera** (f) **di neve**	['bufera di 'neve]

208. Noises. Sounds

silence (quiet)	**silenzio** (m)	[si'lentsio]
sound	**suono** (m)	[su'ono]

noise	**rumore** (m)	[ru'more]
to make noise	**far rumore**	[far ru'more]
noisy (adj)	**rumoroso**	[rumo'rozo]
loudly (to speak, etc.)	**forte, alto**	['forte], ['alto]
loud (voice, etc.)	**alto, forte**	['alto], ['forte]
constant (e.g., ~ noise)	**costante**	[ko'stante]
cry, shout (n)	**grido** (m)	['grido]
to cry, to shout (vi)	**gridare** (vi)	[gri'dare]
whisper	**sussurro** (m)	[sus'surro]
to whisper (vi, vt)	**sussurrare** (vi, vt)	[sussur'rare]
barking (dog's ~)	**abbaiamento** (m)	[abaja'mento]
to bark (vi)	**abbaiare** (vi)	[abba'jare]
groan (of pain, etc.)	**gemito** (m)	['dʒemito]
to groan (vi)	**gemere** (vi)	['dʒemere]
cough	**tosse** (f)	['tosse]
to cough (vi)	**tossire** (vi)	[tos'sire]
whistle	**fischio** (m)	['fiskio]
to whistle (vi)	**fischiare** (vi)	[fis'kjare]
knock (at the door)	**bussata** (f)	[bus'sata]
to knock (on the door)	**bussare** (vi)	[bus'sare]
to crack (vi)	**crepitare** (vi)	[krepi'tare]
crack (cracking sound)	**crepitio** (m)	[krepi'tio]
siren	**sirena** (f)	[si'rena]
whistle (factory ~, etc.)	**sirena** (f) **di fabbrica**	[si'rena di 'fabbrika]
to whistle (ab. train)	**emettere un fischio**	[e'mettere un 'fiskio]
honk (car horn sound)	**colpo** (m) **di clacson**	['kolpo di 'klakson]
to honk (vi)	**clacsonare** (vi)	[klakso'nare]

209. Winter

winter (n)	**inverno** (m)	[in'verno]
winter (as adj)	**invernale**	[inver'nale]
in winter	**d'inverno**	[din'verno]
snow	**neve** (f)	['neve]
it's snowing	**nevica**	['nevika]
snowfall	**nevicata** (f)	[nevi'kata]
snowdrift	**mucchio** (m) **di neve**	['mukkio di 'neve]
snowflake	**fiocco** (m) **di neve**	[fjokko di 'neve]
snowball	**palla** (f) **di neve**	['palla di 'neve]
snowman	**pupazzo** (m) **di neve**	[pu'pattso di 'neve]
icicle	**ghiacciolo** (m)	[gja'tʃolo]

December	**dicembre** (m)	[di'tʃembre]
January	**gennaio** (m)	[dʒen'najo]
February	**febbraio** (m)	[feb'brajo]
frost (severe ~, freezing cold)	**gelo** (m)	['dʒelo]
frosty (weather, air)	**gelido**	['dʒelido]
below zero (adv)	**sotto zero**	['sotto 'dzero]
first frost	**primi geli** (m pl)	['primi 'dʒeli]
hoarfrost	**brina** (f)	['brina]
cold (cold weather)	**freddo** (m)	['freddo]
it's cold	**fa freddo**	[fa 'freddo]
fur coat	**pelliccia** (f)	[pel'litʃa]
mittens	**manopole** (f pl)	[ma'nopole]
to get sick	**ammalarsi** (vr)	[amma'larsi]
cold (illness)	**raffreddore** (m)	[raffred'dore]
to catch a cold	**raffreddarsi** (vr)	[raffred'darsi]
ice	**ghiaccio** (m)	['gjatʃo]
black ice	**ghiaccio** (m) **trasparente**	['gjatʃo traspa'rente]
to freeze over (ab. river, etc.)	**ghiacciarsi** (vr)	[gja'tʃarsi]
ice floe	**banco** (m) **di ghiaccio**	['banko di 'gjatʃo]
skis	**sci** (m pl)	[ʃi]
skier	**sciatore** (m)	[ʃia'tore]
to ski (vi)	**sciare** (vi)	[ʃi'are]
to skate (vi)	**pattinare** (vi)	[patti'nare]

Fauna

210. Mammals. Predators

predator	**predatore** (m)	[preda'tore]
tiger	**tigre** (f)	['tigre]
lion	**leone** (m)	[le'one]
wolf	**lupo** (m)	['lupo]
fox	**volpe** (m)	['volpe]
jaguar	**giaguaro** (m)	[ʤa'gwaro]
leopard	**leopardo** (m)	[leo'pardo]
cheetah	**ghepardo** (m)	[ge'pardo]
black panther	**pantera** (f)	[pan'tera]
puma	**puma** (f)	['puma]
snow leopard	**leopardo** (m) **delle nevi**	[leo'pardo 'delle 'nevi]
lynx	**lince** (f)	['linʧe]
coyote	**coyote** (m)	[ko'jote]
jackal	**sciacallo** (m)	[ʃa'kallo]
hyena	**iena** (f)	['jena]

211. Wild animals

animal	**animale** (m)	[ani'male]
beast (animal)	**bestia** (f)	['bestia]
squirrel	**scoiattolo** (m)	[sko'jattolo]
hedgehog	**riccio** (m)	['riʧo]
hare	**lepre** (f)	['lepre]
rabbit	**coniglio** (m)	[ko'niʎʎo]
badger	**tasso** (m)	['tasso]
raccoon	**procione** (f)	[pro'ʧone]
hamster	**criceto** (m)	[kri'ʧeto]
marmot	**marmotta** (f)	[mar'motta]
mole	**talpa** (f)	['talpa]
mouse	**topo** (m)	['topo]
rat	**ratto** (m)	['ratto]
bat	**pipistrello** (m)	[pipi'strello]
ermine	**ermellino** (m)	[ermel'lino]
sable	**zibellino** (m)	[ʣibel'lino]

marten	**martora** (f)	['martora]
weasel	**donnola** (f)	['donnola]
mink	**visone** (m)	[vi'zone]
beaver	**castoro** (m)	[kas'toro]
otter	**lontra** (f)	['lontra]
horse	**cavallo** (m)	[ka'vallo]
moose	**alce** (m)	['altʃe]
deer	**cervo** (m)	['tʃervo]
camel	**cammello** (m)	[kam'mello]
bison	**bisonte** (m) **americano**	[bi'zonte ameri'kano]
wisent	**bisonte** (m) **europeo**	[bi'zonte euro'peo]
buffalo	**bufalo** (m)	['bufalo]
zebra	**zebra** (f)	['dzebra]
antelope	**antilope** (f)	[an'tilope]
roe deer	**capriolo** (m)	[kapri'olo]
fallow deer	**daino** (m)	['daino]
chamois	**camoscio** (m)	[ka'moʃo]
wild boar	**cinghiale** (m)	[tʃin'gjale]
whale	**balena** (f)	[ba'lena]
seal	**foca** (f)	['foka]
walrus	**tricheco** (m)	[tri'keko]
fur seal	**otaria** (f)	[o'taria]
dolphin	**delfino** (m)	[del'fino]
bear	**orso** (m)	['orso]
polar bear	**orso** (m) **bianco**	['orso 'bjanko]
panda	**panda** (m)	['panda]
monkey	**scimmia** (f)	['ʃimmia]
chimpanzee	**scimpanzè** (m)	[ʃimpan'dze]
orangutan	**orango** (m)	[o'rango]
gorilla	**gorilla** (m)	[go'rilla]
macaque	**macaco** (m)	[ma'kako]
gibbon	**gibbone** (m)	[dʒib'bone]
elephant	**elefante** (m)	[ele'fante]
rhinoceros	**rinoceronte** (m)	[rinotʃe'ronte]
giraffe	**giraffa** (f)	[dʒi'raffa]
hippopotamus	**ippopotamo** (m)	[ippo'potamo]
kangaroo	**canguro** (m)	[kan'guro]
koala (bear)	**koala** (m)	[ko'ala]
mongoose	**mangusta** (f)	[man'gusta]
chinchilla	**cincillà** (f)	[tʃintʃil'la]
skunk	**moffetta** (f)	[mof'fetta]
porcupine	**istrice** (m)	['istritʃe]

212. Domestic animals

cat	**gatta** (f)	['gatta]
tomcat	**gatto** (m)	['gatto]
dog	**cane** (m)	['kane]
horse	**cavallo** (m)	[ka'vallo]
stallion (male horse)	**stallone** (m)	[stal'lone]
mare	**giumenta** (f)	[dʒu'menta]
cow	**mucca** (f)	['mukka]
bull	**toro** (m)	['toro]
ox	**bue** (m)	['bue]
sheep (ewe)	**pecora** (f)	['pekora]
ram	**montone** (m)	[mon'tone]
goat	**capra** (f)	['kapra]
billy goat, he-goat	**caprone** (m)	[kap'rone]
donkey	**asino** (m)	['azino]
mule	**mulo** (m)	['mulo]
pig, hog	**porco** (m)	['porko]
piglet	**porcellino** (m)	[portʃel'lino]
rabbit	**coniglio** (m)	[ko'niʎʎo]
hen (chicken)	**gallina** (f)	[gal'lina]
rooster	**gallo** (m)	['gallo]
duck	**anatra** (f)	['anatra]
drake	**maschio** (m) **dell'anatra**	['maskio dell 'anatra]
goose	**oca** (f)	['oka]
tom turkey, gobbler	**tacchino** (m)	[tak'kino]
turkey (hen)	**tacchina** (f)	[tak'kina]
domestic animals	**animali** (m pl) **domestici**	[ani'mali do'mestitʃi]
tame (e.g., ~ hamster)	**addomesticato**	[addomesti'kato]
to tame (vt)	**addomesticare** (vt)	[addomesti'kare]
to breed (vt)	**allevare** (vt)	[alle'vare]
farm	**fattoria** (f)	[fatto'ria]
poultry	**pollame** (m)	[pol'lame]
cattle	**bestiame** (m)	[bes'tjame]
herd (cattle)	**branco** (m), **mandria** (f)	['branko], ['mandria]
stable	**scuderia** (f)	[skude'ria]
pigpen	**porcile** (m)	[por'tʃile]
cowshed	**stalla** (f)	['stalla]
rabbit hutch	**conigliera** (f)	[koniʎ'ʎera]
hen house	**pollaio** (m)	[pol'lajo]

213. Dogs. Dog breeds

dog	**cane** (m)	['kane]
sheepdog	**cane** (m) **da pastore**	['kane da pas'tore]
German shepherd	**battaglia** (f)	[bat'taʎʎa]
poodle	**barbone** (m)	[bar'bone]
dachshund	**bassotto** (m)	[bas'sotto]
bulldog	**bulldog** (m)	[bull'dog]
boxer	**boxer** (m)	['bokser]
mastiff	**mastino** (m)	[ma'stino]
Rottweiler	**rottweiler** (m)	[rot'vajler]
Doberman	**dobermann** (m)	[dober'mann]
basset	**bassotto** (m)	[bas'sotto]
bobtail	**bobtail** (m)	['bobtejl]
Dalmatian	**dalmata** (m)	['dalmata]
cocker spaniel	**cocker** (m)	['kokker]
Newfoundland	**terranova** (m)	[terra'nova]
Saint Bernard	**sanbernardo** (m)	[sanber'nardo]
husky	**husky** (m)	['aski]
Chow Chow	**chow chow** (m)	['ʧau 'ʧau]
spitz	**volpino** (m)	[vol'pino]
pug	**carlino** (m)	[kar'lino]

214. Sounds made by animals

barking (n)	**abbaiamento** (m)	[abaja'mento]
to bark (vi)	**abbaiare** (vi)	[abba'jare]
to meow (vi)	**miagolare** (vi)	[mjago'lare]
to purr (vi)	**fare le fusa**	['fare le 'fuza]
to moo (vi)	**muggire** (vi)	[mu'ʤire]
to bellow (bull)	**muggire** (vi)	[mu'ʤire]
to growl (vi)	**ringhiare** (vi)	[rin'gjare]
howl (n)	**ululato** (m)	[ulu'lato]
to howl (vi)	**ululare** (vi)	[ulu'lare]
to whine (vi)	**guaire** (vi)	[gwa'ire]
to bleat (sheep)	**belare** (vi)	[be'lare]
to oink, to grunt (pig)	**grugnire** (vi)	[gru'ɲıre]
to squeal (vi)	**squittire** (vi)	[skwit'tire]
to croak (vi)	**gracidare** (vi)	[graʧi'dare]
to buzz (insect)	**ronzare** (vi)	[ron'ʣare]
to chirp (crickets, grasshopper)	**frinire** (vi)	[fri'nire]

215. Young animals

cub	**cucciolo** (m)	['kuʧolo]
kitten	**micino** (m)	[mi'ʧino]
baby mouse	**topolino** (m)	[topo'lino]
puppy	**cucciolo** (m) **di cane**	['kuʧolo di 'kane]
leveret	**leprotto** (m)	[le'protto]
baby rabbit	**coniglietto** (m)	[koniʎ'ʎetto]
wolf cub	**cucciolo** (m) **di lupo**	['kuʧolo di 'lupo]
fox cub	**cucciolo** (m) **di volpe**	['kuʧolo di 'volpe]
bear cub	**cucciolo** (m) **di orso**	['kuʧolo di 'orso]
lion cub	**cucciolo** (m) **di leone**	['kuʧolo di le'one]
tiger cub	**cucciolo** (m) **di tigre**	[ku'ʧolo di 'tigre]
elephant calf	**elefantino** (m)	[elefan'tino]
piglet	**porcellino** (m)	[porʧel'lino]
calf (young cow, bull)	**vitello** (m)	[vi'tello]
kid (young goat)	**capretto** (m)	[ka'pretto]
lamb	**agnello** (m)	[a'ɲello]
fawn (young deer)	**cerbiatto** (m)	[ʧer'bjatto]
young camel	**cucciolo** (m) **di cammello**	['kuʧolo di kam'mello]
snakelet (baby snake)	**piccolo** (m) **di serpente**	['pikkolo di ser'pente]
froglet (baby frog)	**piccolo** (m) **di rana**	['pikkolo di 'rana]
baby bird	**uccellino** (m)	[uʧel'lino]
chick (of chicken)	**pulcino** (m)	[pul'ʧino]
duckling	**anatroccolo** (m)	[ana'trokkolo]

216. Birds

bird	**uccello** (m)	[u'ʧello]
pigeon	**colombo** (m), **piccione** (m)	[kolombo], [pi'ʧone]
sparrow	**passero** (m)	['passero]
tit (great tit)	**cincia** (f)	['ʧinʧa]
magpie	**gazza** (f)	['gattsa]
raven	**corvo** (m)	['korvo]
crow	**cornacchia** (f)	[kor'nakkia]
jackdaw	**taccola** (f)	['takkola]
rook	**corvo** (m) **nero**	['korvo 'nero]
duck	**anatra** (f)	['anatra]
goose	**oca** (f)	['oka]
pheasant	**fagiano** (m)	[fa'ʤano]
eagle	**aquila** (f)	['akwila]

hawk	**astore** (m)	[a'store]
falcon	**falco** (m)	['falko]
vulture	**grifone** (m)	[gri'fone]
condor (Andean ~)	**condor** (m)	['kondor]
swan	**cigno** (m)	['ʧiɲo]
crane	**gru** (f)	[gru]
stork	**cicogna** (f)	[ʧi'koɲa]
parrot	**pappagallo** (m)	[pappa'gallo]
hummingbird	**colibrì** (m)	[koli'bri]
peacock	**pavone** (m)	[pa'vone]
ostrich	**struzzo** (m)	['struttso]
heron	**airone** (m)	[ai'rone]
flamingo	**fenicottero** (m)	[feni'kottero]
pelican	**pellicano** (m)	[pelli'kano]
nightingale	**usignolo** (m)	[uzi'ɲolo]
swallow	**rondine** (f)	['rondine]
thrush	**tordo** (m)	['tordo]
song thrush	**tordo** (m) **sasello**	['tordo sa'zello]
blackbird	**merlo** (m)	['merlo]
swift	**rondone** (m)	[ron'done]
lark	**allodola** (f)	[al'lodola]
quail	**quaglia** (f)	['kwaʎʎa]
woodpecker	**picchio** (m)	['pikkio]
cuckoo	**cuculo** (m)	['kukulo]
owl	**civetta** (f)	[ʧi'vetta]
eagle owl	**gufo** (m) **reale**	['gufo re'ale]
wood grouse	**urogallo** (m)	[uro'gallo]
black grouse	**fagiano** (m) **di monte**	[fa'ʤano di 'monte]
partridge	**pernice** (f)	[per'niʧe]
starling	**storno** (m)	['storno]
canary	**canarino** (m)	[kana'rino]
hazel grouse	**francolino** (m) **di monte**	[franko'lino di 'monte]
chaffinch	**fringuello** (m)	[frin'gwello]
bullfinch	**ciuffolotto** (m)	[ʧuffo'lotto]
seagull	**gabbiano** (m)	[gab'bjano]
albatross	**albatro** (m)	['albatro]
penguin	**pinguino** (m)	[pin'gwino]

217. Birds. Singing and sounds

to sing (vi)	**cantare** (vi)	[kan'tare]
to call (animal, bird)	**gridare** (vi)	[gri'dare]

to crow (rooster)	**cantare, chicchiriare**	[kan'tare], [kikki'rjare]
cock-a-doodle-doo	**chicchirichì** (m)	[kikkiri'ki]
to cluck (hen)	**chiocciare** (vi)	[kio'ʧare]
to caw (crow call)	**gracchiare** (vi)	[grak'kjare]
to quack (duck call)	**fare qua qua**	['fare kwa kwa]
to cheep (vi)	**pigolare** (vi)	[pigo'lare]
to chirp, to twitter	**cinguettare** (vi)	[ʧingwet'tare]

218. Fish. Marine animals

bream	**abramide** (f)	[a'bramide]
carp	**carpa** (f)	['karpa]
perch	**perca** (f)	['perka]
catfish	**pesce** (m) **gatto**	['peʃe 'gatto]
pike	**luccio** (m)	['luʧo]
salmon	**salmone** (m)	[sal'mone]
sturgeon	**storione** (m)	[sto'rjone]
herring	**aringa** (f)	[a'ringa]
Atlantic salmon	**salmone** (m)	[sal'mone]
mackerel	**scombro** (m)	['skombro]
flatfish	**sogliola** (f)	['soʎʎoʎa]
zander, pike perch	**lucioperca** (f)	[luʧo'perka]
cod	**merluzzo** (m)	[mer'luttso]
tuna	**tonno** (m)	['tonno]
trout	**trota** (f)	['trota]
eel	**anguilla** (f)	[an'gwilla]
electric ray	**torpedine** (f)	[tor'pedine]
moray eel	**murena** (f)	[mu'rena]
piranha	**piranha, piragna** (f)	[pi'rania]
shark	**squalo** (m)	['skwalo]
dolphin	**delfino** (m)	[del'fino]
whale	**balena** (f)	[ba'lena]
crab	**granchio** (m)	['graŋkio]
jellyfish	**medusa** (f)	[me'duza]
octopus	**polpo** (m)	['polpo]
starfish	**stella** (f) **marina**	['stella ma'rina]
sea urchin	**riccio** (m) **di mare**	['riʧo di 'mare]
seahorse	**cavalluccio** (m) **marino**	[kaval'luʧo ma'rino]
oyster	**ostrica** (f)	['ostrika]
shrimp	**gamberetto** (m)	[gambe'retto]
lobster	**astice** (m)	['astiʧe]
spiny lobster	**aragosta** (f)	[ara'gosta]

219. Amphibians. Reptiles

snake	**serpente** (m)	[ser'pente]
venomous (snake)	**velenoso**	[vele'nozo]
viper	**vipera** (f)	['vipera]
cobra	**cobra** (m)	['kobra]
python	**pitone** (m)	[pi'tone]
boa	**boa** (m)	['boa]
grass snake	**biscia** (f)	['biʃa]
rattle snake	**serpente** (m) **a sonagli**	[ser'pente a so'naʎʎi]
anaconda	**anaconda** (f)	[ana'konda]
lizard	**lucertola** (f)	[lu'ʧertola]
iguana	**iguana** (f)	[i'gwana]
monitor lizard	**varano** (m)	[va'rano]
salamander	**salamandra** (f)	[sala'mandra]
chameleon	**camaleonte** (m)	[kamale'onte]
scorpion	**scorpione** (m)	[skor'pjone]
turtle	**tartaruga** (f)	[tarta'ruga]
frog	**rana** (f)	['rana]
toad	**rospo** (m)	['rospo]
crocodile	**coccodrillo** (m)	[kokko'drillo]

220. Insects

insect, bug	**insetto** (m)	[in'setto]
butterfly	**farfalla** (f)	[far'falla]
ant	**formica** (f)	[for'mika]
fly	**mosca** (f)	['moska]
mosquito	**zanzara** (f)	[ʣan'ʣara]
beetle	**scarabeo** (m)	[skara'beo]
wasp	**vespa** (f)	['vespa]
bee	**ape** (f)	['ape]
bumblebee	**bombo** (m)	['bombo]
gadfly (botfly)	**tafano** (m)	[ta'fano]
spider	**ragno** (m)	['raɲo]
spiderweb	**ragnatela** (f)	[raɲa'tela]
dragonfly	**libellula** (f)	[li'bellula]
grasshopper	**cavalletta** (f)	[kaval'letta]
moth (night butterfly)	**farfalla** (f) **notturna**	[far'falla not'turna]
cockroach	**scarafaggio** (m)	[skara'faʤo]
tick	**zecca** (f)	['tsekka]

flea	**pulce** (f)	['pultʃe]
midge	**moscerino** (m)	[moʃe'rino]
locust	**locusta** (f)	[lo'kusta]
snail	**lumaca** (f)	[lu'maka]
cricket	**grillo** (m)	['grillo]
lightning bug	**lucciola** (f)	['lutʃola]
ladybug	**coccinella** (f)	[kotʃi'nella]
cockchafer	**maggiolino** (m)	[madʒo'lino]
leech	**sanguisuga** (f)	[sangwi'zuga]
caterpillar	**bruco** (m)	['bruko]
earthworm	**verme** (m)	['verme]
larva	**larva** (m)	['larva]

221. Animals. Body parts

beak	**becco** (m)	['bekko]
wings	**ali** (f pl)	['ali]
foot (of bird)	**zampa** (f)	['dzampa]
feathers (plumage)	**piumaggio** (m)	[pju'madʒo]
feather	**penna** (f), **piuma** (f)	['penna], ['pjuma]
crest	**cresta** (f)	['kresta]
gills	**branchia** (f)	['brankia]
spawn	**uova** (f pl)	[u'ova]
larva	**larva** (f)	['larva]
fin	**pinna** (f)	['pinna]
scales (of fish, reptile)	**squama** (f)	['skwama]
fang (canine)	**zanna** (f)	['tzanna]
paw (e.g., cat's ~)	**zampa** (f)	['dzampa]
muzzle (snout)	**muso** (m)	['muzo]
maw (mouth)	**bocca** (f)	['bokka]
tail	**coda** (f)	['koda]
whiskers	**baffi** (m pl)	['baffi]
hoof	**zoccolo** (m)	['dzokkolo]
horn	**corno** (m)	['korno]
carapace	**carapace** (f)	[kara'patʃe]
shell (of mollusk)	**conchiglia** (f)	[kon'kiʎʎa]
eggshell	**guscio** (m) **dell'uovo**	['guʃo dell u'ovo]
animal's hair (pelage)	**pelo** (m)	['pelo]
pelt (hide)	**pelle** (f)	['pelle]

222. Actions of animals

to fly (vi)	**volare** (vi)	[vo'lare]
to fly in circles	**volteggiare** (vi)	[volte'dʒare]
to fly away	**volare via**	[vo'lare 'via]
to flap (~ the wings)	**battere le ali**	['battere le 'ali]
to peck (vi)	**beccare** (vi)	[bek'kare]
to sit on eggs	**covare** (vt)	[ko'vare]
to hatch out (vi)	**sgusciare** (vi)	[zgu'ʃare]
to build a nest	**fare il nido**	['fare il 'nido]
to slither, to crawl	**strisciare** (vi)	[stri'ʃare]
to sting, to bite (insect)	**pungere** (vt)	['pundʒere]
to bite (ab. animal)	**mordere** (vt)	['mordere]
to sniff (vt)	**fiutare** (vt)	[fju'tare]
to bark (vi)	**abbaiare** (vi)	[abba'jare]
to hiss (snake)	**sibilare** (vi)	[sibi'lare]
to scare (vt)	**spaventare** (vt)	[spaven'tare]
to attack (vt)	**attaccare** (vt)	[attak'kare]
to gnaw (bone, etc.)	**rodere** (vt)	['rodere]
to scratch (with claws)	**graffiare** (vt)	[graf'fjare]
to hide (vi)	**nascondersi** (vr)	[na'skondersi]
to play (kittens, etc.)	**giocare** (vi)	[dʒo'kare]
to hunt (vi, vt)	**cacciare** (vt)	[ka'tʃare]
to hibernate (vi)	**ibernare** (vi)	[iber'nare]
to go extinct	**estinguersi** (vr)	[e'stinguersi]

223. Animals. Habitats

habitat	**ambiente** (m) **naturale**	[am'bjente natu'rale]
migration	**migrazione** (f)	[migra'tsjone]
mountain	**monte** (m), **montagna** (f)	['monte], [mon'taɲa]
reef	**scogliera** (f)	[skoʎ'ʎera]
cliff	**falesia** (f)	[fa'lezia]
forest	**foresta** (f)	[fo'resta]
jungle	**giungla** (f)	['dʒungla]
savanna	**savana** (f)	[sa'vana]
tundra	**tundra** (f)	['tundra]
steppe	**steppa** (f)	['steppa]
desert	**deserto** (m)	[de'zerto]
oasis	**oasi** (f)	['oazi]
sea	**mare** (m)	['mare]

lake	**lago** (m)	['lago]
ocean	**oceano** (m)	[o'tʃeano]
swamp (marshland)	**palude** (f)	[pa'lude]
freshwater (adj)	**di acqua dolce**	[di 'akwa 'doltʃe]
pond	**stagno** (m)	['staɲo]
river	**fiume** (m)	['fjume]
den (bear's ~)	**tana** (f)	['tana]
nest	**nido** (m)	['nido]
tree hollow	**cavità** (f)	[kavi'ta]
burrow (animal hole)	**tana** (f)	['tana]
anthill	**formicaio** (m)	[formi'kajo]

224. Animal care

zoo	**zoo** (m)	['dzoo]
nature preserve	**riserva** (f) **naturale**	[ri'zerva natu'rale]
breeder (cattery, kennel, etc.)	**allevatore** (m)	[alleva'tore]
open-air cage	**gabbia** (f) **all'aperto**	['gabbja all a'perto]
cage	**gabbia** (f)	['gabbia]
doghouse (kennel)	**canile** (m)	[ka'nile]
dovecot	**piccionaia** (f)	[pitʃo'naja]
aquarium (fish tank)	**acquario** (m)	[a'kwario]
dolphinarium	**delfinario** (m)	[delfi'nario]
to breed (animals)	**allevare** (vt)	[alle'vare]
brood, litter	**cucciolata** (f)	[kutʃio'lata]
to tame (vt)	**addomesticare** (vt)	[addomesti'kare]
to train (animals)	**ammaestrare** (vt)	[ammae'strare]
feed (fodder, etc.)	**mangime** (m)	[man'dʒime]
to feed (vt)	**dare da mangiare**	['dare da man'dʒare]
pet store	**negozio** (m) **di animali**	[ne'gotsio di ani'mali]
muzzle (for dog)	**museruola** (f)	[muzeru'ola]
collar (e.g., dog ~)	**collare** (m)	[kol'lare]
name (of animal)	**nome** (m)	['nome]
pedigree (of dog)	**pedigree** (m)	['pedigri]

225. Animals. Miscellaneous

pack (wolves)	**branco** (m)	['branko]
flock (birds)	**stormo** (m)	['stormo]
shoal, school (fish)	**banco** (m)	['banko]
herd (horses)	**mandria** (f)	['mandria]

male (n)	**maschio** (m)	['maskio]
female (n)	**femmina** (f)	['femmina]
hungry (adj)	**affamato**	[affa'mato]
wild (adj)	**selvatico**	[sel'vatiko]
dangerous (adj)	**pericoloso**	[periko'lozo]

226. Horses

horse	**cavallo** (m)	[ka'vallo]
breed (race)	**razza** (f)	['rattsa]
foal	**puledro** (m)	[pu'ledro]
mare	**giumenta** (f)	[dʒu'menta]
mustang	**mustang** (m)	['mustang]
pony	**pony** (m)	['poni]
draft horse	**cavallo** (m) **da tiro pesante**	[ka'vallo da 'tiro pe'zante]
mane	**criniera** (f)	[kri'njera]
tail	**coda** (f)	['koda]
hoof	**zoccolo** (m)	['dzokkolo]
horseshoe	**ferro** (m) **di cavallo**	['ferro di ka'vallo]
to shoe (vt)	**ferrare** (vt)	[fer'rare]
blacksmith	**fabbro** (m)	['fabbro]
saddle	**sella** (f)	['sella]
stirrup	**staffa** (f)	['staffa]
bridle	**briglia** (f)	['briʎʎa]
reins	**redini** (m pl)	['redini]
whip (for riding)	**frusta** (f)	['frusta]
rider	**fantino** (m)	[fan'tino]
to saddle up (vt)	**sellare** (vt)	[sel'lare]
to mount a horse	**montare in sella**	[mon'tare in 'sella]
gallop	**galoppo** (m)	[ga'loppo]
to gallop (vi)	**galoppare** (vi)	[galop'pare]
trot (n)	**trotto** (m)	['trotto]
at a trot (adv)	**al trotto**	[al 'trotto]
to go at a trot	**andare al trotto**	[an'dare al 'trotto]
racehorse	**cavallo** (m) **da corsa**	[ka'vallo da 'korsa]
horse racing	**corse** (f pl)	['korse]
stable	**scuderia** (f)	[skude'ria]
to feed (vt)	**dare da mangiare**	['dare da man'dʒare]
hay	**fieno** (m)	['fjeno]

to water (animals)	**abbeverare** (vt)	[abbeve'rare]
to wash (horse)	**lavare** (vt)	[la'vare]
horse-drawn cart	**carro** (m)	['karro]
to graze (vi)	**pascolare** (vi)	[pasko'lare]
to neigh (vi)	**nitrire** (vi)	[ni'trire]
to kick (to buck)	**dare un calcio**	['dare un 'kaltʃo]

Flora

227. Trees

tree	**albero** (m)	['albero]
deciduous (adj)	**deciduo**	[de'tʃiduo]
coniferous (adj)	**conifero**	[ko'nifero]
evergreen (adj)	**sempreverde**	[sempre'verde]
apple tree	**melo** (m)	['melo]
pear tree	**pero** (m)	['pero]
sweet cherry tree	**ciliegio** (m)	[tʃi'ljedʒo]
sour cherry tree	**amareno** (m)	[ama'reno]
plum tree	**prugno** (m)	['pruɲo]
birch	**betulla** (f)	[be'tulla]
oak	**quercia** (f)	['kwertʃa]
linden tree	**tiglio** (m)	['tiʎʎo]
aspen	**pioppo** (m) **tremolo**	['pjoppo 'tremolo]
maple	**acero** (m)	['atʃero]
spruce	**abete** (m)	[a'bete]
pine	**pino** (m)	['pino]
larch	**larice** (m)	['laritʃe]
fir tree	**abete** (m) **bianco**	[a'bete 'bjanko]
cedar	**cedro** (m)	['tʃedro]
poplar	**pioppo** (m)	['pjoppo]
rowan	**sorbo** (m)	['sorbo]
willow	**salice** (m)	['salitʃe]
alder	**alno** (m)	['alno]
beech	**faggio** (m)	['fadʒo]
elm	**olmo** (m)	['olmo]
ash (tree)	**frassino** (m)	['frassino]
chestnut	**castagno** (m)	[ka'staɲo]
magnolia	**magnolia** (f)	[ma'ɲolia]
palm tree	**palma** (f)	['palma]
cypress	**cipresso** (m)	[tʃi'presso]
mangrove	**mangrovia** (f)	[man'growia]
baobab	**baobab** (m)	[bao'bab]
eucalyptus	**eucalipto** (m)	[ewka'lipto]
sequoia	**sequoia** (f)	[se'kwoja]

228. Shrubs

bush	**cespuglio** (m)	[tʃes'puʎʎo]
shrub	**arbusto** (m)	[ar'busto]
grapevine	**vite** (f)	['vite]
vineyard	**vigneto** (m)	[vi'ɲeto]
raspberry bush	**lampone** (m)	[lam'pone]
redcurrant bush	**ribes** (m) **rosso**	['ribes 'rosso]
gooseberry bush	**uva** (f) **spina**	['uva 'spina]
acacia	**acacia** (f)	[a'katʃa]
barberry	**crespino** (m)	[kres'pino]
jasmine	**gelsomino** (m)	[dʒelso'mino]
juniper	**ginepro** (m)	[dʒi'nepro]
rosebush	**roseto** (m)	[ro'zeto]
dog rose	**rosa** (f) **canina**	['roza ka'nina]

229. Mushrooms

mushroom	**fungo** (m)	['fungo]
edible mushroom	**fungo** (m) **commestibile**	['fungo komme'stibile]
poisonous mushroom	**fungo** (m) **velenoso**	['fungo vele'nozo]
cap (of mushroom)	**cappello** (m)	[kap'pello]
stipe (of mushroom)	**gambo** (m)	['gambo]
cep (Boletus edulis)	**porcino** (m)	[por'tʃino]
orange-cap boletus	**boleto** (m) **rufo**	[bo'leto 'rufo]
birch bolete	**porcinello** (m)	[portʃi'nello]
chanterelle	**gallinaccio** (m)	[galli'natʃo]
russula	**rossola** (f)	['rossola]
morel	**spugnola** (f)	['spuɲola]
fly agaric	**ovolaccio** (m)	[ovo'latʃo]
death cap	**fungo** (m) **moscario**	['fungo mos'kario]

230. Fruits. Berries

fruit	**frutto** (m)	['frutto]
fruits	**frutti** (m pl)	['frutti]
apple	**mela** (f)	['mela]
pear	**pera** (f)	['pera]
plum	**prugna** (f)	['pruɲa]
strawberry (garden ~)	**fragola** (f)	['fragola]
sour cherry	**amarena** (f)	[ama'rena]

sweet cherry	**ciliegia** (f)	[tʃi'ljedʒa]
grape	**uva** (f)	['uva]
raspberry	**lampone** (m)	[lam'pone]
blackcurrant	**ribes** (m) **nero**	['ribes 'nero]
redcurrant	**ribes** (m) **rosso**	['ribes 'rosso]
gooseberry	**uva** (f) **spina**	['uva 'spina]
cranberry	**mirtillo** (m) **di palude**	[mir'tillo di pa'lude]
orange	**arancia** (f)	[a'rantʃa]
mandarin	**mandarino** (m)	[manda'rino]
pineapple	**ananas** (m)	[ana'nas]
banana	**banana** (f)	[ba'nana]
date	**dattero** (m)	['dattero]
lemon	**limone** (m)	[li'mone]
apricot	**albicocca** (f)	[albi'kokka]
peach	**pesca** (f)	['peska]
kiwi	**kiwi** (m)	['kiwi]
grapefruit	**pompelmo** (m)	[pom'pelmo]
berry	**bacca** (f)	['bakka]
berries	**bacche** (f pl)	['bakke]
cowberry	**mirtillo** (m) **rosso**	[mir'tillo 'rosso]
wild strawberry	**fragola** (f) **di bosco**	['fragola di 'bosko]
bilberry	**mirtillo** (m)	[mir'tillo]

231. Flowers. Plants

flower	**fiore** (m)	['fjore]
bouquet (of flowers)	**mazzo** (m) **di fiori**	['mattso di 'fjori]
rose (flower)	**rosa** (f)	['roza]
tulip	**tulipano** (m)	[tuli'pano]
carnation	**garofano** (m)	[ga'rofano]
gladiolus	**gladiolo** (m)	[gla'djolo]
cornflower	**fiordaliso** (m)	[fjorda'lizo]
harebell	**campanella** (f)	[kampa'nella]
dandelion	**soffione** (m)	[sof'fjone]
camomile	**camomilla** (f)	[kamo'milla]
aloe	**aloe** (m)	['aloe]
cactus	**cactus** (m)	['kaktus]
rubber plant, ficus	**ficus** (m)	['fikus]
lily	**giglio** (m)	['dʒiʎʎo]
geranium	**geranio** (m)	[dʒe'ranio]
hyacinth	**giacinto** (m)	[dʒa'tʃinto]
mimosa	**mimosa** (f)	[mi'moza]

narcissus	**narciso** (m)	[nar'ʧizo]
nasturtium	**nasturzio** (m)	[na'sturtsio]
orchid	**orchidea** (f)	[orki'dea]
peony	**peonia** (f)	[pe'onia]
violet	**viola** (f)	[vi'ola]
pansy	**viola** (f) **del pensiero**	[vi'ola del pen'sjero]
forget-me-not	**nontiscordardimè** (m)	[non·ti·skordar·di'me]
daisy	**margherita** (f)	[marge'rita]
poppy	**papavero** (m)	[pa'pavero]
hemp	**canapa** (f)	['kanapa]
mint	**menta** (f)	['menta]
lily of the valley	**mughetto** (m)	[mu'getto]
snowdrop	**bucaneve** (m)	[buka'neve]
nettle	**ortica** (f)	[or'tika]
sorrel	**acetosa** (f)	[aʧe'toza]
water lily	**ninfea** (f)	[nin'fea]
fern	**felce** (f)	['felʧe]
lichen	**lichene** (m)	[li'kene]
conservatory (greenhouse)	**serra** (f)	['serra]
lawn	**prato** (m) **erboso**	['prato er'bozo]
flowerbed	**aiuola** (f)	[aju'ola]
plant	**pianta** (f)	['pjanta]
grass	**erba** (f)	['erba]
blade of grass	**filo** (m) **d'erba**	['filo 'derba]
leaf	**foglia** (f)	['foʎʎa]
petal	**petalo** (m)	['petalo]
stem	**stelo** (m)	['stelo]
tuber	**tubero** (m)	['tubero]
young plant (shoot)	**germoglio** (m)	[ʤer'moʎʎo]
thorn	**spina** (f)	['spina]
to blossom (vi)	**fiorire** (vi)	[fjo'rire]
to fade, to wither	**appassire** (vi)	[appas'sire]
smell (odor)	**odore** (m), **profumo** (m)	[o'dore], [pro'fumo]
to cut (flowers)	**tagliare** (vt)	[taʎ'ʎare]
to pick (a flower)	**cogliere** (vt)	['koʎʎere]

232. Cereals, grains

grain	**grano** (m)	['grano]
cereal crops	**cereali** (m pl)	[ʧere'ali]

ear (of barley, etc.)	**spiga** (f)	['spiga]
wheat	**frumento** (m)	[fru'mento]
rye	**segale** (f)	['segale]
oats	**avena** (f)	[a'vena]
millet	**miglio** (m)	['miʎʎo]
barley	**orzo** (m)	['ortso]
corn	**mais** (m)	['mais]
rice	**riso** (m)	['rizo]
buckwheat	**grano** (m) **saraceno**	['grano sara'ʧeno]
pea plant	**pisello** (m)	[pi'zello]
kidney bean	**fagiolo** (m)	[fa'ʤolo]
soy	**soia** (f)	['soja]
lentil	**lenticchie** (f pl)	[len'tikkje]
beans (pulse crops)	**fave** (f pl)	['fave]

233. Vegetables. Greens

vegetables	**ortaggi** (m pl)	[or'taʤi]
greens	**verdura** (f)	[ver'dura]
tomato	**pomodoro** (m)	[pomo'doro]
cucumber	**cetriolo** (m)	[ʧetri'olo]
carrot	**carota** (f)	[ka'rota]
potato	**patata** (f)	[pa'tata]
onion	**cipolla** (f)	[ʧi'polla]
garlic	**aglio** (m)	['aʎʎo]
cabbage	**cavolo** (m)	['kavolo]
cauliflower	**cavolfiore** (m)	[kavol'fjore]
Brussels sprouts	**cavoletti** (m pl) **di Bruxelles**	[kavo'letti di bruk'sel]
broccoli	**broccolo** (m)	['brokkolo]
beet	**barbabietola** (f)	[barba'bjetola]
eggplant	**melanzana** (f)	[melan'tsana]
zucchini	**zucchina** (f)	[ʣuk'kina]
pumpkin	**zucca** (f)	['ʣukka]
turnip	**rapa** (f)	['rapa]
parsley	**prezzemolo** (m)	[pret'tsemolo]
dill	**aneto** (m)	[a'neto]
lettuce	**lattuga** (f)	[lat'tuga]
celery	**sedano** (m)	['sedano]
asparagus	**asparago** (m)	[a'sparago]
spinach	**spinaci** (m pl)	[spi'naʧi]
pea	**pisello** (m)	[pi'zello]
beans	**fave** (f pl)	['fave]

corn (maize)	**mais** (m)	['mais]
kidney bean	**fagiolo** (m)	[fa'dʒolo]
pepper	**peperone** (m)	[pepe'rone]
radish	**ravanello** (m)	[rava'nello]
artichoke	**carciofo** (m)	[kar'tʃofo]

REGIONAL GEOGRAPHY

Countries. Nationalities

234. Western Europe

Europe	**Europa** (f)	[eu'ropa]
European Union	**Unione** (f) **Europea**	[uni'one euro'pea]
European (n)	**europeo** (m)	[euro'peo]
European (adj)	**europeo**	[euro'peo]
Austria	**Austria** (f)	['austria]
Austrian (masc.)	**austriaco** (m)	[au'striako]
Austrian (fem.)	**austriaca** (f)	[au'striaka]
Austrian (adj)	**austriaco**	[au'striako]
Great Britain	**Gran Bretagna** (f)	[gran bre'taɲa]
England	**Inghilterra** (f)	[ingil'terra]
British (masc.)	**britannico** (m), **inglese** (m)	[bri'taniko], [in'gleze]
British (fem.)	**britannica** (f), **inglese** (f)	[bri'tanika], [in'gleze]
English, British (adj)	**inglese**	[in'gleze]
Belgium	**Belgio** (m)	['beldʒo]
Belgian (masc.)	**belga** (m)	['belga]
Belgian (fem.)	**belga** (f)	['belga]
Belgian (adj)	**belga** (agg)	['belga]
Germany	**Germania** (f)	[dʒer'mania]
German (masc.)	**tedesco** (m)	[te'desko]
German (fem.)	**tedesca** (f)	[te'deska]
German (adj)	**tedesco** (agg)	[te'desko]
Netherlands	**Paesi Bassi** (m pl)	[pa'ezi 'bassi]
Holland	**Olanda** (f)	[o'landa]
Dutch (masc.)	**olandese** (m)	[olan'deze]
Dutch (fem.)	**olandese** (f)	[olan'deze]
Dutch (adj)	**olandese** (agg)	[olan'deze]
Greece	**Grecia** (f)	['gretʃa]
Greek (masc.)	**greco** (m)	['greko]
Greek (fem.)	**greca** (f)	['greka]
Greek (adj)	**greco** (agg)	['greko]
Denmark	**Danimarca** (f)	[dani'marka]
Dane (masc.)	**danese** (m)	[da'neze]

Dane (fem.)	**danese** (f)	[da'neze]
Danish (adj)	**danese** (agg)	[da'neze]
Ireland	**Irlanda** (f)	[ir'landa]
Irish (masc.)	**irlandese** (m)	[irlan'deze]
Irish (fem.)	**irlandese** (f)	[irlan'deze]
Irish (adj)	**irlandese** (agg)	[irlan'deze]
Iceland	**Islanda** (f)	[iz'landa]
Icelander (masc.)	**islandese** (m)	[izlan'deze]
Icelander (fem.)	**islandese** (f)	[izlan'deze]
Icelandic (adj)	**islandese** (agg)	[izlan'deze]
Spain	**Spagna** (f)	['spaɲa]
Spaniard (masc.)	**spagnolo** (m)	[spa'ɲolo]
Spaniard (fem.)	**spagnola** (f)	[spa'ɲola]
Spanish (adj)	**spagnolo** (agg)	[spa'ɲolo]
Italy	**Italia** (f)	[i'talia]
Italian (masc.)	**italiano** (m)	[ita'ljano]
Italian (fem.)	**italiana** (f)	[ita'ljana]
Italian (adj)	**italiano** (agg)	[ita'ljano]
Cyprus	**Cipro** (m)	['ʧipro]
Cypriot (masc.)	**cipriota** (m)	[ʧipri'ota]
Cypriot (fem.)	**cipriota** (f)	[ʧipri'ota]
Cypriot (adj)	**cipriota** (agg)	[ʧipri'ota]
Malta	**Malta** (f)	['malta]
Maltese (masc.)	**maltese** (m)	[mal'teze]
Maltese (fem.)	**maltese** (f)	[mal'teze]
Maltese (adj)	**maltese** (agg)	[mal'teze]
Norway	**Norvegia** (f)	[nor'veʤa]
Norwegian (masc.)	**norvegese** (m)	[norve'ʤeze]
Norwegian (fem.)	**norvegese** (f)	[norve'ʤeze]
Norwegian (adj)	**norvegese** (agg)	[norve'ʤeze]
Portugal	**Portogallo** (f)	[porto'gallo]
Portuguese (masc.)	**portoghese** (m)	[porto'geze]
Portuguese (fem.)	**portoghese** (f)	[porto'geze]
Portuguese (adj)	**portoghese** (agg)	[porto'geze]
Finland	**Finlandia** (f)	[fin'landia]
Finn (masc.)	**finlandese** (m)	[finlan'deze]
Finn (fem.)	**finlandese** (f)	[finlan'deze]
Finnish (adj)	**finlandese** (agg)	[finlan'deze]
France	**Francia** (f)	['franʧa]
French (masc.)	**francese** (m)	[fran'ʧeze]
French (fem.)	**francese** (f)	[fran'ʧeze]
French (adj)	**francese** (agg)	[fran'ʧeze]

Sweden	**Svezia** (f)	['zvetsia]
Swede (masc.)	**svedese** (m)	[zve'deze]
Swede (fem.)	**svedese** (f)	[zve'deze]
Swedish (adj)	**svedese** (agg)	[zve'deze]
Switzerland	**Svizzera** (f)	['zvittsera]
Swiss (masc.)	**svizzero** (m)	['zvittsero]
Swiss (fem.)	**svizzera** (f)	['zvittsera]
Swiss (adj)	**svizzero** (agg)	['zvittsero]
Scotland	**Scozia** (f)	['skotsia]
Scottish (masc.)	**scozzese** (m)	[skot'tseze]
Scottish (fem.)	**scozzese** (f)	[skot'tseze]
Scottish (adj)	**scozzese** (agg)	[skot'tseze]
Vatican	**Vaticano** (m)	[vati'kano]
Liechtenstein	**Liechtenstein** (m)	['liktenstajn]
Luxembourg	**Lussemburgo** (m)	[lussem'burgo]
Monaco	**Monaco** (m)	['monako]

235. Central and Eastern Europe

Albania	**Albania** (f)	[alba'nia]
Albanian (masc.)	**albanese** (m)	[alba'neze]
Albanian (fem.)	**albanese** (f)	[alba'neze]
Albanian (adj)	**albanese** (agg)	[alba'neze]
Bulgaria	**Bulgaria** (f)	[bulga'ria]
Bulgarian (masc.)	**bulgaro** (m)	['bulgaro]
Bulgarian (fem.)	**bulgara** (f)	['bulgara]
Bulgarian (adj)	**bulgaro** (agg)	['bulgaro]
Hungary	**Ungheria** (f)	[unge'ria]
Hungarian (masc.)	**ungherese** (m)	[unge'reze]
Hungarian (fem.)	**ungherese** (f)	[unge'reze]
Hungarian (adj)	**ungherese** (agg)	[unge'reze]
Latvia	**Lettonia** (f)	[let'tonia]
Latvian (masc.)	**lettone** (m)	['lettone]
Latvian (fem.)	**lettone** (f)	['lettone]
Latvian (adj)	**lettone** (agg)	['lettone]
Lithuania	**Lituania** (f)	[litu'ania]
Lithuanian (masc.)	**lituano** (m)	[litu'ano]
Lithuanian (fem.)	**lituana** (f)	[litu'ana]
Lithuanian (adj)	**lituano** (agg)	[litu'ano]
Poland	**Polonia** (f)	[po'lonia]
Pole (masc.)	**polacco** (m)	[po'lakko]
Pole (fem.)	**polacca** (f)	[po'lakka]

Polish (adj)	**polacco** (agg)	[po'lakko]
Romania	**Romania** (f)	[roma'nia]
Romanian (masc.)	**rumeno** (m)	[ru'meno]
Romanian (fem.)	**rumena** (f)	[ru'mena]
Romanian (adj)	**rumeno** (agg)	[ru'meno]
Serbia	**Serbia** (f)	['serbia]
Serbian (masc.)	**serbo** (m)	['serbo]
Serbian (fem.)	**serba** (f)	['serba]
Serbian (adj)	**serbo** (agg)	['serbo]
Slovakia	**Slovacchia** (f)	[zlo'vakkia]
Slovak (masc.)	**slovacco** (m)	[zlo'vakko]
Slovak (fem.)	**slovacca** (f)	[zlo'vakka]
Slovak (adj)	**slovacco** (agg)	[zlo'vakko]
Croatia	**Croazia** (f)	[kro'atsia]
Croatian (masc.)	**croato** (m)	[kro'ato]
Croatian (fem.)	**croata** (f)	[kro'ata]
Croatian (adj)	**croato** (agg)	[kro'ato]
Czech Republic	**Repubblica** (f) **Ceca**	[re'pubblika 'ʧeka]
Czech (masc.)	**ceco** (m)	['ʧeko]
Czech (fem.)	**ceca** (f)	['ʧeka]
Czech (adj)	**ceco** (agg)	['ʧeko]
Estonia	**Estonia** (f)	[es'tonia]
Estonian (masc.)	**estone** (m)	['estone]
Estonian (fem.)	**estone** (f)	['estone]
Estonian (adj)	**estone** (agg)	['estone]
Bosnia and Herzegovina	**Bosnia-Erzegovina** (f)	['boznia-ertse'govina]
Macedonia (Republic of ~)	**Macedonia** (f)	[maʧe'donia]
Slovenia	**Slovenia** (f)	[zlo'venia]
Montenegro	**Montenegro** (m)	[monte'negro]

236. Former USSR countries

Azerbaijan	**Azerbaigian** (m)	[azerbaj'ʤan]
Azerbaijani (masc.)	**azerbaigiano** (m)	[azerbaj'ʤano]
Azerbaijani (fem.)	**azerbaigiana** (f)	[azerbaj'ʤana]
Azerbaijani, Azeri (adj)	**azerbaigiano** (agg)	[azerbaj'ʤano]
Armenia	**Armenia** (f)	[ar'menia]
Armenian (masc.)	**armeno** (m)	[ar'meno]
Armenian (fem.)	**armena** (f)	[ar'mena]
Armenian (adj)	**armeno** (agg)	[ar'meno]
Belarus	**Bielorussia** (f)	[bjelo'russia]
Belarusian (masc.)	**bielorusso** (m)	[bjelo'russo]

Belarusian (fem.)	**bielorussa** (f)	[bjelo'russa]
Belarusian (adj)	**bielorusso** (agg)	[bjelo'russo]
Georgia	**Georgia** (f)	[ʤe'orʤa]
Georgian (masc.)	**georgiano** (m)	[ʤeor'ʤano]
Georgian (fem.)	**georgiana** (f)	[ʤeor'ʤana]
Georgian (adj)	**georgiano** (agg)	[ʤeor'ʤano]
Kazakhstan	**Kazakistan** (m)	[ka'zakistan]
Kazakh (masc.)	**kazaco** (m)	[ka'zako]
Kazakh (fem.)	**kazaca** (f)	[ka'zaka]
Kazakh (adj)	**kazaco** (agg)	[ka'zako]
Kirghizia	**Kirghizistan** (m)	[kir'gizistan]
Kirghiz (masc.)	**kirghiso** (m)	[kir'gizo]
Kirghiz (fem.)	**kirghisa** (f)	[kir'giza]
Kirghiz (adj)	**kirghiso** (agg)	[kir'gizo]
Moldova, Moldavia	**Moldavia** (f)	[mol'davia]
Moldavian (masc.)	**moldavo** (m)	[mol'davo]
Moldavian (fem.)	**moldava** (f)	[mol'dava]
Moldavian (adj)	**moldavo** (agg)	[mol'davo]
Russia	**Russia** (f)	['russia]
Russian (masc.)	**russo** (m)	['russo]
Russian (fem.)	**russa** (f)	['russa]
Russian (adj)	**russo** (agg)	['russo]
Tajikistan	**Tagikistan** (m)	[ta'ʤikistan]
Tajik (masc.)	**tagico** (m)	['taʤiko]
Tajik (fem.)	**tagica** (f)	['taʤika]
Tajik (adj)	**tagico** (agg)	['taʤiko]
Turkmenistan	**Turkmenistan** (m)	[turk'menistan]
Turkmen (masc.)	**turkmeno** (m)	[turk'meno]
Turkmen (fem.)	**turkmena** (f)	[turk'mena]
Turkmenian (adj)	**turkmeno** (agg)	[turk'meno]
Uzbekistan	**Uzbekistan** (m)	[uz'bekistan]
Uzbek (masc.)	**usbeco** (m)	[uz'beko]
Uzbek (fem.)	**usbeca** (f)	[uz'beka]
Uzbek (adj)	**usbeco** (agg)	[uz'beko]
Ukraine	**Ucraina** (f)	[uk'raina]
Ukrainian (masc.)	**ucraino** (m)	[u'kraino]
Ukrainian (fem.)	**ucraina** (f)	[uk'raina]
Ukrainian (adj)	**ucraino** (agg)	[u'kraino]

237. Asia

Asia	**Asia** (f)	['azia]
Asian (adj)	**asiatico** (agg)	[azi'atiko]

Vietnam	**Vietnam** (m)	['vjetnam]
Vietnamese (masc.)	**vietnamita** (m)	[vjetna'mita]
Vietnamese (fem.)	**vietnamita** (f)	[vjetna'mita]
Vietnamese (adj)	**vietnamita** (agg)	[vjetna'mita]
India	**India** (f)	['india]
Indian (masc.)	**indiano** (m)	[indi'ano]
Indian (fem.)	**indiana** (f)	[indi'ana]
Indian (adj)	**indiano** (agg)	[indi'ano]
Israel	**Israele** (m)	[izra'ele]
Israeli (masc.)	**israeliano** (m)	[izrae'ljano]
Israeli (fem.)	**israeliana** (f)	[izrae'ljana]
Israeli (adj)	**israeliano** (agg)	[izraeljano]
Jew (n)	**ebreo** (m)	[e'breo]
Jewess (n)	**ebrea** (f)	[eb'rea]
Jewish (adj)	**ebraico** (agg)	[eb'raiko]
China	**Cina** (f)	['ʧina]
Chinese (masc.)	**cinese** (m)	[ʧi'neze]
Chinese (fem.)	**cinese** (f)	[ʧi'neze]
Chinese (adj)	**cinese** (agg)	[ʧi'neze]
Korean (masc.)	**coreano** (m)	[kore'ano]
Korean (fem.)	**coreana** (f)	[kore'ana]
Korean (adj)	**coreano** (agg)	[kore'ano]
Lebanon	**Libano** (m)	['libano]
Lebanese (masc.)	**libanese** (m)	[liba'neze]
Lebanese (fem.)	**libanese** (f)	[liba'neze]
Lebanese (adj)	**libanese** (agg)	[liba'neze]
Mongolia	**Mongolia** (f)	[mo'ngolia]
Mongolian (masc.)	**mongolo** (m)	['mongolo]
Mongolian (fem.)	**mongola** (f)	['mongola]
Mongolian (adj)	**mongolo** (agg)	['mongolo]
Malaysia	**Malesia** (f)	[ma'lezia]
Malaysian (masc.)	**malese** (m)	[ma'leze]
Malaysian (fem.)	**malese** (f)	[ma'leze]
Malaysian (adj)	**malese** (agg)	[ma'leze]
Pakistan	**Pakistan** (m)	['pakistan]
Pakistani (masc.)	**pakistano** (m)	[paki'stano]
Pakistani (fem.)	**pakistana** (f)	[paki'stana]
Pakistani (adj)	**pakistano** (agg)	[paki'stano]
Saudi Arabia	**Arabia Saudita** (f)	[a'rabia sau'dita]
Arab (masc.)	**arabo** (m), **saudita** (m)	['arabo], [sau'dita]
Arab (fem.)	**araba** (f)	['araba]
Arab, Arabic (adj)	**arabo** (agg)	['arabo]

Thailand	**Tailandia** (f)	[taj'landia]
Thai (masc.)	**tailandese** (m)	[tajlan'deze]
Thai (fem.)	**tailandese** (f)	[tajlan'deze]
Thai (adj)	**tailandese** (agg)	[tajlan'deze]
Taiwan	**Taiwan** (m)	[taj'van]
Taiwanese (masc.)	**taiwanese** (m)	[tajva'neze]
Taiwanese (fem.)	**taiwanese** (f)	[tajva'neze]
Taiwanese (adj)	**taiwanese** (agg)	[tajva'neze]
Turkey	**Turchia** (f)	[tur'kia]
Turk (masc.)	**turco** (m)	['turko]
Turk (fem.)	**turca** (f)	['turka]
Turkish (adj)	**turco** (agg)	['turko]
Japan	**Giappone** (m)	[ʤap'pone]
Japanese (masc.)	**giapponese** (m)	[ʤappo'neze]
Japanese (fem.)	**giapponese** (f)	[ʤappo'neze]
Japanese (adj)	**giapponese** (agg)	[ʤappo'neze]
Afghanistan	**Afghanistan** (m)	[af'ganistan]
Bangladesh	**Bangladesh** (m)	['bangladeʃ]
Indonesia	**Indonesia** (f)	[indo'nezia]
Jordan	**Giordania** (f)	[ʤor'dania]
Iraq	**Iraq** (m)	['irak]
Iran	**Iran** (m)	['iran]
Cambodia	**Cambogia** (f)	[kam'boʤa]
Kuwait	**Kuwait** (m)	[ku'vejt]
Laos	**Laos** (m)	['laos]
Myanmar	**Birmania** (f)	[bir'mania]
Nepal	**Nepal** (m)	[ne'pal]
United Arab Emirates	**Emirati** (m pl) **Arabi**	[emi'rati 'arabi]
Syria	**Siria** (f)	['siria]
Palestine	**Palestina** (f)	[pale'stina]
South Korea	**Corea** (f) **del Sud**	[ko'rea del sud]
North Korea	**Corea** (f) **del Nord**	[ko'rea del nord]

238. North America

United States of America	**Stati** (m pl) **Uniti d'America**	['stati u'niti da'merika]
American (masc.)	**americano** (m)	[ameri'kano]
American (fem.)	**americana** (f)	[ameri'kana]
American (adj)	**americano** (agg)	[ameri'kano]
Canada	**Canada** (m)	['kanada]
Canadian (masc.)	**canadese** (m)	[kana'deze]
Canadian (fem.)	**canadese** (f)	[kana'deze]

Canadian (adj)	**canadese** (agg)	[kana'deze]
Mexico	**Messico** (m)	['messiko]
Mexican (masc.)	**messicano** (m)	[messi'kano]
Mexican (fem.)	**messicana** (f)	[messi'kana]
Mexican (adj)	**messicano** (agg)	[messi'kano]

239. Central and South America

Argentina	**Argentina** (f)	[arʤen'tina]
Argentinian (masc.)	**argentino** (m)	[arʤen'tino]
Argentinian (fem.)	**argentina** (f)	[arʤen'tina]
Argentinian (adj)	**argentino** (agg)	[arʤen'tino]
Brazil	**Brasile** (m)	[bra'zile]
Brazilian (masc.)	**brasiliano** (m)	[brazi'ljano]
Brazilian (fem.)	**brasiliana** (f)	[brazi'ljana]
Brazilian (adj)	**brasiliano** (agg)	[brazi'ljano]
Colombia	**Colombia** (f)	[ko'lombia]
Colombian (masc.)	**colombiano** (m)	[kolom'bjano]
Colombian (fem.)	**colombiana** (f)	[kolom'bjana]
Colombian (adj)	**colombiano** (agg)	[kolom'bjano]
Cuba	**Cuba** (f)	['kuba]
Cuban (masc.)	**cubano** (m)	[ku'bano]
Cuban (fem.)	**cubana** (f)	[ku'bana]
Cuban (adj)	**cubano** (agg)	[ku'bano]
Chile	**Cile** (m)	['ʧile]
Chilean (masc.)	**cileno** (m)	[ʧi'leno]
Chilean (fem.)	**cilena** (f)	[ʧi'lena]
Chilean (adj)	**cileno** (agg)	[ʧi'leno]
Bolivia	**Bolivia** (f)	[bo'livia]
Venezuela	**Venezuela** (f)	[venetsu'ela]
Paraguay	**Paraguay** (m)	[para'gwaj]
Peru	**Perù** (m)	[pe'ru]
Suriname	**Suriname** (m)	[suri'name]
Uruguay	**Uruguay** (m)	[uru'gwaj]
Ecuador	**Ecuador** (m)	[ekva'dor]
The Bahamas	**le Bahamas**	[le ba'amas]
Haiti	**Haiti** (m)	[a'iti]
Dominican Republic	**Repubblica** (f) **Dominicana**	[re'pubblika domini'kana]
Panama	**Panama** (m)	['panama]
Jamaica	**Giamaica** (f)	[ʤa'majka]

240. Africa

Egypt	**Egitto** (m)	[e'ʤitto]
Egyptian (masc.)	**egiziano** (m)	[eʤi'tsjano]
Egyptian (fem.)	**egiziana** (f)	[eʤi'tsjana]
Egyptian (adj)	**egiziano** (agg)	[eʤi'tsjano]
Morocco	**Marocco** (m)	[ma'rokko]
Moroccan (masc.)	**marocchino** (m)	[marok'kino]
Moroccan (fem.)	**marocchina** (f)	[marok'kina]
Moroccan (adj)	**marocchino** (agg)	[marok'kino]
Tunisia	**Tunisia** (f)	[tuni'zia]
Tunisian (masc.)	**tunisino** (m)	[tuni'zino]
Tunisian (fem.)	**tunisina** (f)	[tuni'zina]
Tunisian (adj)	**tunisino** (agg)	[tuni'zino]
Ghana	**Ghana** (m)	['gana]
Zanzibar	**Zanzibar**	['ʣanʣibar]
Kenya	**Kenya** (m)	['kenia]
Libya	**Libia** (f)	['libia]
Madagascar	**Madagascar** (m)	[madagas'kar]
Namibia	**Namibia** (f)	[na'mibia]
Senegal	**Senegal** (m)	[sene'gal]
Tanzania	**Tanzania** (f)	[tan'ʣania]
South Africa	**Repubblica** (f) **Sudafricana**	[re'pubblika sudafri'kana]
African (masc.)	**africano** (m)	[afri'kano]
African (fem.)	**africana** (f)	[afri'kana]
African (adj)	**africano** (agg)	[afri'kano]

241. Australia. Oceania

Australia	**Australia** (f)	[au'stralia]
Australian (masc.)	**australiano** (m)	[austra'ljano]
Australian (fem.)	**australiana** (f)	[austra'ljana]
Australian (adj)	**australiano** (agg)	[austra'ljano]
New Zealand	**Nuova Zelanda** (f)	[nu'ova ʣe'landa]
New Zealander (masc.)	**neozelandese** (m)	[neoʣelan'deze]
New Zealander (fem.)	**neozelandese** (f)	[neoʣelan'deze]
New Zealand (as adj)	**neozelandese** (agg)	[neoʣelan'deze]
Tasmania	**Tasmania** (f)	[taz'mania]
French Polynesia	**Polinesia** (f) **Francese**	[poli'nezia fran'ʧeze]

242. Cities

Amsterdam	**Amsterdam**	['amsterdam]
Ankara	**Ankara**	['ankara]
Athens	**Atene**	[a'tene]
Baghdad	**Baghdad**	[bag'dad]
Bangkok	**Bangkok**	[baŋ'kok]
Barcelona	**Barcellona**	[bartʃel'lona]
Beijing	**Pechino**	[pe'kino]
Beirut	**Beirut**	['bejrut]
Berlin	**Berlino**	[ber'lino]
Mumbai (Bombay)	**Bombay, Mumbai**	[bom'bej], [mum'baj]
Bonn	**Bonn**	[bonn]
Bordeaux	**Bordeaux**	[bor'do]
Bratislava	**Bratislava**	[brati'zlava]
Brussels	**Bruxelles**	[bruk'sel]
Bucharest	**Bucarest**	['bukarest]
Budapest	**Budapest**	['budapest]
Cairo	**Il Cairo**	[il 'kairo]
Kolkata (Calcutta)	**Calcutta**	[kal'kutta]
Chicago	**Chicago**	[tʃi'kago]
Copenhagen	**Copenaghen**	[kope'nagen]
Dar-es-Salaam	**Dar es Salaam**	[dar es sala'am]
Delhi	**Delhi**	['deli]
Dubai	**Dubai**	[du'bai]
Dublin	**Dublino**	[du'blino]
Düsseldorf	**Düsseldorf**	['dysseldorf]
Florence	**Firenze**	[fi'rentse]
Frankfurt	**Francoforte**	[franko'forte]
Geneva	**Ginevra**	[dʒi'nevra]
The Hague	**L'Aia**	['laja]
Hamburg	**Amburgo**	[am'burgo]
Hanoi	**Hanoi**	[a'noj]
Havana	**L'Avana**	[la'vana]
Helsinki	**Helsinki**	['elsinki]
Hiroshima	**Hiroshima**	[iro'ʃima]
Hong Kong	**Hong Kong**	[on'kong]
Istanbul	**Istanbul**	['istanbul]
Jerusalem	**Gerusalemme**	[dʒeruza'lemme]
Kyiv	**Kiev**	['kiev]
Kuala Lumpur	**Kuala Lumpur**	[ku'ala 'lumpur]
Lisbon	**Lisbona**	[liz'bona]
London	**Londra**	['londra]
Los Angeles	**Los Angeles**	[los 'endʒeles]

Lyons	**Lione**	[li'one]
Madrid	**Madrid**	[ma'drid]
Marseille	**Marsiglia**	[mar'siʎʎa]
Mexico City	**Città del Messico**	[ʧit'ta del 'messiko]
Miami	**Miami**	[ma'jami]
Montreal	**Montreal**	[monre'al]
Moscow	**Mosca**	['moska]
Munich	**Monaco di Baviera**	['monako di ba'vjera]
Nairobi	**Nairobi**	[naj'robi]
Naples	**Napoli**	['napoli]
New York	**New York**	[nju 'jork]
Nice	**Nizza**	['nittsa]
Oslo	**Oslo**	['ozlo]
Ottawa	**Ottawa**	[ot'tava]
Paris	**Parigi**	[pa'riʤi]
Prague	**Praga**	['praga]
Rio de Janeiro	**Rio de Janeiro**	['rio de ʒa'nejro]
Rome	**Roma**	['roma]
Saint Petersburg	**San Pietroburgo**	[san pjetro'burgo]
Seoul	**Seoul**	[se'ul]
Shanghai	**Shanghai**	[ʃan'gaj]
Singapore	**Singapore**	[singa'pore]
Stockholm	**Stoccolma**	[stok'kolma]
Sydney	**Sidney**	[sid'nej]
Taipei	**Taipei**	[taj'pej]
Tokyo	**Tokio**	['tokio]
Toronto	**Toronto**	[to'ronto]
Venice	**Venezia**	[ve'netsia]
Vienna	**Vienna**	['vjenna]
Warsaw	**Varsavia**	[var'savia]
Washington	**Washington**	['woʃinton]

243. Politics. Government. Part 1

politics	**politica** (f)	[po'litika]
political (adj)	**politico** (agg)	[po'litiko]
politician	**politico** (m)	[po'litiko]
state (country)	**stato** (m)	['stato]
citizen	**cittadino** (m)	[ʧitta'dino]
citizenship	**cittadinanza** (f)	[ʧittadi'nantsa]
national emblem	**emblema** (m) **nazionale**	[em'blema natsjo'nale]
national anthem	**inno** (m) **nazionale**	['inno natsjo'nale]
government	**governo** (m)	[go'verno]

head of state	**capo** (m) **di Stato**	['kapo di 'stato]
parliament	**parlamento** (m)	[parla'mento]
party	**partito** (m)	[par'tito]
capitalism	**capitalismo** (m)	[kapita'lizmo]
capitalist (adj)	**capitalistico**	[kapita'listiko]
socialism	**socialismo** (m)	[sotʃia'lizmo]
socialist (adj)	**socialista**	[sotʃia'lista]
communism	**comunismo** (m)	[komu'nizmo]
communist (adj)	**comunista**	[komu'nista]
communist (n)	**comunista** (m)	[komu'nista]
democracy	**democrazia** (f)	[demokra'tsia]
democrat	**democratico** (m)	[demo'kratiko]
democratic (adj)	**democratico**	[demo'kratiko]
Democratic party	**partito** (m) **democratico**	[par'tito demo'kratiko]
liberal (n)	**liberale** (m)	[libe'rale]
liberal (adj)	**liberale** (agg)	[libe'rale]
conservative (n)	**conservatore** (m)	[konserva'tore]
conservative (adj)	**conservatore** (agg)	[konserva'tore]
republic (n)	**repubblica** (f)	[re'pubblika]
republican (n)	**repubblicano** (m)	[repubbli'kano]
Republican party	**partito** (m) **repubblicano**	[par'tito repubbli'kano]
elections	**elezioni** (f pl)	[ele'tsjoni]
to elect (vt)	**eleggere** (vt)	[e'ledʒere]
elector, voter	**elettore** (m)	[elet'tore]
election campaign	**campagna** (f) **elettorale**	[kam'paɲa eletto'rale]
voting (n)	**votazione** (f)	[vota'tsjone]
to vote (vi)	**votare** (vi)	[vo'tare]
suffrage, right to vote	**diritto** (m) **di voto**	[di'ritto di 'voto]
candidate	**candidato** (m)	[kandi'dato]
to be a candidate	**candidarsi** (vr)	[kandi'darsi]
campaign	**campagna** (f)	[kam'paɲa]
opposition (as adj)	**d'opposizione**	[doppozi'tsjone]
opposition (n)	**opposizione** (f)	[oppozi'tsjone]
visit	**visita** (f)	['vizita]
official visit	**visita** (f) **ufficiale**	['vizita uffi'tʃale]
international (adj)	**internazionale**	[internatsjo'nale]
negotiations	**trattative** (f pl)	[tratta'tive]
to negotiate (vi)	**negoziare** (vi)	[nego'tsjare]

244. Politics. Government. Part 2

society	**società** (f)	[sotʃie'ta]
constitution	**costituzione** (f)	[kostitu'tsjone]
power (political control)	**potere** (m)	[po'tere]
corruption	**corruzione** (f)	[korru'tsjone]
law (justice)	**legge** (f)	['ledʒe]
legal (legitimate)	**legittimo**	[le'dʒittimo]
justice (fairness)	**giustizia** (f)	[dʒu'stitsia]
just (fair)	**giusto**	['dʒusto]
committee	**comitato** (m)	[komi'tato]
bill (draft law)	**disegno** (m) **di legge**	[di'zeɲo di 'ledʒe]
budget	**bilancio** (m)	[bi'lantʃo]
policy	**politica** (f)	[po'litika]
reform	**riforma** (f)	[ri'forma]
radical (adj)	**radicale**	[radi'kale]
power (strength, force)	**forza** (f), **potenza** (f)	['fortsa], [po'tentsa]
powerful (adj)	**potente**	[po'tente]
supporter	**sostenitore** (m)	[sosteni'tore]
influence	**influenza** (f)	[influ'entsa]
regime (e.g., military ~)	**regime** (m)	[re'dʒime]
conflict	**conflitto** (m)	[kon'flitto]
conspiracy (plot)	**complotto** (m)	[kom'plotto]
provocation	**provocazione** (f)	[provoka'tsjone]
to overthrow (regime, etc.)	**rovesciare** (vt)	[rove'ʃare]
overthrow (of government)	**rovesciamento** (m)	[roveʃa'mento]
revolution	**rivoluzione** (f)	[rivolu'tsjone]
coup d'état	**colpo** (m) **di Stato**	['kolpo di 'stato]
military coup	**golpe** (m) **militare**	['golpe mili'tare]
crisis	**crisi** (f)	['krizi]
economic recession	**recessione** (f) **economica**	[retʃes'sjone eko'nomika]
demonstrator (protester)	**manifestante** (m)	[manife'stante]
demonstration	**manifestazione** (f)	[manifesta'tsjone]
martial law	**legge** (f) **marziale**	['ledʒe mar'tsjale]
military base	**base** (f) **militare**	['baze mili'tare]
stability	**stabilità** (f)	[stabili'ta]
stable (adj)	**stabile**	['stabile]
exploitation	**sfruttamento** (m)	[sfrutta'mento]
to exploit (workers)	**sfruttare** (vt)	[sfrut'tare]
racism	**razzismo** (m)	[rat'tsizmo]
racist	**razzista** (m)	[rat'tsista]

fascism	**fascismo** (m)	[fa'ʃizmo]
fascist	**fascista** (m)	[fa'ʃista]

245. Countries. Miscellaneous

foreigner	**straniero** (m)	[stra'njero]
foreign (adj)	**straniero** (agg)	[stra'njero]
abroad (in a foreign country)	**all'estero**	[all 'estero]
emigrant	**emigrato** (m)	[emi'grato]
emigration	**emigrazione** (f)	[emigra'tsjone]
to emigrate (vi)	**emigrare** (vi)	[emi'grare]
the West	**Ovest** (m)	['ovest]
the East	**Est** (m)	[est]
the Far East	**Estremo Oriente** (m)	[e'stremo o'rjente]
civilization	**civiltà** (f)	[ʧivil'ta]
humanity (mankind)	**umanità** (f)	[umani'ta]
the world (earth)	**mondo** (m)	['mondo]
peace	**pace** (f)	['paʧe]
worldwide (adj)	**mondiale**	[mon'djale]
homeland	**patria** (f)	['patria]
people (population)	**popolo** (m)	['popolo]
population	**popolazione** (f)	[popola'tsjone]
people (a lot of ~)	**gente** (f)	['ʤente]
nation (people)	**nazione** (f)	[na'tsjone]
generation	**generazione** (f)	[ʤenera'tsjone]
territory (area)	**territorio** (m)	[terri'torio]
region	**regione** (f)	[re'ʤone]
state (part of a country)	**stato** (m)	['stato]
tradition	**tradizione** (f)	[tradi'tsjone]
custom (tradition)	**costume** (m)	[ko'stume]
ecology	**ecologia** (f)	[ekolo'ʤia]
Indian (Native American)	**indiano** (m)	[indi'ano]
Gypsy (masc.)	**zingaro** (m)	['tsingaro]
Gypsy (fem.)	**zingara** (f)	['tsingara]
Gypsy (adj)	**di zingaro**	[di 'tsingaro]
empire	**impero** (m)	[im'pero]
colony	**colonia** (f)	[ko'lonia]
slavery	**schiavitù** (f)	[skjavi'tu]
invasion	**invasione** (f)	[inva'zjone]
famine	**carestia** (f)	[kare'stia]

246. Major religious groups. Confessions

religion	**religione** (f)	[reli'dʒone]
religious (adj)	**religioso**	[reli'dʒozo]
faith, belief	**fede** (f)	['fede]
to believe (in God)	**credere** (vi)	['kredere]
believer	**credente** (m)	[kre'dente]
atheism	**ateismo** (m)	[ate'izmo]
atheist	**ateo** (m)	['ateo]
Christianity	**cristianesimo** (m)	[kristja'nezimo]
Christian (n)	**cristiano** (m)	[kri'stjano]
Christian (adj)	**cristiano** (agg)	[kri'stjano]
Catholicism	**Cattolicesimo** (m)	[kattoli'tʃezimo]
Catholic (n)	**cattolico** (m)	[kat'toliko]
Catholic (adj)	**cattolico** (agg)	[kat'toliko]
Protestantism	**Protestantesimo** (m)	[protestan'tesimo]
Protestant Church	**Chiesa** (f) **protestante**	['kjeza protes'tante]
Protestant (n)	**protestante** (m)	[prote'stante]
Orthodoxy	**Ortodossia** (f)	[ortodos'sia]
Orthodox Church	**Chiesa** (f) **ortodossa**	['kjeza orto'dossa]
Orthodox (n)	**ortodosso** (m)	[orto'dosso]
Presbyterianism	**Presbiterianesimo** (m)	[presbiterja'nezimo]
Presbyterian Church	**Chiesa** (f) **presbiteriana**	['kjeza presbite'rjana]
Presbyterian (n)	**presbiteriano** (m)	[presbite'rjano]
Lutheranism	**Luteranesimo** (m)	[lutera'nezimo]
Lutheran (n)	**luterano** (m)	[lute'rano]
Baptist Church	**confessione** (f) **battista**	[konfes'sjone bat'tista]
Baptist (n)	**battista** (m)	[bat'tista]
Anglican Church	**Chiesa** (f) **anglicana**	['kjeza angli'kana]
Anglican (n)	**anglicano** (m)	[angli'kano]
Mormonism	**Mormonismo** (m)	[mormo'nizmo]
Mormon (n)	**mormone** (m)	[mor'mone]
Judaism	**giudaismo** (m)	[dʒuda'izmo]
Jew (n)	**ebreo** (m)	[e'breo]
Buddhism	**buddismo** (m)	[bud'dizmo]
Buddhist (n)	**buddista** (m)	[bud'dista]
Hinduism	**Induismo** (m)	[indu'izmo]
Hindu (n)	**induista** (m)	[indu'ista]

Islam	**Islam** (m)	['izlam]
Muslim (n)	**musulmano** (m)	[musul'mano]
Muslim (adj)	**musulmano**	[musul'mano]
Shiah Islam	**sciismo** (m)	[ʃi'izmo]
Shiite (n)	**sciita** (m)	[ʃi'ita]
Sunni Islam	**sunnismo** (m)	[sun'nizmo]
Sunnite (n)	**sunnita** (m)	[sun'nita]

247. Religions. Priests

priest	**prete** (m)	['prete]
the Pope	**Papa** (m)	['papa]
monk, friar	**monaco** (m)	['monako]
nun	**monaca** (f)	['monaka]
pastor	**pastore** (m)	[pa'store]
abbot	**abate** (m)	[a'bate]
vicar (parish priest)	**vicario** (m)	[vi'kario]
bishop	**vescovo** (m)	['veskovo]
cardinal	**cardinale** (m)	[kardi'nale]
preacher	**predicatore** (m)	[predika'tore]
preaching	**predica** (f)	['predika]
parishioners	**parrocchiani** (m)	[parrok'kjani]
believer	**credente** (m)	[kre'dente]
atheist	**ateo** (m)	['ateo]

248. Faith. Christianity. Islam

Adam	**Adamo**	[a'damo]
Eve	**Eva**	['eva]
God	**Dio** (m)	['dio]
the Lord	**Signore** (m)	[si'ɲore]
the Almighty	**Onnipotente** (m)	[onnipo'tente]
sin	**peccato** (m)	[pek'kato]
to sin (vi)	**peccare** (vi)	[pek'kare]
sinner (masc.)	**peccatore** (m)	[pekka'tore]
sinner (fem.)	**peccatrice** (f)	[pekka'tritʃe]
hell	**inferno** (m)	[in'ferno]
paradise	**paradiso** (m)	[para'dizo]
Jesus	**Gesù**	[dʒe'su]

Jesus Christ	**Gesù Cristo**	[dʒe'su 'kristo]
the Holy Spirit	**Spirito** (m) **Santo**	['spirito 'santo]
the Savior	**Salvatore** (m)	[salva'tore]
the Virgin Mary	**Madonna**	[ma'donna]
the Devil	**Diavolo** (m)	['djavolo]
devil's (adj)	**del diavolo**	[del 'djavolo]
Satan	**Satana** (m)	['satana]
satanic (adj)	**satanico**	[sa'taniko]
angel	**angelo** (m)	['andʒelo]
guardian angel	**angelo** (m) **custode**	['andʒelo kus'tode]
angelic (adj)	**angelico**	[an'dʒeliko]
apostle	**apostolo** (m)	[a'postolo]
archangel	**arcangelo** (m)	[ar'kandʒelo]
the Antichrist	**Anticristo** (m)	[anti'kristo]
Church	**Chiesa** (f)	['kjeza]
Bible	**Bibbia** (f)	['bibbia]
biblical (adj)	**biblico**	['bibliko]
Old Testament	**Vecchio Testamento** (m)	['vekkio testa'mento]
New Testament	**Nuovo Testamento** (m)	[nu'ovo testa'mento]
Gospel	**Vangelo** (m)	[van'dʒelo]
Holy Scripture	**Sacra Scrittura** (f)	['sakra skrit'tura]
Heaven	**Il Regno dei Cieli**	[il 'reɲo dei 'tʃeli]
Commandment	**comandamento** (m)	[komanda'mento]
prophet	**profeta** (m)	[pro'feta]
prophecy	**profezia** (f)	[profe'tsia]
Allah	**Allah**	[al'la]
Mohammed	**Maometto**	[mao'meto]
the Koran	**Corano** (m)	[ko'rano]
mosque	**moschea** (f)	[mos'kea]
mullah	**mullah** (m)	[mul'la]
prayer	**preghiera** (f)	[pre'gjera]
to pray (vi, vt)	**pregare** (vi, vt)	[pre'gare]
pilgrimage	**pellegrinaggio** (m)	[pellegri'nadʒo]
pilgrim	**pellegrino** (m)	[pelle'grino]
Mecca	**La Mecca** (f)	[la 'mekka]
church	**chiesa** (f)	['kjeza]
temple	**tempio** (m)	['tempjo]
cathedral	**cattedrale** (f)	[katte'drale]
Gothic (adj)	**gotico**	['gotiko]
synagogue	**sinagoga** (f)	[sina'goga]
mosque	**moschea** (f)	[mos'kea]
chapel	**cappella** (f)	[kap'pella]

abbey	**abbazia** (f)	[abba'tsia]
convent	**convento** (m) **di suore**	[kon'vento di su'ore]
monastery	**monastero** (m)	[mona'stero]
bell (church ~s)	**campana** (f)	[kam'pana]
bell tower	**campanile** (m)	[kampa'nile]
to ring (ab. bells)	**suonare** (vi)	[suo'nare]
cross	**croce** (f)	['krotʃe]
cupola (roof)	**cupola** (f)	['kupola]
icon	**icona** (f)	[i'kona]
soul	**anima** (f)	['anima]
fate (destiny)	**destino** (m), **sorte** (f)	[de'stino], ['sorte]
evil (n)	**male** (m)	['male]
good (n)	**bene** (m)	['bene]
vampire	**vampiro** (m)	[vam'piro]
witch (evil ~)	**strega** (f)	['strega]
demon	**demone** (m)	['demone]
spirit	**spirito** (m)	['spirito]
redemption (giving us ~)	**redenzione** (f)	[reden'tsjone]
to redeem (vt)	**redimere** (vt)	[re'dimere]
church service, mass	**messa** (f)	['messa]
to say mass	**dire la messa**	['dire la 'messa]
confession	**confessione** (f)	[konfes'sjone]
to confess (vi)	**confessarsi** (vr)	[konfes'sarsi]
saint (n)	**santo** (m)	['santo]
sacred (holy)	**sacro**	['sakro]
holy water	**acqua** (f) **santa**	['akwa 'santa]
ritual (n)	**rito** (m)	['rito]
ritual (adj)	**rituale**	[ritu'ale]
sacrifice	**sacrificio** (m)	[sakri'fitʃo]
superstition	**superstizione** (f)	[supersti'tsjone]
superstitious (adj)	**superstizioso**	[supersti'tsjozo]
afterlife	**vita** (f) **dell'oltretomba**	['vita dell oltre'tomba]
eternal life	**vita** (f) **eterna**	['vita e'terna]

MISCELLANEOUS

249. Various useful words

background (green ~)	**sfondo** (m)	['sfondo]
balance (of situation)	**bilancio** (m)	[bi'lantʃo]
barrier (obstacle)	**barriera** (f)	[bar'rjera]
base (basis)	**base** (f)	['baze]
beginning	**inizio** (m)	[i'nitsio]
category	**categoria** (f)	[katego'ria]
cause (reason)	**causa** (f)	['kauza]
choice	**scelta** (f)	['ʃelta]
coincidence	**coincidenza** (f)	[kojntʃi'dentsa]
comfortable (~ chair)	**comodo**	['komodo]
comparison	**confronto** (m)	[kon'fronto]
compensation	**compenso** (m)	[kom'penso]
degree (extent, amount)	**grado** (m)	['grado]
development	**sviluppo** (m)	[zvi'luppo]
difference	**differenza** (f)	[diffe'rentsa]
effect (e.g., of drugs)	**effetto** (m)	[ef'fetto]
effort (exertion)	**sforzo** (m)	['sfortso]
element	**elemento** (m)	[ele'mento]
end (finish)	**termine** (m)	['termine]
example (illustration)	**esempio** (m)	[e'zempjo]
fact	**fatto** (m)	['fatto]
frequent (adj)	**frequente**	[fre'kwente]
growth (development)	**crescita** (f)	['kreʃita]
help	**aiuto** (m)	[a'juto]
ideal	**ideale** (m)	[ide'ale]
kind (sort, type)	**genere** (m)	['dʒenere]
labyrinth	**labirinto** (m)	[labi'rinto]
mistake, error	**errore** (m)	[er'rore]
moment	**momento** (m)	[mo'mento]
object (thing)	**oggetto** (m)	[o'dʒetto]
obstacle	**ostacolo** (m)	[os'takolo]
original (original copy)	**originale** (m)	[oridʒi'nale]
part (~ of sth)	**parte** (f)	['parte]
particle, small part	**particella** (f)	[parti'tʃella]
pause (break)	**pausa** (f)	['pauza]

position	**posizione** (f)	[pozi'tsjone]
principle	**principio** (m)	[prin'ʧipjo]
problem	**problema** (m)	[pro'blema]
process	**processo** (m)	[pro'ʧesso]
progress	**progresso** (m)	[pro'gresso]
property (quality)	**proprietà** (f)	[proprie'ta]
reaction	**reazione** (f)	[rea'tsjone]
risk	**rischio** (m)	['riskio]
secret	**segreto** (m)	[se'greto]
series	**serie** (f)	['serie]
shape (outer form)	**forma** (f)	['forma]
situation	**situazione** (f)	[situa'tsjone]
solution	**soluzione** (f)	[solu'tsjone]
standard (adj)	**standard**	['standar]
standard (level of quality)	**standard** (m)	['standar]
stop (pause)	**pausa** (f)	['pauza]
style	**stile** (m)	['stile]
system	**sistema** (m)	[si'stema]
table (chart)	**tabella** (f)	[ta'bella]
tempo, rate	**ritmo** (m)	['ritmo]
term (word, expression)	**termine** (m)	['termine]
thing (object, item)	**cosa** (f)	['koza]
truth (e.g., moment of ~)	**verità** (f)	[veri'ta]
turn (please wait your ~)	**turno** (m)	['turno]
type (sort, kind)	**tipo** (m)	['tipo]
urgent (adj)	**urgente**	[ur'ʤente]
urgently (adv)	**urgentemente**	[urʤente'mente]
utility (usefulness)	**utilità** (f)	[utili'ta]
variant (alternative)	**variante** (f)	[vari'ante]
way (means, method)	**modo** (m)	['modo]
zone	**zona** (f)	['ʣona]

250. Modifiers. Adjectives. Part 1

additional (adj)	**supplementare**	[supplemen'tare]
ancient (~ civilization)	**antico**	[an'tiko]
artificial (adj)	**artificiale**	[artifi'ʧale]
back, rear (adj)	**posteriore**	[poste'rjore]
bad (adj)	**cattivo**	[kat'tivo]
beautiful (~ palace)	**magnifico**	[ma'ɲifiko]
beautiful (person)	**bello**	['bello]
big (in size)	**grande**	['grande]

bitter (taste)	**amaro**	[a'maro]
blind (sightless)	**cieco**	['ʧeko]
calm, quiet (adj)	**tranquillo**	[tran'kwillo]
careless (negligent)	**noncurante**	[nonku'rante]
caring (~ father)	**premuroso**	[premu'rozo]
central (adj)	**centrale**	[ʧen'trale]
cheap (low-priced)	**a buon mercato**	[a bu'on mer'kato]
cheerful (adj)	**allegro**	[al'legro]
children's (adj)	**per bambini**	[per bam'bini]
civil (~ law)	**civile**	[ʧi'vile]
clandestine (secret)	**clandestino**	[klande'stino]
clean (free from dirt)	**pulito**	[pu'lito]
clear (explanation, etc.)	**chiaro**	['kjaro]
clever (smart)	**intelligente**	[intelli'ʤente]
closed (adj)	**chiuso**	['kjuzo]
cloudless (sky)	**sereno**	[se'reno]
cold (drink, weather)	**freddo**	['freddo]
compatible (adj)	**compatibile**	[kompa'tibile]
contented (satisfied)	**contento**	[kon'tento]
continuous (uninterrupted)	**ininterrotto**	[ininte'rotto]
cool (weather)	**fresco**	['fresko]
dangerous (adj)	**pericoloso**	[periko'lozo]
dark (room)	**buio, scuro**	['bujo], ['skuro]
dead (not alive)	**morto**	['morto]
dense (fog, smoke)	**denso**	['denso]
destitute (extremely poor)	**molto povero**	['molto 'povero]
different (not the same)	**diverso**	[di'verso]
difficult (decision)	**difficile**	[dif'fiʧile]
difficult (problem, task)	**complicato**	[kompli'kato]
dim, faint (light)	**fievole**	['fjevole]
dirty (not clean)	**sporco**	['sporko]
distant (in space)	**lontano**	[lon'tano]
dry (clothes, etc.)	**secco**	['sekko]
easy (not difficult)	**facile**	['faʧile]
empty (glass, room)	**vuoto**	[vu'oto]
even (e.g., ~ surface)	**piatto**	['pjatto]
exact (amount)	**preciso**	[pre'ʧizo]
excellent (adj)	**eccellente**	[eʧel'lente]
excessive (adj)	**eccessivo**	[eʧes'sivo]
expensive (adj)	**caro**	['karo]
exterior (adj)	**esterno**	[e'sterno]
far (the ~ East)	**distante**	[di'stante]
fast (quick)	**veloce, rapido**	[veloʧe], ['rapido]

fatty (food)	**grasso**	['grasso]
fertile (land, soil)	**fertile**	['fertile]
flat (~ panel display)	**piatto**	['pjatto]
foreign (adj)	**straniero**	[stra'njero]
fragile (china, glass)	**fragile**	['fradʒile]
free (at no cost)	**gratuito**	[gratu'ito]
free (unrestricted)	**libero**	['libero]
fresh (~ water)	**dolce**	['doltʃe]
fresh (e.g., ~ bread)	**fresco**	['fresko]
frozen (food)	**surgelato**	[surdʒe'lato]
full (completely filled)	**pieno**	['pjeno]
gloomy (house, forecast)	**fosco**	['fosko]
good (book, etc.)	**buono**	[bu'ono]
good, kind (kindhearted)	**buono**	[bu'ono]
grateful (adj)	**grato**	['grato]
happy (adj)	**felice**	[fe'litʃe]
hard (not soft)	**duro**	['duro]
heavy (in weight)	**pesante**	[pe'zante]
hostile (adj)	**ostile**	[o'stile]
hot (adj)	**caldo**	['kaldo]
huge (adj)	**enorme**	[e'norme]
humid (adj)	**umido**	['umido]
hungry (adj)	**affamato**	[affa'mato]
ill (sick, unwell)	**malato**	[ma'lato]
immobile (adj)	**immobile**	[im'mobile]
important (adj)	**importante**	[impor'tante]
impossible (adj)	**impossibile**	[impos'sibile]
incomprehensible	**incomprensibile**	[inkompren'sibile]
indispensable (adj)	**indispensabile**	[indispen'sabile]
inexperienced (adj)	**inesperto**	[ine'sperto]
insignificant (adj)	**insignificante**	[insiɲifi'kante]
interior (adj)	**interno**	[in'terno]
joint (~ decision)	**collegiale**	[kolle'dʒale]
last (e.g., ~ week)	**scorso**	['skorso]
last (final)	**ultimo**	['ultimo]
left (e.g., ~ side)	**sinistro**	[si'nistro]
legal (legitimate)	**legale**	[le'gale]
light (in weight)	**leggero**	[le'dʒero]
light (pale color)	**chiaro, tenue**	['kjaro], ['tenue]
limited (adj)	**limitato**	[limi'tato]
liquid (fluid)	**liquido**	['likwido]
long (e.g., ~ hair)	**lungo**	['lungo]
loud (voice, etc.)	**alto, forte**	['alto], ['forte]
low (voice)	**basso**	['basso]

251. Modifiers. Adjectives. Part 2

main (principal)	**principale**	[printʃi'pale]
matt, matte	**opaco**	[o'pako]
meticulous (job)	**meticoloso, accurato**	[metiko'lozo], [akku'rato]
mysterious (adj)	**misterioso**	[miste'rjozo]
narrow (street, etc.)	**stretto**	['stretto]
native (~ country)	**nativo**	[na'tivo]
nearby (adj)	**vicino, accanto**	[vi'tʃino], [a'kanto]
nearsighted (adj)	**miope**	['miope]
needed (necessary)	**necessario**	[netʃes'sarjo]
negative (~ response)	**negativo**	[nega'tivo]
neighboring (adj)	**vicino, prossimo**	[vi'tʃino], ['prossimo]
nervous (adj)	**nervoso**	[ner'vozo]
new (adj)	**nuovo**	[nu'ovo]
next (e.g., ~ week)	**successivo**	[sutʃes'sivo]
nice (agreeable)	**gentile**	[dʒen'tile]
pleasant (voice)	**gradevole**	[gra'devole]
normal (adj)	**normale**	[nor'male]
not big (adj)	**non molto grande**	[non 'molto 'grande]
not difficult (adj)	**non difficile**	[non dif'fitʃile]
obligatory (adj)	**obbligatorio**	[obbliga'torio]
old (house)	**vecchio**	['vekkio]
open (adj)	**aperto**	[a'perto]
opposite (adj)	**opposto**	[op'posto]
ordinary (usual)	**comune, normale**	[ko'mune], [nor'male]
original (unusual)	**originale**	[oridʒi'nale]
past (recent)	**passato**	[pas'sato]
permanent (adj)	**permanente**	[perma'nente]
personal (adj)	**personale**	[perso'nale]
polite (adj)	**gentile**	[dʒen'tile]
poor (not rich)	**povero**	['povero]
possible (adj)	**possibile**	[pos'sibile]
present (current)	**presente**	[pre'zente]
previous (adj)	**precedente**	[pretʃe'dente]
principal (main)	**principale**	[printʃi'pale]
private (~ jet)	**privato**	[pri'vato]
probable (adj)	**probabile**	[pro'babile]
prolonged (e.g., ~ applause)	**continuo**	[kon'tinuo]
public (open to all)	**pubblico**	['pubbliko]
punctual (person)	**puntuale**	[puntu'ale]
quiet (tranquil)	**calmo**	['kalmo]

rare (adj)	**raro**	['raro]
raw (uncooked)	**crudo**	['krudo]
right (not left)	**destro**	['destro]
right, correct (adj)	**giusto**	['ʤusto]
ripe (fruit)	**maturo**	[ma'turo]
risky (adj)	**rischioso**	[ris'kjozo]
sad (~ look)	**triste**	['triste]
sad (depressing)	**triste, mesto**	['triste], ['mesto]
safe (not dangerous)	**sicuro**	[si'kuro]
salty (food)	**salato**	[sa'lato]
satisfied (customer)	**soddisfatto**	[soddi'sfatto]
second hand (adj)	**di seconda mano**	[di se'konda 'mano]
shallow (water)	**poco profondo**	['poko pro'fondo]
sharp (blade, etc.)	**affilato**	[affi'lato]
short (in length)	**corto**	['korto]
short, short-lived (adj)	**breve**	['breve]
significant (notable)	**notevole**	[no'tevole]
similar (adj)	**simile**	['simile]
simple (easy)	**semplice**	['sempliʧe]
skinny	**molto magro**	['molto 'magro]
small (in size)	**piccolo**	['pikkolo]
smooth (surface)	**liscio**	['liʃo]
soft (~ toys)	**morbido**	['morbido]
solid (~ wall)	**solido**	['solido]
sour (flavor, taste)	**acido, agro**	['aʧido], ['agro]
spacious (house, etc.)	**spazioso**	[spa'tsjozo]
special (adj)	**speciale**	[spe'ʧale]
straight (line, road)	**dritto**	['dritto]
strong (person)	**forte**	['forte]
stupid (foolish)	**stupido**	['stupido]
suitable (e.g., ~ for drinking)	**idoneo**	[i'doneo]
sunny (day)	**di sole**	[di 'sole]
superb, perfect (adj)	**perfetto**	[per'fetto]
swarthy (adj)	**bruno**	['bruno]
sweet (sugary)	**dolce**	['dolʧe]
tan (adj)	**abbronzato**	[abbron'ʣato]
tasty (delicious)	**buono, gustoso**	[bu'ono], [gu'stozo]
tender (affectionate)	**dolce, tenero**	['dolʧe], ['tenero]
the highest (adj)	**il più alto**	[il pju 'alto]
the most important	**il più importante**	[il pju impor'tante]
the nearest	**il più vicino**	[il pju vi'ʧino]
the same, equal (adj)	**uguale**	[u'gwale]

thick (e.g., ~ fog)	**fitto**	['fitto]
thick (wall, slice)	**spesso**	['spesso]
thin (person)	**magro**	['magro]
tight (~ shoes)	**stretto**	['stretto]
tired (exhausted)	**stanco**	['stanko]
tiring (adj)	**faticoso**	[fati'kozo]
transparent (adj)	**trasparente**	[traspa'rente]
unclear (adj)	**poco chiaro**	['poko 'kjaro]
unique (exceptional)	**unico**	['uniko]
various (adj)	**differente**	[diffe'rente]
warm (moderately hot)	**caldo**	['kaldo]
wet (e.g., ~ clothes)	**bagnato**	[ba'ɲato]
whole (entire, complete)	**intero**	[in'tero]
wide (e.g., ~ road)	**largo**	['largo]
young (adj)	**giovane**	['ʤovane]

MAIN 500 VERBS

252. Verbs A-C

to accompany (vt)	**accompagnare** (vt)	[akkompa'ɲare]
to accuse (vt)	**accusare** (vt)	[akku'zare]
to acknowledge (admit)	**ammettere** (vt)	[am'mettere]
to act (take action)	**agire** (vi)	[a'dʒire]
to add (supplement)	**aggiungere** (vt)	[a'dʒundʒare]
to address (speak to)	**rivolgersi a ...**	[ri'voldʒersi a]
to admire (vi)	**ammirare** (vi)	[ammi'rare]
to advertise (vt)	**pubblicizzare** (vt)	[pubblitʃid'dzare]
to advise (vt)	**consigliare** (vt)	[konsiʎ'ʎare]
to affirm (assert)	**affermare** (vt)	[affer'mare]
to agree (say yes)	**essere d'accordo**	['essere dak'kordo]
to aim (to point a weapon)	**mirare, puntare**	[mi'rare], [pun'tare]
to allow (sb to do sth)	**autorizzare** (vt)	[autorid'dzare]
to amputate (vt)	**amputare** (vt)	[ampu'tare]
to answer (vi, vt)	**rispondere** (vi, vt)	[ris'pondere]
to apologize (vi)	**scusarsi** (vr)	[sku'zarsi]
to appear (come into view)	**apparire** (vi)	[appa'rire]
to applaud (vi, vt)	**applaudire** (vi, vt)	[applau'dire]
to appoint (assign)	**nominare** (vt)	[nomi'nare]
to approach (come closer)	**avvicinarsi** (vr)	[avvitʃi'narsi]
to arrive (ab. train)	**arrivare** (vi)	[arri'vare]
to ask (~ sb to do sth)	**chiedere, domandare**	['kjedere], [doman'dare]
to aspire to ...	**aspirare** (vi)	[aspi'rare]
to assist (help)	**assistere** (vt)	[as'sistere]
to attack (mil.)	**attaccare** (vt)	[attak'kare]
to attain (objectives)	**raggiungere** (vt)	[ra'dʒundʒere]
to avenge (get revenge)	**vendicare** (vt)	[vendi'kare]
to avoid (danger, task)	**evitare** (vt)	[evi'tare]
to award (give medal to)	**decorare qn**	[deko'rare]
to battle (vi)	**combattere** (vi)	[kom'battere]
to be (vi)	**essere** (vi)	['essere]
to be a cause of ...	**essere causa di ...**	['essere 'kauza di]
to be afraid	**avere paura**	[a'vere pa'ura]
to be angry (with ...)	**essere arrabbiato con ...**	['essere arrab'bjato kon]

to be at war	**essere in guerra**	['essere in 'gwerra]
to be based (on ...)	**basarsi su ...**	[ba'zarsi su]
to be bored	**annoiarsi** (vr)	[anno'jarsi]
to be convinced	**convincersi** (vr)	[kon'vintʃersi]
to be enough	**bastare** (vi)	[bas'tare]
to be envious	**invidiare** (vt)	[invi'djare]
to be indignant	**indignarsi** (vr)	[indi'ɲarsi]
to be interested in ...	**interessarsi di ...**	[interes'sarsi di]
to be lost in thought	**diventare pensieroso**	[diven'tare pensje'rozo]
to be lying (~ on the table)	**stare** (vi)	['stare]
to be needed	**essere necessario**	['essere netʃes'sario]
to be perplexed (puzzled)	**essere perplesso**	['essere per'plesso]
to be preserved	**essere conservato**	['essere konser'vato]
to be required	**occorrere** (vi)	[ok'korrere]
to be surprised	**stupirsi** (vr)	[stu'pirsi]
to be worried	**essere preoccupato**	['essere preokku'pato]
to beat (to hit)	**picchiare** (vt)	[pik'kjare]
to become (e.g., ~ old)	**diventare, divenire**	[diven'tare], [deve'nire]
to behave (vi)	**comportarsi** (vr)	[kompor'tarsi]
to believe (think)	**credere** (vt)	['kredere]
to belong to ...	**appartenere** (vi)	[apparte'nere]
to berth (moor)	**ormeggiarsi** (vr)	[orme'dʒarsi]
to blind (other drivers)	**abbagliare** (vt)	[abbaʎ'ʎare]
to blow (wind)	**soffiare** (vi)	[sof'fjare]
to blush (vi)	**arrossire** (vi)	[arros'sire]
to boast (vi)	**vantarsi** (vr)	[van'tarsi]
to borrow (money)	**prendere in prestito**	['prendere in 'prestito]
to break (branch, toy, etc.)	**rompere** (vt)	['rompere]
to breathe (vi)	**respirare** (vi)	[respi'rare]
to bring (sth)	**portare** (vt)	[por'tare]
to burn (paper, logs)	**bruciare** (vt)	[bru'tʃare]
to buy (purchase)	**comprare** (vt)	[kom'prare]
to call (~ for help)	**chiamare** (vt)	[kja'mare]
to call (yell for sb)	**chiamare** (vt)	[kja'mare]
to calm down (vt)	**calmare** (vt)	[kal'mare]
can (v aux)	**potere** (vi)	[po'tere]
to cancel (call off)	**annullare** (vt)	[annul'lare]
to cast off (of a boat or ship)	**salpare** (vi)	[sal'pare]
to catch (e.g., ~ a ball)	**afferrare** (vt)	[affer'rare]
to change (~ one's opinion)	**cambiare** (vt)	[kam'bjare]
to change (exchange)	**scambiare** (vt)	[skam'bjare]
to charm (vt)	**incantare** (vt)	[iŋkan'tare]
to choose (select)	**scegliere** (vt)	['ʃeʎʎere]

to chop off (with an ax)	**tagliare** (vt)	[taʎ'ʎare]
to clean (e.g., kettle from scale)	**pulirsi** (vr)	[pu'lirsi]
to clean (shoes, etc.)	**pulire** (vt)	[pu'lire]
to clean up (tidy)	**fare le pulizie**	['fare le puli'tsie]
to close (vt)	**chiudere** (vt)	['kjudere]
to comb one's hair	**pettinarsi** (vr)	[petti'narsi]
to come down (the stairs)	**scendere** (vi)	['ʃendere]
to come out (book)	**uscire** (vi)	[u'ʃire]
to compare (vt)	**confrontare** (vt)	[konfron'tare]
to compensate (vt)	**compensare** (vt)	[kompen'sare]
to compete (vi)	**competere** (vi)	[kom'petere]
to compile (~ a list)	**compilare** (vt)	[kompi'lare]
to complain (vi, vt)	**lamentarsi** (vr)	[lamen'tarsi]
to complicate (vt)	**complicare** (vt)	[kompli'kare]
to compose (music, etc.)	**comporre** (vt)	[kom'porre]
to compromise (reputation)	**compromettere** (vt)	[kompro'mettere]
to concentrate (vi)	**concentrarsi** (vr)	[kontʃen'trarsi]
to confess (criminal)	**confessarsi** (vr)	[konfes'sarsi]
to confuse (mix up)	**confondere** (vt)	[kon'fondere]
to congratulate (vt)	**congratularsi** (vr)	[kongratu'larsi]
to consult (doctor, expert)	**consultare** (vt)	[konsul'tare]
to continue (~ to do sth)	**continuare** (vt)	[kontinu'are]
to control (vt)	**controllare** (vt)	[kontrol'lare]
to convince (vt)	**convincere** (vt)	[kon'vintʃere]
to cooperate (vi)	**collaborare** (vi)	[kollabo'rare]
to coordinate (vt)	**coordinare** (vt)	[koordi'nare]
to correct (an error)	**correggere** (vt)	[kor'redʒere]
to cost (vt)	**costare** (vt)	[ko'stare]
to count (money, etc.)	**contare** (vt)	[kon'tare]
to count on ...	**contare su ...**	[kon'tare su]
to crack (ceiling, wall)	**screpolarsi** (vi)	[skrepo'larsi]
to create (vt)	**creare** (vt)	[kre'are]
to crush, to squash (~ a bug)	**schiacciare** (vt)	[skia'tʃare]
to cry (weep)	**piangere** (vi)	['pjandʒere]
to cut off (with a knife)	**tagliare** (vt)	[taʎ'ʎare]

253. Verbs D-G

to dare (~ to do sth)	**osare** (vt)	[o'zare]
to date from ...	**risalire a ...**	[resa'lire a]

to deceive (vi, vt)	**ingannare** (vt)	[ingan'nare]
to decide (~ to do sth)	**decidere** (vt)	[de'ʧidere]
to decorate (tree, street)	**decorare** (vt)	[deko'rare]
to dedicate (book, etc.)	**dedicare** (vt)	[dedi'kare]
to defend (a country, etc.)	**difendere** (vt)	[di'fendere]
to defend oneself	**difendersi** (vr)	[di'fendersi]
to demand (request firmly)	**esigere** (vt)	[e'ziʤere]
to denounce (vt)	**denunciare** (vt)	[denun'ʧare]
to deny (vt)	**negare** (vt)	[ne'gare]
to depend on ...	**dipendere da ...**	[di'pendere da]
to deprive (vt)	**privare** (vt)	[pri'vare]
to deserve (vt)	**meritare** (vt)	[meri'tare]
to design (machine, etc.)	**progettare** (vt)	[proʤet'tare]
to desire (want, wish)	**desiderare** (vt)	[dezide'rare]
to despise (vt)	**disprezzare** (vt)	[dispret'tsare]
to destroy (documents, etc.)	**distruggere** (vt)	[di'struʤere]
to differ (from sth)	**essere diverso da ...**	['essere di'verso da]
to dig (tunnel, etc.)	**scavare** (vt)	[ska'vare]
to direct (point the way)	**indirizzare** (vt)	[indirit'tsare]
to disappear (vi)	**sparire** (vi)	[spa'rire]
to discover (new land, etc.)	**scoprire** (vt)	[sko'prire]
to discuss (vt)	**discutere** (vt)	[di'skutere]
to distribute (leaflets, etc.)	**distribuire** (vt)	[distribu'ire]
to disturb (vt)	**disturbare** (vt)	[distur'bare]
to dive (vi)	**tuffarsi** (vr)	[tuf'farsi]
to divide (math)	**dividere** (vt)	[di'videre]
to do (vt)	**fare** (vt)	['fare]
to do the laundry	**fare il bucato**	['fare il bu'kato]
to double (increase)	**raddoppiare** (vt)	[raddop'pjare]
to doubt (have doubts)	**dubitare** (vi)	[dubi'tare]
to draw a conclusion	**trarre una conclusione**	['trarre 'una konklu'zjone]
to dream (daydream)	**sognare** (vi)	[so'ɲare]
to dream (in sleep)	**sognare** (vi)	[so'ɲare]
to drink (vi, vt)	**bere** (vi, vt)	['bere]
to drive a car	**guidare, condurre**	[gwi'dare], [kon'durre]
to drive away (scare away)	**cacciare via**	[ka'ʧare 'via]
to drop (let fall)	**lasciar cadere**	[la'ʃar ka'dere]
to drown (ab. person)	**annegare** (vi)	[anne'gare]
to dry (clothes, hair)	**asciugare** (vt)	[aʃu'gare]
to eat (vi, vt)	**mangiare** (vi, vt)	[man'ʤare]
to eavesdrop (vi)	**origliare** (vi)	[oriʎ'ʎare]

to emit (diffuse - odor, etc.)	**emanare** (vt)	[ema'nare]
to enjoy oneself	**divertirsi** (vr)	[diver'tirsi]
to enter (on the list)	**iscrivere** (vt)	[I'skrivere]
to enter (room, house, etc.)	**entrare** (vi)	[en'trare]
to entertain (amuse)	**divertire** (vt)	[diver'tire]
to equip (fit out)	**equipaggiare** (vt)	[ekwipa'ʤare]
to examine (proposal)	**esaminare** (vt)	[ezami'nare]
to exchange (sth)	**scambiarsi** (vr)	[skam'bjarsi]
to excuse (forgive)	**scusare** (vt)	[sku'zare]
to exist (vi)	**esistere** (vi)	[e'zistere]
to expect (anticipate)	**aspettarsi** (vr)	[aspet'tarsi]
to expect (foresee)	**prevedere** (vt)	[preve'dere]
to expel (from school, etc.)	**escludere** (vt)	[e'skludere]
to explain (vt)	**spiegare** (vt)	[spje'gare]
to express (vt)	**esprimere** (vt)	[e'sprimere]
to extinguish (a fire)	**estinguere** (vt)	[e'stingwere]
to fall in love (with ...)	**innamorarsi di ...**	[innamo'rarsi di]
to feed (provide food)	**dare da mangiare**	['dare da man'ʤare]
to fight (against the enemy)	**battersi** (vr)	['battersi]
to fight (vi)	**picchiarsi** (vr)	[pik'kjarsi]
to fill (glass, bottle)	**riempire** (vt)	[riem'pire]
to find (~ lost items)	**trovare** (vt)	[tro'vare]
to finish (vt)	**finire, terminare** (vt)	[fi'nire], [termi'nare]
to fish (angle)	**pescare** (vi)	[pe'skare]
to fit (ab. dress, etc.)	**stare bene**	['stare 'bene]
to flatter (vt)	**adulare** (vt)	[adu'lare]
to fly (bird, plane)	**volare** (vi)	[vo'lare]
to follow ... (come after)	**seguire** (vt)	[se'gwire]
to forbid (vt)	**vietare** (vt)	[vje'tare]
to force (compel)	**costringere** (vt)	[ko'strinʤere]
to forget (vi, vt)	**dimenticare** (vt)	[dimenti'kare]
to forgive (pardon)	**perdonare** (vt)	[perdo'nare]
to form (constitute)	**formare** (vt)	[for'mare]
to get dirty (vi)	**sporcarsi** (vr)	[spor'karsi]
to get infected (with ...)	**contagiarsi** (vr)	[konta'ʤarsi]
to get irritated	**irritarsi** (vr)	[irri'tarsi]
to get married	**sposarsi** (vr)	[spo'zarsi]
to get rid of ...	**liberarsi** (vr)	[libe'rarsi]
to get tired	**stancarsi** (vr)	[stan'karsi]
to get up (arise from bed)	**alzarsi** (vr)	[al'tsarsi]

to give (vt)	**dare** (vt)	['dare]
to give a bath (to bath)	**far fare il bagno**	[far 'fare il 'baɲo]
to give a hug, to hug (vt)	**abbracciare** (vt)	[abbra'ʧare]
to give in (yield to)	**arrendersi** (vr)	[ar'rendersi]
to glimpse (vt)	**intravedere** (vt)	[intrave'dere]
to go (by car, etc.)	**andare** (vi)	[an'dare]
to go (on foot)	**camminare** (vi)	[kammi'nare]
to go for a swim	**fare il bagno**	['fare il 'baɲo]
to go out (for dinner, etc.)	**uscire** (vi)	[u'ʃire]
to go to bed (go to sleep)	**andare a letto**	[an'dare a 'letto]
to greet (vt)	**salutare** (vt)	[salu'tare]
to grow (plants)	**coltivare** (vt)	[kolti'vare]
to guarantee (vt)	**garantire** (vt)	[garan'tire]
to guess (the answer)	**indovinare** (vt)	[indovi'nare]

254. Verbs H-M

to hand out (distribute)	**distribuire** (vt)	[distribu'ire]
to hang (curtains, etc.)	**appendere** (vt)	[ap'pendere]
to have (vt)	**avere** (vt)	[a'vere]
to have a try	**tentare** (vt)	[ten'tare]
to have breakfast	**fare colazione**	['fare kola'tsjone]
to have dinner	**cenare** (vi)	[ʧe'nare]
to have lunch	**pranzare** (vi)	[pran'tsare]
to head (group, etc.)	**capeggiare** (vt)	[kape'ʤare]
to hear (vt)	**sentire** (vt)	[sen'tire]
to heat (vt)	**scaldare** (vt)	[skal'dare]
to help (vt)	**aiutare** (vt)	[aju'tare]
to hide (vt)	**nascondere** (vt)	[na'skondere]
to hire (e.g., ~ a boat)	**noleggiare** (vt)	[nole'ʤare]
to hire (staff)	**assumere** (vt)	[as'sumere]
to hope (vi, vt)	**sperare** (vi, vt)	[spe'rare]
to hunt (for food, sport)	**cacciare** (vt)	[ka'ʧare]
to hurry (vi)	**avere fretta**	[a'vere 'fretta]
to imagine (to picture)	**immaginare** (vt)	[immaʤi'nare]
to imitate (vt)	**imitare** (vt)	[imi'tare]
to implore (vt)	**supplicare** (vt)	[suppli'kare]
to import (vt)	**importare** (vt)	[impor'tare]
to increase (vi)	**aumentare** (vi)	[aumen'tare]
to increase (vt)	**aumentare** (vt)	[aumen'tare]
to infect (vt)	**contagiare** (vt)	[konta'ʤare]
to influence (vt)	**influire** (vt)	[influ'ire]
to inform (e.g., ~ the police about)	**informare di ...**	[infor'mare di]

to inform (vt)	**informare** (vt)	[infor'mare]
to inherit (vt)	**ereditare** (vt)	[eredi'tare]
to inquire (about ...)	**scoprire** (vt)	[sko'prire]
to insert (put in)	**inserire** (vt)	[inse'rire]
to insinuate (imply)	**alludere** (vi)	[al'ludere]
to insist (vi, vt)	**insistere** (vi)	[in'sistere]
to inspire (vt)	**ispirare** (vt)	[ispi'rare]
to instruct (teach)	**dare istruzioni**	['dare istru'tsjoni]
to insult (offend)	**insultare** (vt)	[insul'tare]
to interest (vt)	**interessare** (vt)	[interes'sare]
to intervene (vi)	**intervenire** (vi)	[interve'nire]
to introduce (sb to sb)	**far conoscere**	[far ko'noʃere]
to invent (machine, etc.)	**inventare** (vt)	[inven'tare]
to invite (vt)	**invitare** (vt)	[invi'tare]
to iron (clothes)	**stirare** (vt)	[sti'rare]
to irritate (annoy)	**irritare** (vt)	[irri'tare]
to isolate (vt)	**isolare** (vt)	[izo'lare]
to join (political party, etc.)	**aderire a ...**	[ade'rire]
to joke (be kidding)	**scherzare** (vi)	[sker'tsare]
to keep (old letters, etc.)	**tenere** (vt)	[te'nere]
to keep silent, to hush	**tacere** (vi)	[ta'ʧere]
to kill (vt)	**uccidere** (vt)	[u'ʧidere]
to knock (on the door)	**bussare** (vi)	[bus'sare]
to know (sb)	**conoscere** (vt)	[ko'noʃere]
to know (sth)	**sapere** (vt)	[sa'pere]
to laugh (vi)	**ridere** (vi)	['ridere]
to launch (start up)	**avviare** (vt)	[av'vjare]
to leave (~ for Mexico)	**partire** (vi)	[par'tire]
to leave (forget sth)	**lasciare** (vt)	[la'ʃare]
to leave (spouse)	**lasciare** (vt)	[la'ʃare]
to liberate (city, etc.)	**liberare** (vt)	[libe'rare]
to lie (~ on the floor)	**essere sdraiato**	['essere zdra'jato]
to lie (tell untruth)	**mentire** (vi)	[men'tire]
to light (campfire, etc.)	**accendere** (vt)	[a'ʧendere]
to light up (illuminate)	**illuminare** (vt)	[illumi'nare]
to like (I like ...)	**piacere** (vi)	[pja'ʧere]
to limit (vt)	**limitare** (vt)	[limi'tare]
to listen (vi)	**ascoltare** (vi)	[askol'tare]
to live (~ in France)	**abitare** (vi)	[abi'tare]
to live (exist)	**vivere** (vi)	['vivere]
to load (gun)	**caricare** (vt)	[kari'kare]
to load (vehicle, etc.)	**caricare** (vt)	[kari'kare]
to look (I'm just ~ing)	**guardare** (vi)	[gwar'dare]
to look for ... (search)	**cercare** (vt)	[ʧer'kare]

to look like (resemble)	**assomigliare a ...**	[assomiʎ'ʎare a]
to lose (umbrella, etc.)	**perdere** (vt)	['perdere]
to love (e.g., ~ dancing)	**gradire** (vt)	[gra'dire]
to love (sb)	**amare** (vt)	[a'mare]
to lower (blind, head)	**abbassare** (vt)	[abbas'sare]
to make (~ dinner)	**fare, preparare**	['fare], [prepa'rare]
to make a mistake	**sbagliare** (vi)	[zbaʎ'ʎare]
to make angry	**far arrabbiare**	[far arrab'bjare]
to make easier	**semplificare** (vt)	[semplifi'kare]
to make multiple copies	**fare copie**	['fare 'kopje]
to make the acquaintance	**fare la conoscenza di ...**	['fare la kono'ʃentsa di]
to make use (of ...)	**usare** (vt)	[u'zare]
to manage, to run	**dirigere** (vt)	[di'riʤere]
to mark (make a mark)	**segnare** (vt)	[se'ɲare]
to mean (signify)	**significare** (vt)	[siɲifi'kare]
to memorize (vt)	**memorizzare** (vt)	[memorid'ʣare]
to mention (talk about)	**menzionare** (vt)	[mentsjo'nare]
to miss (school, etc.)	**mancare le lezioni**	[man'kare le le'tsjoni]
to mix (combine, blend)	**mescolare** (vt)	[mesko'lare]
to mock (make fun of)	**canzonare** (vt)	[kantso'nare]
to move (to shift)	**spostare** (vt)	[spo'stare]
to multiply (math)	**moltiplicare** (vt)	[moltipli'kare]
must (v aux)	**dovere** (v aus)	[do'vere]

255. Verbs N-R

to name, to call (vt)	**chiamare** (vt)	[kja'mare]
to negotiate (vi)	**negoziare** (vi)	[nego'tsjare]
to note (write down)	**prendere nota**	['prendere 'nota]
to notice (see)	**accorgersi** (vr)	[ak'korʤersi]
to obey (vi, vt)	**obbedire** (vi)	[obbe'dire]
to object (vi, vt)	**obiettare** (vt)	[objet'tare]
to observe (see)	**osservare** (vt)	[osser'vare]
to offend (vt)	**offendere** (vt)	[of'fendere]
to omit (word, phrase)	**omettere** (vt)	[o'mettere]
to open (vt)	**aprire** (vt)	[a'prire]
to order (in restaurant)	**ordinare** (vt)	[ordi'nare]
to order (mil.)	**comandare**	[koman'dare]
to organize (concert, party)	**organizzare** (vt)	[organid'ʣare]
to overestimate (vt)	**sopravvalutare** (vt)	[sopravvalu'tare]
to own (possess)	**possedere** (vt)	[posse'dere]
to participate (vi)	**partecipare** (vi)	[partetʃi'pare]
to pass through (by car, etc.)	**sorpassare** (vt)	[sorpas'sare]

to pay (vi, vt)	**pagare** (vi, vt)	[pa'gare]
to peep, spy on	**spiare** (vt)	[spi'are]
to penetrate (vt)	**penetrare** (vi)	[pene'trare]
to permit (vt)	**permettere** (vt)	[per'mettere]
to pick (flowers)	**cogliere** (vt)	['koʎʎere]
to place (put, set)	**collocare** (vt)	[kollo'kare]
to plan (~ to do sth)	**pianificare** (vt)	[pjanifi'kare]
to play (actor)	**recitare** (vt)	[retʃi'tare]
to play (children)	**giocare** (vi)	[dʒo'kare]
to point (~ the way)	**indicare** (vt)	[indi'kare]
to pour (liquid)	**versare** (vt)	[ver'sare]
to pray (vi, vt)	**pregare** (vi, vt)	[pre'gare]
to prefer (vt)	**preferire** (vt)	[prefe'rire]
to prepare (~ a plan)	**preparare** (vt)	[prepa'rare]
to present (sb to sb)	**presentare** (vt)	[prezen'tare]
to preserve (peace, life)	**preservare** (vt)	[prezer'vare]
to prevail (vt)	**prevalere** (vi)	[preva'lere]
to progress (move forward)	**avanzare** (vi)	[avan'tsare]
to promise (vt)	**promettere** (vt)	[pro'mettere]
to pronounce (vt)	**pronunciare** (vt)	[pronun'tʃare]
to propose (vt)	**proporre** (vt)	[pro'porre]
to protect (e.g., ~ nature)	**proteggere** (vt)	[pro'tedʒere]
to protest (vi)	**protestare** (vi)	[prote'stare]
to prove (vt)	**provare** (vt)	[pro'vare]
to provoke (vt)	**provocare** (vt)	[provo'kare]
to pull (~ the rope)	**tirare** (vt)	[ti'rare]
to punish (vt)	**punire** (vt)	[pu'nire]
to push (~ the door)	**spingere** (vt)	['spindʒere]
to put away (vt)	**mettere via**	['mettere 'via]
to put in order	**mettere in ordine**	['mettere in 'ordine]
to put, to place	**mettere** (vt)	['mettere]
to quote (cite)	**citare** (vt)	[tʃi'tare]
to reach (arrive at)	**raggiungere** (vt)	[ra'dʒundʒere]
to read (vi, vt)	**leggere** (vi, vt)	['ledʒere]
to realize (a dream)	**realizzare** (vt)	[realid'dzare]
to recognize (identify sb)	**riconoscere** (vt)	[riko'noʃere]
to recommend (vt)	**raccomandare** (vt)	[rakkoman'dare]
to recover (~ from flu)	**guarire** (vi)	[gwa'rire]
to redo (do again)	**rifare** (vt)	[ri'fare]
to reduce (speed, etc.)	**ridurre** (vt)	[ri'durre]
to refuse (~ sb)	**rifiutare** (vt)	[rifju'tare]
to regret (be sorry)	**rammaricarsi** (vr)	[ramari'karsi]

to reinforce (vt)	**rafforzare** (vt)	[raffor'tsare]
to remember (Do you ~ me?)	**ricordare** (vt)	[rikor'dare]
to remember (I can't ~ her name)	**ricordarsi di**	[rikor'darsi di]
to remind of ...	**ricordare** (vt)	[rikor'dare]
to remove (~ a stain)	**rimuovere** (vt)	[rimu'overe]
to remove (~ an obstacle)	**eliminare** (vt)	[elimi'nare]
to rent (sth from sb)	**affittare** (vt)	[affit'tare]
to repair (mend)	**riparare** (vt)	[ripa'rare]
to repeat (say again)	**ripetere** (vt)	[ri'petere]
to report (make a report)	**fare un rapporto**	['fare un rap'porto]
to reproach (vt)	**rimproverare** (vt)	[rimprove'rare]
to reserve, to book	**prenotare** (vt)	[preno'tare]
to restrain (hold back)	**trattenere** (vt)	[tratte'nere]
to return (come back)	**ritornare** (vi)	[ritor'nare]
to risk, to take a risk	**rischiare** (vi, vt)	[ris'kjare]
to rub out (erase)	**cancellare** (vt)	[kantʃel'lare]
to run (move fast)	**correre** (vi)	['korrere]
to rush (hurry sb)	**mettere fretta a ...**	['mettere 'fretta a]

256. Verbs S-W

to satisfy (please)	**soddisfare** (vt)	[soddi'sfare]
to save (rescue)	**salvare** (vt)	[sal'vare]
to say (~ thank you)	**dire** (vt)	['dire]
to scold (vt)	**sgridare** (vt)	[zgri'dare]
to scratch (with claws)	**graffiare** (vt)	[graf'fjare]
to select (to pick)	**selezionare** (vt)	[seletsjo'nare]
to sell (goods)	**vendere** (vt)	['vendere]
to send (a letter)	**inviare** (vt)	[in'vjare]
to send back (vt)	**rimandare** (vt)	[riman'dare]
to sense (~ danger)	**sentire** (vt)	[sen'tire]
to sentence (vt)	**condannare** (vt)	[kondan'nare]
to serve (in restaurant)	**servire** (vt)	[ser'vire]
to settle (a conflict)	**regolare** (vt)	[rego'lare]
to shake (vt)	**scuotere** (vt)	[sku'otere]
to shave (vi)	**rasarsi** (vr)	[ra'zarsi]
to shine (gleam)	**splendere** (vi)	['splendere]
to shiver (with cold)	**tremare** (vi)	[tre'mare]
to shoot (vi)	**sparare** (vi)	[spa'rare]
to shout (vi)	**gridare** (vi)	[gri'dare]

to show (to display)	**mostrare** (vt)	[mo'strare]
to shudder (vi)	**sussultare** (vi)	[sussul'tare]
to sigh (vi)	**sospirare** (vi)	[sospi'rare]
to sign (document)	**firmare** (vt)	[fir'mare]
to signify (mean)	**significare** (vt)	[siɲifi'kare]
to simplify (vt)	**semplificare** (vt)	[semplifi'kare]
to sin (vi)	**peccare** (vi)	[pek'kare]
to sit (be sitting)	**sedere** (vi)	[se'dere]
to sit down (vi)	**sedersi** (vr)	[se'dersi]
to smell (emit an odor)	**emanare odore**	[ema'nare o'dore]
to smell (inhale the odor)	**odorare** (vt)	[odo'rare]
to smile (vi)	**sorridere** (vi)	[sor'ridere]
to snap (vi, ab. rope)	**scoppiare** (vi)	[skop'pjare]
to solve (problem)	**risolvere** (vt)	[ri'zolvere]
to sow (seed, crop)	**seminare** (vt)	[semi'nare]
to spill (liquid)	**rovesciare** (vt)	[rove'ʃare]
to spill out, scatter (flour, etc.)	**spargersi** (vr)	['spardʒersi]
to spit (vi)	**sputare** (vi)	[spu'tare]
to stand (toothache, cold)	**sopportare** (vt)	[soppor'tare]
to start (begin)	**cominciare** (vt)	[komin'tʃare]
to steal (money, etc.)	**rubare** (vt)	[ru'bare]
to stop (for pause, etc.)	**fermarsi** (vr)	[fer'marsi]
to stop (please ~ calling me)	**cessare** (vt)	[tʃes'sare]
to stop talking	**smettere di parlare**	['zmettere di par'lare]
to stroke (caress)	**accarezzare** (vt)	[akkaret'tsare]
to study (vt)	**studiare** (vt)	[stu'djare]
to suffer (feel pain)	**soffrire** (vt)	[sof'frire]
to support (cause, idea)	**sostenere** (vt)	[soste'nere]
to suppose (assume)	**supporre** (vt)	[sup'porre]
to surface (ab. submarine)	**emergere** (vi)	[e'merdʒere]
to surprise (amaze)	**sorprendere** (vt)	[sor'prendere]
to suspect (vt)	**sospettare** (vt)	[sospet'tare]
to swim (vi)	**nuotare** (vi)	[nuo'tare]
to take (get hold of)	**prendere** (vt)	['prendere]
to take a bath	**fare un bagno**	['fare un 'baɲo]
to take a rest	**riposarsi** (vr)	[ripo'zarsi]
to take away (e.g., about waiter)	**portare via**	[por'tare 'via]
to take off (airplane)	**decollare** (vi)	[dekol'lare]
to take off (painting, curtains, etc.)	**togliere** (vt)	['toʎʎere]

to take pictures	**fare foto**	['fare 'foto]
to talk to ...	**parlare con ...**	[par'lare kon]
to teach (give lessons)	**insegnare** (vt)	[inse'ɲare]
to tear off, to rip off (vt)	**strappare** (vt)	[strap'pare]
to tell (story, joke)	**raccontare** (vt)	[rakkon'tare]
to thank (vt)	**ringraziare** (vt)	[ringra'tsjare]
to think (believe)	**pensare** (vi)	[pen'sare]
to think (vi, vt)	**pensare** (vi, vt)	[pen'sare]
to threaten (vt)	**minacciare** (vt)	[mina'ʧare]
to throw (stone, etc.)	**gettare** (vt)	[ʤet'tare]
to tie to ...	**legare** (vt)	[le'gare]
to tie up (prisoner)	**legare** (vt)	[le'gare]
to tire (make tired)	**stancare** (vt)	[sta'nakre]
to touch (one's arm, etc.)	**toccare** (vt)	[tok'kare]
to tower (over ...)	**sovrastare** (vi)	[sovra'stare]
to train (animals)	**ammaestrare** (vt)	[ammae'strare]
to train (sb)	**allenare** (vt)	[alle'nare]
to train (vi)	**allenarsi** (vr)	[alle'narsi]
to transform (vt)	**trasformare** (vt)	[trasfor'mare]
to translate (vt)	**tradurre** (vt)	[tra'durre]
to treat (illness)	**curare** (vt)	[ku'rare]
to trust (vt)	**fidarsi** (vt)	[fi'darsi]
to try (attempt)	**tentare** (vt)	[ten'tare]
to turn (e.g., ~ left)	**girare** (vi)	[ʤi'rare]
to turn away (vi)	**girare lo sguardo**	[ʤi'rare lo 'zgwardo]
to turn off (the light)	**spegnere** (vt)	['speɲere]
to turn on (computer, etc.)	**accendere** (vt)	[a'ʧendere]
to turn over (stone, etc.)	**capovolgere** (vt)	[kapo'volʤere]
to underestimate (vt)	**sottovalutare** (vt)	[sottovalu'tare]
to underline (vt)	**sottolineare** (vt)	[sottoline'are]
to understand (vt)	**capire** (vt)	[ka'pire]
to undertake (vt)	**intraprendere** (vt)	[intra'prendere]
to unite (vt)	**unire** (vt)	[u'nire]
to untie (vt)	**slegare** (vt)	[zle'gare]
to use (phrase, word)	**utilizzare** (vt)	[utilid'ʣare]
to vaccinate (vt)	**vaccinare** (vt)	[vaʧi'nare]
to vote (vi)	**votare** (vi)	[vo'tare]
to wait (vt)	**aspettare** (vt)	[aspet'tare]
to wake (sb)	**svegliare** (vt)	[zveʎ'ʎare]
to want (wish, desire)	**volere** (vt)	[vo'lere]
to warn (of the danger)	**avvertire** (vt)	[avver'tire]
to wash (clean)	**lavare** (vt)	[la'vare]

to water (plants)	**innaffiare** (vt)	[innaf'fjare]
to wave (the hand)	**agitare la mano**	[adʒi'tare la 'mano]
to weigh (have weight)	**pesare** (vi)	[pe'zare]
to work (vi)	**lavorare** (vi)	[lavo'rare]
to worry (make anxious)	**preoccupare** (vt)	[preokku'pare]
to worry (vi)	**preoccuparsi** (vr)	[preokku'parsi]
to wrap (parcel, etc.)	**incartare** (vt)	[inkar'tare]
to wrestle (sport)	**lottare** (vi)	[lot'tare]
to write (vt)	**scrivere** (vi, vt)	['skrivere]
to write down	**annotare** (vt)	[anno'tare]

Printed in Great Britain
by Amazon

69790960R00156